Analytic Philosophy

AN HISTORICAL INTRODUCTION

This book is one of a series, Traditions in Philosophy, published by Pegasus in cooperation with Educational Resources Corporation, which has created and developed the series under the direction of Nicholas Capaldi, Professor of Philosophy, Queens College, New York.

Analytic Philosophy
AN HISTORICAL INTRODUCTION

by *Barry R. Gross*

PEGASUS NEW YORK

ACKNOWLEDGMENTS

Vendler: *Linguistics in Philosophy.* Reprinted from Zeno Vendler: *Linguistics in Philosophy.* Copyright © 1967 by Cornell University. Used by permission of Cornell University Press.

Russell: *Our Knowledge of the External World.* Used by permission of George Allen and Unwin Ltd., London.

Russell: *Introduction to Mathematical Philosophy.* Used by permission of The Macmillan Co.

Russell: *Logic and Knowledge.* Used by permission of George Allen and Unwin Ltd., London.

Wittgenstein: *Philosophical Investigation.* Used by permission of Basil Blackwell, Oxford.

Carnap: *Logical Structure of the World and Pseudoproblems in Philosophy.* Used by permission of Routledge and Kegan Paul Ltd., London and The Regents of the University of California.

Carnap: *Logical Syntax and Language.* Used by permission of the Orthological Institution, London.

Ryle: *Concept of Mind.* Used by permission of Hutchinson Publishing Group Ltd., London and Barnes and Noble, Inc.

Austin: *A Plea for Excuses.* Used by permission of The Aristolelian Society, London.

Schilpp: *The Philosophy of G. E. Moore.* 3rd Edition, 1968. Used by permission of The Open Court Publishing Co., LaSalle, Illinois.

Moore: *Some Main Problems of Philosophy.* 1953. Used by permission of The Macmillan Co.

Quine: *From a Logical Point of View.* Used by permission of Harvard University Press.

Ayer: *Language, Truth and Logic.* Used by permission of Dover Publications, Inc.

Ayer: *Logical Positivism.* 1959. Used by permission of The Macmillan Co.

Library of Congress Catalogue Card Number 74–101078

Contents

Preface   vii

ONE ☐ Introduction   9

TWO ☐ G. E. Moore: 21
Sense Data

THREE ☐ G. E. Moore: 44
Meaning and Reference

FOUR ☐ Bertrand Russell: 66
Meaning and Reference

FIVE ☐ Bertrand Russell: 83
Sense Data

SIX ☐ Logical Positivism: 106
Meaning and Reference

SEVEN ☐ Logical Positivism: 123
Sense Data—The Basis of Knowledge

EIGHT ☐ Ludwig Wittgenstein: 141
Meaning and Reference

NINE ☐ Ludwig Wittgenstein: 159
Sensations and Mental Acts

TEN ☐ Other Directions   180
1. Gilbert Ryle: Sense Data
2. John Austin: Sense Data
3. W.V.O. Quine: Meaning and Reference
4. Peter Strawson: Meaning and Reference

ELEVEN ☐ Epilogue   223

Notes   229

Selected Bibliography   235

Index   241

Preface

This book is meant to introduce the reader to the historical development of the movement called analytic philosophy. It does this by taking him through some positions and arguments in moderate detail as they developed out of one another. It is thus neither a complete historical account of the movement nor a sketch of major views. It occupies a position somewhere between the two.

Because of the vastness of the topic and the limitations of space the book is organized around two principal themes, which have in various guises appeared throughout the history of philosophy: sense data and meaning and reference. They are both central to twentieth-century analysis. It seemed to me that an in-depth treatment of a limited number of topics was preferable to a more superficial treatment of a great many. Because of this structure it happens that some important views of the thinkers included could not be mentioned. This is regrettable, but unavoidable.

I wish to thank Albert Borgman, Nicholas Capaldi, Laila Gross, Gerald Kauvar, and Arnold Levison, each of whom read a draft of the manuscript and made important suggestions. My thanks also to the Rev. Thomas Munson, S.J., who read a draft of Chapters 8 and 9. I am particularly indebted to Professor Capaldi, who is the editor of this series, and to Professor Levison for innumerable conversations about topics covered in the book. I alone am responsible for any remaining errors and infelicities, for they are of my own construction.

Barry R. Gross
York College, City University of New York

1

Introduction

What is called analytic philosophy grew up around the work of G. E. Moore and Bertrand Russell. Both of them began doing philosophy as a comprehensive description of the whole of reality. But one of the chief characteristics of the development of analytic philosophy was that it came to concern itself less and less with giving such a description (here it had been in a sort of competition with science, which also offers such a comprehensive description) and more and more with the analysis of particular concepts and notions. Among these are the concepts and notions of philosophy itself, of language, both natural and artificial, and of science. Though analytic philosophers continued to try to understand the world as before, they turned more often toward attempts to understand our talk about the world, whether that talk was philosophic or scientific. Of course it is inevitable that this should turn into a preoccupation with language.

Three areas of concern about language may be singled out. Historically the earliest was the concern to use words precisely so as to formulate problems clearly and unambiguously. This is effected by a careful scrutiny of what one is saying. The next was the construction of artificial or mathematical languages. This is effected by the development of symbolic logic. The last was the systematic analysis of 'ordinary' or natural language as philosophers usually speak it. This is effected by making up situations and analyzing what we would or should be likely to say when confronted by them. Naturally these areas of concern did not appear so neatly separated out and ordered in time as talking about them makes it seem. Various strands of each may be found in the work of one thinker, and they overlap in time from thinker to thinker. Like many generalizations, this one is convenient, though not precisely accurate.

To a certain extent analytic philosophy is continuous in style and method with the ways philosophy has been done since antiquity. Russell and Wittgenstein pointed out that one phase of their joint efforts may be compared to Plato's work in the *Theatetus,* and other phases of Russell's work may be compared to Plato's analyses in the *Sophist.* In the joint attempt of Russell and the logical positivists to construct an artificial language comprehensive enough to contain both science and philosophy we may see a reflection of Leibnitz' notion of a *mathesis universalis*—a universal formal language. Leibnitz himself had written, "I truly believe that languages are the best mirror of the human mind, and that an exact analysis of the meanings of words would reveal the operations of the understanding far better than anything else."[1] Other analysts have noted similarities in style and method between their work and that of Aristotle, or the work of Locke, Berkeley, and Hume. Indeed, it is to these latter, and especially to Hume, that the analysts owe a great debt, not only of style and method, but of outlook as well.

But if analytic philosophy is continuous with large portions of our philosophic traditions, why has it seemed to many to be so very revolutionary? The answer might be given in three parts. First, it developed in reaction to a very different philosophy which was dominant in Great Britain during the later half of the nineteenth century. Second, it came to be misunderstood as the complete rejection of the possibility of any metaphysics. Third, it has identified itself with certain techniques, methods, and outlooks of natural science, even though it has given up philosophy's old claim to comprehensiveness. We turn first to an account of its immediate background.

It is probably safe to say that British philosophy has been dominated by the empirical tradition. The long and distinguished line of British philosophers down to Bertrand Russell has more often than not believed that knowledge, at least knowledge of the world, insofar as it was possible, was given through the senses. Russell was born in 1872. John Stuart Mill was born in 1806 and died in 1873. His empiricistic work, *A System of Logic,* was published in 1843. He was literally and figuratively Russell's godfather. Between the end of Mill's influence and the time when Russell entered Cambridge there arose in England a very different sort of philosophy called British Idealism. Against this alien philosophy, largely dominated by the thought of F. H. Bradley, Moore and Russell, first its advocates, reacted.

Very roughly, Bradley argued that the empiricistic picture of the world was wrong on at least two counts. First he argued that the empiricists had too psychological a notion of what thinking was. They were in need of logic to complete that notion. Empiricists like Locke had conceived of thinking as a kind of activity of picturing or having conceptions in one's mind. These were called true or false according as they did or did not correspond to what they were supposed to be pictures or conceptions of. But for Bradley, thinking could not be just the having of ideas, images, or conceptions. There was also the problem of what our thoughts or mental contents mean. This he found to be the province of logic. And in this dichotomy, if not in its details, the analytic tradition followed him. But, second, he also argued that though things may seem separate and discrete they really are one unified whole, in Reality. This was rejected by the analytic tradition. For Bradley the universe was a unified whole where things were organically related. Things were not related to each other externally by means of such relations as 'to the left of', 'behind', and the like, but rather they were related to each other, as he called it, 'internally'. If their relations were changed, then they themselves changed and would not be precisely the things that they had been. In some important sense they would be different. Moreover, since things were an organic whole, to analyze them was to destroy them. The rose of the lover is forever destroyed by the plant physiologist's examination.

Against this organic or wholistic view Moore and Russell began to argue. Though the world appeared to be in discrete bits and pieces, for the British Idealists it was really one unified thing. This led them to the distinction between appearance and reality which is also the title of Bradley's most famous book. What *appeared* discrete was just that: an appearance. What you reasoned to as an organic whole was real. Moore and Russell picked up and revitalized the traditional British empiricism emphasizing the notion of the reality of discrete things. They borrowed freely from Hume's thought, though with a new emphasis on logic.

Hume considered that the senses give us our only real knowledge. All our knowledge of the external world arises from sense perception. Every meaningful expression about the world refers to experience. Every idea in our minds derives ultimately from an impression received from the external world, or from some relation between ideas so received. Derived from Locke this is the doctrine of *unem nomen, unem nominatum:* one name, one thing. Hume wrote, "First, when we analyze our thoughts or ideas, however compounded or sublime, we always find that they resolve themselves into such simple ideas as were copied from a similar impression."[2] To refute Hume you must produce some idea which cannot be traced back to a preceding sense impression, and this, Hume holds, you cannot do. He divides our knowledge into what we know by means of impressions of sense and what we know by means of comparison of ideas. Our ideas are copies of sense impressions, being less strong, or lively, or vivacious. Whatever piece of knowledge we think that we have which cannot be traced back either to a sense impression or to a comparison of relations of ideas, is fraudulent and not knowledge at all.

Hume argued further that all reasoning concerning the world was based upon the relation of cause and effect. We discover what causes what by means of experience, and not by reason alone. But how do we discover the relation of cause and effect? In discovering that X causes Y we do not, in fact, experience the *relation* of cause and effect itself. We experience only the fact that certain events appear in a temporal and spatial sequence which induces us to call the first the cause and the second the effect.

With this background let us turn to the analysts themselves. On page 1 above I distinguished three areas of concern about language: 1) concern to use words precisely so as to make one's point clearly and unambiguously; 2) concern with artificial languages; 3) concern with 'ordinary' philosophic language. Using these three areas and borrowing freely from Mr. J. O. Urmson,[3] the history of analytic philosophy can be divided into five stages. The first stage is called early realism and analysis, and Moore and Russell practiced it at first. Their concern was with putting questions precisely and with getting clear answers. The task was to dig out the meaning of a philosophic proposition by reformulating it so as to make it plain. The second stage is concerned with constructing formal languages and is associated with the work of Russell from 1914–19, and the early work of Wittgenstein. It is called logical atomism. The task of the logical atomist was to construct a language whose syntax mirrored the relations of the basic entities of which the world was made up. Such a language describes the structure of the world by mirroring it. In contradistinction to these two stages which not only countenance metaphysics but join in the attempt to construct one, the third stage attempts to abandon metaphysics as meaningless. This is logical positivism and it, too, is concerned with formal languages. But the concern has now changed. On the one hand there is the desire to construct a formal language such that no metaphysical sentence can be constructed in it, and, joining with it on the other, is the desire to construct a formal language adequate for science to be carried on in it. The fourth stage concerns the performance of analyses of what philosophers usually say in natural languages and is a repudiation, direct or implicit, of stages two and three. It was practiced by Ryle and Wittgenstein, who now came to believe that philosophic problems were not so much solved as dissolved by discovering the linguistic traps into which philosophers have fallen. The fifth and last stage was initiated by Austin and it, too, deals with what we ordinarily say. But now the concern is not necessarily with dissolving problems or untangling puzzles, but with the diversity of language in its own right. The subtleties and nuances of language are catalogued, laid out, and shown to be rather less a matter of different or misleading ways of saying the same thing, than subtle ways of saying different things. It is an intellectual exercise which has results.

Once again one must be careful not to take the idealized terms used in description as if they marked off the precise paths of a philosophy or its precise characteristics. Exact history is always complicated both in detail and in outline. Many philosophers, for example, showed characteristics of several phases at one time, or at different times, and each member of a phase exhibited some of its characteristics but not others. Even where the thought of two men had similar characteristics, it was of necessity also different.

The beginning of analytic philosophy can be dated from the work of G. E. Moore (though some begin it with Frege). He attended a good classically oriented college (our secondary school) prior to his entrance to Cambridge. At the college his main occupation was translating prose and poetry out of and into Greek and Latin. He also read the German commentators on those works. The attention to detail necessary for such work left its mark upon his philosophy.

When he attended Cambridge he barely knew that there was such a subject as philosophy. But he met Russell there and soon became interested in philosophical discussion. Moore's devastating naïveté and persistence made a strong impression. Though he questioned critically, he accepted Idealist doctrines and his first philosophical writings supported them. He gradually began to move from Idealist to common-sense Realist positions. When the Idealists said that Time was unreal, Moore wanted to know whether that meant that he had not, after all, had breakfast before lunch, and lunched before he dined. When they said that matter was not real he asked about the chairs upon which they sat.

Since he came to feel that he knew perfectly well that there were chairs and tables, he abandoned Idealism. But though he knew that chairs and tables existed, what he did not know, and what he tried hard to discover, was the correct way to analyze propositions stating that chairs and tables existed. His philosophic style is marked by an insistence that one pay close attention to detail; what had been thought alternative ways of formulating questions or propositions Moore showed were really different propositions and questions. Moore began his philosophic life as a metaphysician and ended it as one. His analyses were always meant to find what was real.

Bertrand Russell came to philosophy through his interest in mathematics. Russell, too, was brought up in the Idealistic tradition at Cambridge. From there he turned to a kind of modern Platonism where numbers and universals existed in some Ideal heaven. His decisive move away from Platonism came in 1905 with the publication of his theory of descriptions in "On Denoting" in the journal, *Mind*. The insistence here is that the grammatical form of a sentence may not mirror its logical form. In collaboration with A. N. Whitehead he developed a large portion of modern logic. In their *Principia Mathematica* Russell and Whitehead attempted to show that all of mathematics could be derived from logic by means of a few elementary axioms and operations. Although Russell was a logician and always retained his interest in logic, he was also a metaphysician and never ceased to believe that once you had cleared up which questions you wanted to ask, you could and should go on to ask metaphysical questions. Russell tried not to destroy metaphysics, but to discover metaphysical truths.

Moore and Russell, the two founders of analytic philosophy, were born, came to philosophic young manhood, and published their first works during the reign of Queen Victoria. Thus, this movement, which has a deserved reputation for scientific philosophy and philosophic modernity, was begun in that old and bygone era whose very name is a synonym for the stuffy, out-of-date, and old-fashioned.

Inspired by the work of Russell and the young Wittgenstein, who was both his pupil and also exerted an influence on him, a group of philosophically oriented scientists and scientifically oriented philosophers, known as the Vienna Circle, began to work out philosophic positions which attempted to work out the logic of the sciences. These positions had in common the view that metaphysics was to be eliminated altogether from philosophy. They tried to maintain that outside of mathematics and logic what characterized the propositions of science was the fact that they spoke about the world, made statements which could be checked about what would or would not happen. This was no feature of philosophic propositions as philosophy had traditionally been practiced. The positivists held that the metaphysical statements of philosophy were neither true nor false, but meaningless, and they attempted with little success to construct a verifiability principle by means of which sentences could be tested.

Side by side with this attempt they also tried to construct artificial languages. These were of interest not for their own sake but because the positivists believed that these highly precise languages could replace idiomatic and imprecise ordinary language in which science had been done. The ambiguities of our grammar and the many meanings of our words would be exchanged for a logical grammar which was unambiguous and words with unique meanings. The task of philosophy was, in their eyes, to develop such a language and refine it. If this language was adequate to the formulation of the substantive theses of science it would also, they thought, not be adequate to the formulation of metaphysical theses and hence, if we did our important work in such a language, metaphysical problems, psuedo-problems, would no longer plague us.

Meanwhile, Ludwig Wittgenstein, who had formulated a bold logically oriented metaphysical thesis and then left philosophy, returned in 1929 and gradually sketched out a position which was a radical critique of his and Russell's earlier work. It was published in 1953 as *Philosophical Investigations.* According to his disciples and biographers, Wittgenstein must have been a haunted and haunting character. The son of a wealthy Viennese family, he first studied engineering, became interested in mathematics, and from there became interested in philosophy. He led a solitary life giving away his fortune and living in great simplicity at various times in a small Austrian village, on the seacoast of Norway, in a small Irish fishing village, and in bare rooms at Cambridge. He seems to have been a man driven by the philosophic problems which plagued him. When these problems appeared solved, as they did in his early days, he simply abandoned philosophy. Such an appearance of simplicity and devotion attracted a great many disciples. It helps to explain the highly personal and idiosyncratic character of his thought, the latent mysticism that some find in his early work, and the strange methods of exposition that he chose.

In his later work, with which we are here concerned, Wittgenstein argues that language is basically imprecise but that this is not necessarily a drawback, but merely one of its properties. In order to work with it you had to understand what it could and could not do. Philosophy has for its activity the clearing up of conceptual puzzles which the incorrect use of language brings about. When one speaks of mental processes as if they were physical ones, of the essential properties of things, of the unity of all concepts which are called by the same name, then one ends in puzzlement and confusion. The way out is to pay attention to the various functions of language. These functions Wittgenstein sketches in broad strokes, illustrating his points with picturesque questions, exclamations, and turns of phrase. The point of this procedure is to get the reader to realize that he has been held captive by false pictures. Once the hold of those pictures of the workings of language is broken, he is free of his confusion. One solves philosophic problems not by erecting a theory, but by showing how they are dissolved. Clarity results in the elimination of the problem.

In England recent philosophy has by and large tended to stay in the Wittgenstenian mold. Three of the four men, accounts of whom conclude this book, are ordinary language philosophers, yet there are differences to be found among them. Gilbert Ryle is professor of philosophy at Oxford and editor of the influential journal, *Mind.* His major work, *The Concept of Mind,* appeared before Wittgenstein's *Philosophical Investigations,* but is in basic agreement with it. Ryle introduces several novel notions in his attempt to show that the traditional mind-body problem arose through a series of logical errors in thinking about mental and physical phenomena. The analyses of various mental concepts are worked out in detail where Ryle tries to show that the old ways of thinking about mind contain the seeds of their own destruction.

Peter Strawson is also an ordinary language philosopher at Oxford. His attack on one of Russell's key theories, the theory of descriptions, tries to show that Russell forced his logical framework upon language, and that instead of clearing up puzzles, it leaves them intact. For him, in order to understand descriptive or denoting phrases it is necessary to understand that language is lived and spoken, not rigid and written down in logic texts. Once this is understood in some detail, solutions can be provided for Russell's problems which take into account the real nature of language and which, therefore, can do the job they were designed to do.

John Austin was a very influential philosopher at Oxford who published little and died young. He held that ordinary language analysis was one among many ways of doing philosophy. But the results it achieved were not confined to mere puzzle solving, they had intrinsic interest. He catalogued and traced down many minute shades of meaning with a view to showing that they represented different con-

cepts or casts of thought. He was not satisfied with sketch-
ing these in the large, but held that the real interest was in
getting the actual detail down on paper. With his marvelous
ear for language he was often able to show that myriad uses
and meanings of words, when properly considered, made
radical solutions to certain problems untenable, because they
were far too simple. His posthumous work *Sense and Sensibilia*
was, I suspect, so named because the nineteenth-century
novelist Jane Austen had a novel of manners entitled *Sense
and Sensibility,* and her ear for nuances has generally been
considered one of the finest.

W. V. O. Quine comes to philosophy as a famous Harvard
logician. Writing in the pragmatic tradition of Charles Sanders Peirce and William James, Quine tries to show that certain conceptions of language and science are predicated
upon a wrong view—wrong because too rigid. He attempts to
get rid of the analytic-synthetic distinction because he thinks
that it cannot be rigorously made without circularity, and
because holding on to it could impede the way in which he
thinks that science progresses.

Analytic philosophers have as much or as little in common
as the members of other groups. There is probably something
in common between Baptists, Children of the Pillar of Fire,
and Copts, but it is very difficult to say just what that is. It
is the same with analytic philosophers. Any two of them are
apt to disagree at least in detail, if not in principle, about
almost any philosophic issue. What differentiates them from
other groups of philosophers? Linguistic analyists seem to
have at least two views in common: 1) that large numbers of,
if not all, philosophic problems can be understood, solved, or
dissolved only through a close analysis or reform of the way
language works (we shall see in some detail that in their
different ways Moore, Russell, the positivists, Wittgenstein,
Ryle, Austin, Strawson, and Quine all think that this is
true); and 2) the questions of language and how it is to be
construed are far more difficult than non-analytic philosophers realized. Concern with language is not merely some
preliminary to getting things straight, but is very close to the

whole business. Hence, they concentrate their efforts heavily on analyzing ordinary language to see how it functions and what properties it has, or they construct formal languages, hoping to be able to formulate all substantive problems in them. Any purported problem which cannot be so formulated is not a problem at all. The various views of language they put forward raise many questions both of detail and of principle, and hence the analysts are forced back again to linguistic questions of even greater detail and higher levels of abstraction. In the end this becomes for some a full-time occupation—both the beginning and the end of philosophy; but not, as we shall see, for all.

2

G. E. Moore: Sense Data

We may date the beginning of the earliest stage of analysis with the work of G. E. Moore. Moore was interested in asking what appeared to be philosophically naïve questions about the statements of philosophers, though upon close inspection those questions turned out to be rather sophisticated. We might call his sort of question a 'the emperor has no clothes' question—after the fable of the little boy who saw what others wouldn't and who had the courage to tell what he saw. It aimed at showing that opinions thought solidly founded or questions thought well-conceived were faulty because they presumed too much that required further argument, or had been stated misleadingly, or had unacceptable consequences, or required for adequate answer to be divided into several different questions.

What the Problem Is and How It Arises

One of the recurring nests of problems in philosophy is associated with perception. What is it that we really perceive when, as we say, we perceive material objects? Are the things we perceive real? Do we have a good reason for believing in a world outside ourselves? Consider the following sorts of statements, which appear pretentious or profound according to the readers' philosophic predilections and sophistication.

"The things which we see about us are mere shadows and exemplars of things which Truly Exist."

"We never know anything but the ideas in our own minds."

"All Reality is Mental."

"Matter does not Exist."

"To be is to be perceived."

"Matter is the permanent possibility of sensation."

At least since Plato's time philosophers have made these and similar statements while asking what we can know and how it is we know that we know. Many religions, St. Thomas Aquinas' version of Christianity for example, hold that matter is not really real, that it exists only in some secondary sense, that it is not eternal, that mind or spirit or soul exist truly and are eternal.

But these statements are very far from what ordinary men believe and even from what philosophers believe in their ordinary moments. For even philosophers usually believe that what they see exists, and that there is an external world composed of material things outside of themselves. But when they begin to philosophize they seem to leave their ordinary beliefs behind and a great gap opens between what they say is *really* true and what intelligent non-philosophers believe to be true.

Moore found that he was very interested in what men said about such problems, in what their analyses and solutions of them were, and in what arguments they could bring forward to support their analyses and solutions. All this is stated clearly in the lectures which make up his book, *Some Main Problems of Philosophy*. In his *Autobiography* he says:

> I do not think that the world or the sciences would ever have suggested to me any philosophic problems. What has suggested philosophic problems to me is things which other philosophers have said about the world or the sciences. In many problems suggested in this way I have been (and still am) very keenly interested—the problems in question being mainly of two sorts,

namely, first, the problem of trying to get really clear as to what on earth a given philosopher *meant* by something which he said, and, secondly, the problem of discovering what really satisfactory reasons there are for supposing that what he meant was true, or, alternatively, was false. I think I have been trying to solve problems of this sort all my life, and I certainly have not been nearly so successful in solving them as I should have liked to be.[1]

Moore held, as other philosophers before him, that there was a fund of knowledge which men shared, that there were many things which we simply know to be true and that to doubt these things was just to be perverse. According to Moore, we all know, for example, that it is true to say that matter exists, that minds exist, and that other people exist. We can use these sentences to make meaningful, useful, and true assertions, but what we have not been able to do, according to Moore, is to give a correct analysis of what they mean. This is one of the things he tried to do, though, as we shall see in Chapter 3, he did not himself think that he succeeded.

But Moore did not feel comfortable with abstract statements like 'matter does not exist' or 'all reality is mental' and he preferred to reduce them to less inflated statements involving particular objects: this pencil, that table, etc. A charming and doubtless apocryphal story is told that once when a well-known Idealist was giving a lecture intended to demonstrate that matter did not exist, Moore, who was in the audience, became so enraged at this denial of common sense that he stalked to the front of the room and struck the man in order to demonstrate that it did. In his well-known essay, "A Defense of Common Sense,"[2] he begins by listing a set of common-sense beliefs which he claims to know with certainty to be true. He does not say that matter exists or that minds exist but he does say "there exists at present a living human body, which is *my* body. This body was born at a certain time in the past and has existed continuously ever since. . . . I have, at different times since my body was born, had many different experiences. . . . I have often perceived both my own body and other things which formed part of its environment including other bodies. . . ." *(PP,* 33)

Among the things which common sense appears to reveal is that we have or are acquainted with sense data. Whatever sense data are, Moore is led to them by the problem of what we can know. In Chapter 2 of *Some Main Problems of Philosophy*[3] he opens his discussion of sense data by asking what sort of thing our knowledge of material objects is, supposing for the moment that we really do have knowledge of them. If there is such knowledge, it will be at the very least knowledge based upon the senses. In the main he discusses just one sense: sight. Any general point about sight he thinks will be equally valid of the other senses as well. Seeing an object is a mental occurrence. Moore will not be interested in all the physiological processes which accompany and make it possible. These are difficult to discern and highly technical, while seeing itself is known to us simply and directly. His own acts of seeing can be observed by the subject while his physiological processes cannot, at least without special training.

Moore immediately introduces a practical example: ". . . it is, I think, very important for everyone, in these subjects, to consider carefully single concrete instances, so that there may be no mistake as to exactly what it is that is being talked about. Such mistakes are, I think, very apt to happen, if one talks merely in generalities. . . ." *(SMPOP,* 29) He asked his audience to observe an envelope which he held up. Everyone who looked saw the same object occupying one distinct region in space. More exactly, everyone who looked saw a whitish patch of a certain definite size and shape. This whitish patch of a certain definite size and shape Moore calls a sense datum. When we use our vision to look at an object, to see what is around us, to know what is there outside us, it is sense data with which we are first acquainted and which we first come to know. On this view our knowledge of material objects would be first and foremost knowledge of sense data. Moore holds that whenever he knows or judges that some proposition about a material object is true—'here is a hand', 'there is a pen'— ". . . there is always some *sense datum* about which the proposition in question is a proposition— some sense datum which is *a* subject (and, in a certain sense, the principle or ultimate subject) of the proposition in question. . . ." (ADOCS, 54)

This appears quite straightforward and natural. What could be more obvious than that whenever we see some material object, we are seeing, judging about, picking out, or describing what Moore calls a sense datum—that is, its color, size, and shape. Try it. Look at a material object—a chair, a table, a rock, or a house. What do you see? You see its color, its size, and its shape, and although you notice many peculiarities about its color, size, and shape—gradations, variations in shading and outline—it is the color, size, and shape which you do see.

Although the term 'sense data' may be new, the line of thought leading to it is quite old. Similar things were spoken of in the seventeenth and eighteenth centuries by Locke, Berkeley, and Hume though they were called by other names then. In Moore's view, the different uses these philosophers made of what he calls sense data have raised enormous problems which they could not solve. Some of these Moore thought he had put right, but others and newer ones which he raised plagued him always. In later years he wrote that he did not see his way to a solution of many of these.

Berkeley used some lines of argument leading to sense data in order to show that matter did not exist, and Hume used other lines of argument leading to sense data to place into doubt that we could ever know either that it did or that it did not. But Moore was persuaded as an article of common sense both that matter did exist and that we knew that it existed. His problem was to give a correct analysis of propositions about sense data which would show what it meant to say this. If what we are immediately acquainted with when we see a material object is a sense datum, then a number of questions come to mind: 1) what are sense data? 2) how are they related to material objects? 3) how are they related to our minds? Questions 2) and 3) are crucial, for if we cannot answer them, we leave it open whether there are or are not material bodies and must rest content with Hume's position that we cannot show that there are. Should we find that in answering question 3) we are driven to say that sense data are in any way creatures of or dependent upon our minds, then we may have to rest with Berkeley's conclusion that there is no matter and that whatever is is mental. Both of these conclusions deny what any man with the least common sense knows: that there are material bodies independent of us and that we know that there are. Moore strives to avoid the positions of both Berkeley and Hume and any possible variants of them. Although he was certain that material bodies exist independent of minds, Moore had many difficulties about how to account for them. A more detailed description of his position will make this clearer.

Sense Data: What They Are

According to Moore, sense data are the objects of our immediate or direct perception. Confining ourselves to the sense of sight, we may say that sense data are what we actually see when we look at something. What we actually see when we look at something is quite different from what we may infer. If we observe a man walking out of a room in the direction of his front door and observe him returning moments later with envelopes in his hand, then what we have actually seen is just that: his leaving and returning with envelopes. We may or may not have evidence to infer that he answered the postman's ring and now has mail in his hand, but whether we do or do not have evidence for this, we did not actually see it. Now, when we look at something, what we see is a colored patch of a certain size and shape about which we may or may not think we have enough evidence to infer that it either is or is not related to or caused by some material body. According to Moore, we do not directly see the material body, or at least we do not see all of it. This last qualification will be made clearer below.

Moore generally reasons closely about concrete examples in his writings. In "A Defense of Common Sense" *(PP,* 32–59) he asks the reader to look at his own right hand (54). What the reader sees when he does so will be a sense datum. In "The Nature and Reality of Objects of Perception"[4] he describes what is our experience of seeing a red and a blue book "side by side upon a shelf" (68). We notice the two colors each having a certain size and shape and we notice that these two colored patches, as we may call them, have a particular spatial relation to each other and perhaps to other patches which we may happen to be observing. We have directly perceived these things and only these things. Whatever other properties we mean to ascribe to them when we say that the perceived objects are in fact books, they are not properties directly perceived when we view them in the manner described. These things directly seen when we look at physical objects under *normal* conditions are some of the sorts of things that Moore means by sense data. The word *normal* is emphasized because it is very difficult to specify exactly what normal conditions are,[5] and even under such conditions as may roughly be described as normal there are still many problems about sense data. In order to say that normal conditions obtain when an observer is looking at an object, we need at least to have a human being whose color vision is normal and who lacks double vision or blurred vision, we need natural bright daylight, and we need clear air as the intervening medium. We could, of course, substitute any conditions which compensated for the lack of these.

But we are also acquainted with sense data under conditions which are not normal. When we look at a red book we see a patch of a certain size, shape, and color which is spatially related to other patches of different size, shape, and color. If, while looking at the book, we press one eyeball, we will get two patches somewhat superimposed one upon the other. When we place a stick in the water we now see the patch which appeared straight, as crooked. When we put drops in our eyes, a colored patch which had sharp outlines becomes a colored patch with blurred outlines. When we magnify an object sufficiently, the patch or sense datum becomes radically altered so that its color, size, and shape bear little resemblance to those it had before. When we look at a white wall through blue spectacles we have a blue sense datum. Even under *normal* conditions our sense data change shape and size with the distance and the angle at which we view the object.

Moore held that the class of entities which he called sense data contained other things as well. In "The Status Of Sense Data" *(PS,* 168–96) he lists five subclasses of things which are all sense data: 1) images had while awake which are not sensations of objects existing in front of the perceiver—what you would be having if you were away from home and summoned up an image of your room at home, or if you were away from everyone you knew and summoned up an image of someone you loved; 2) dream experiences; 3) hallucinations and illusions; 4) after-images—what you experience when you stare at a bright light and then close your eyes; 5) what you see what you observe an object under *normal* or *abnormal* conditions. In each of these sets of cases there are entities which are experienced. These entities which are experienced and any like them which are not experienced but which could be, Moore designates 'sense data' (in this article he calls them 'sensibles', pp. 168–70). He implies that entities of the sort described in these five classifications have two characteristics in common. One characteristic is that they are all capable of being experienced and the other he thinks is unanalyzable. I think it fair to say that Moore spends much more time in trying to analyze propositions about the entities in the fifth classification—what is directly seen when you observe an object under *normal* or *abnormal* conditions, than he does in analyzing propositions about the other four, although all raise questions which puzzle him greatly.

Sense data, then, have been specified in two ways. First, they are the sorts of entities with which we are acquainted in direct or immediate perception. I assume that Moore means to hold that this is a *necessary* condition for something to be a sense datum. Nothing which cannot be an object of direct or immediate perception can be a sense datum. But we can also have relations with sense data which are not direct or immediate perception. We can think about them and form judgments about them, and this would be quite different from being directly or immediately related to them in any way. I do not think that Moore wants to maintain that having direct or immediate acquaintance with something is a *sufficient* condition for that thing being a sense datum, for he does hold that we can be directly acquainted with our own acts of consciousness and that we directly apprehend propositions. I do not think that he means by sense data any of these things.[6]

Sense data data are also specified as the sorts of things falling in any of the classes 1-5 which were enumerated above. To these two specifications (that they can be directly experienced, and that they are any of the things in classes 1-5) Moore adds a third. Sense data are the ultimate subjects of propositions or judgments about objects of the senses. Since one is always directly acquainted with sense data when one looks at or observes an object, it is in the most fundamental way sense data about which one judges, thinks, or speaks. For example, look at your hand. For Moore, what you see is a sense datum and not either your whole hand or—though he vacillated on this a good deal—any part of it. When you look at your hand and say 'this is a hand', the 'this' refers to the sense datum you are immediately perceiving. For example, Moore says, "that what I know, with regard to this sense datum, when I know 'This is a human hand,' is not that it is *itself* a human hand, seems to me certain because I know that my hand has many parts . . . which are quite certainly *not* parts of this sense datum. . . . I hold it to be quite certain that I do not *directly* perceive *my hand;* and that when I am said (as I may be correctly said) to 'perceive' it, that I 'perceive' it means that I perceive (in a different and more fundamental sense) something which is . . . *representative* of it. . . ." ("A Defense of Common Sense," *PP,* 55)

Sense data, then, are at least the sorts of things of which it is true to say 1) that they are the objects of direct acquaintance or immediate perception; 2) that they are the objects which fall into the classes 1-5; 3) that they are in some sense the ultimate subjects of judgments about objects of the senses.

The Relation of Sense Data to Our Minds

Moore held that sense data were related to our minds in a way in which whole physical objects were not. They are the objects of immediate or direct apprehension or of acquaintance. Furthermore, in his discussion of different modes of sensory experience—seeing, hearing, smelling, and feeling—he said that the same kind of relation is involved in seeing objects, hearing sounds, feeling and smelling things. The relation is the same, but the objects to which we are related—the sense data—are different. He extends this idea to the relation we have to mental images and the like ("The Status of Sense-Data," *PS*, 172-73).

We have come this far; if we are to know anything of the world external to ourselves, we must use our senses to perceive that world. The relation which we have through our senses to their immediate objects of perception, no matter what sense or what sort of object is involved, is the relation of immediate or direct apprehension. When we see, we see something and in the first instance that thing is a sensible or a sense datum. But how do we know that the thing that we perceive directly is not utterly dependent upon our senses having perceived it, an object with no existence apart from our sensing of it, a creature of our own minds? How do we know that there is anything outside of ourselves? How, in a word, do we know that Berkeley may not have been correct?

It is clear that Moore thinks that he does *know* that there is an external material world and that Berkeley was wrong. In addition, he gives arguments to show that sensations must be distinct from the objects of which they are sensations, that our perception of a colored body is distinct from the body itself, that our experience is one thing, and that of which we have experience is another. For him sense data are related to our minds, but not dependent upon them. He wishes to hold that at least those sense data which we generally perceive under normal or abnormal conditions—class 5 in our list—also exist unperceived.

At one time Moore held that a good reason to believe that sense data exist separately and apart from our perceiving them was just that we have a strong propensity to believe that they do ("The Status of Sense-Data," *PS,* 181). This is in itself scarcely conclusive proof. But put in Moore's characteristically strong language and buttressed by arguments designed to show that the usual arguments designed to prove that sense data do not exist apart from our perceiving them are inconclusive, it carries a good deal of force. In "The Refutation of Idealism" *(PS,* 1–30) he uses many arguments to show that it cannot be proven that the statement 'to be is to be perceived', *esse est percipi,* is true in any important sense. He thinks that this proposition is necessary to prove that Idealism—the view that all reality is spiritual or mental—in any form is correct. Therefore he thinks that if he can show this proposition to be false, while Idealism is not refuted, it is rendered unprovable. If he can show this, then he thinks he will have shown that there is a good reason to think that there is a distinction between an object and our experiencing of it. But the object of our experience is a sense datum. Hence he will have shown that there is a good reason to suppose that sense data are not mind-dependent.

The argument showing that *esse est percipi* cannot be proven may be outlined basically in four parts. Three of these concern possible ways of interpreting the statement itself, 'to be is to be perceived'.

I. The 'is' of 'to be is to be perceived' denotes equivalence. 'To be' means just 'to be perceived'. The expressions are synonymous. Moore holds this to be obviously incorrect. What is meant by the words 'to be' is not what is meant by the words 'to be perceived' (8–9).

II. 'To be' is in some way necessarily connected with 'to be perceived'. That is, ". . . 'the object of experience is inconceivable apart from the subject.' " (12) But Moore argues that this is false. If it were the case, then to deny the statement 'to be is to be perceived' would be to make a contradiction. If any statement is a necessary statement, if its subject is necessarily connected with its predicate, then its denial is a contradiction. If you try to deny such statements as 'all bodies are extended,' or 'all bachelors are unmarried males', or 'triangles have three interior angles' you will contradict yourself. You will be asserting something and then denying the very thing you asserted. But it is not at all obvious that to deny the statement 'to be is to be perceived' is to make a contradiction. Indeed, Moore holds that if this were true then there could be no distinction between the object and the experiencing of it. But we all do make such a distinction without ever feeling that we contradict ourselves and a strong part of his argument consists in his developing this distinction, as we will see shortly. Hence, 'to be' is not necessarily connected to 'to be perceived'.

III. The statement 'to be is to be perceived' may be synthetically necessary. That is, to deny it may not cause a contradiction, but that in some unspecified way 'to be' is inseparably connected with 'to be perceived'. But if this were so, there would be no way to prove that it was so. For statements of this kind there is no handy test as there is for analytic statements like 'all bodies are extended.' Why, then, should we believe it?

IV. This is Moore's major argument and to spell it out in detail will give a notion of what Moore considers a sound and detailed argument. There is a distinction, he says, between an object and a sensation, which is a sensation of the object. An experience is one thing and that of which it is an experience is another. The argument proceeds in the following way (17 f.):

1. The sensation of blue differs from the sensation of green.
2. But they are both sensations and therefore must have something in common.
3. What they have in common is called 'consciousness'.
4. There are, then, two distinct terms in every sensation:
   a) what they both have in common—consciousness;

b) whatever it is that makes one sensation differ from another. This is to be called the 'object of sensation'.

5. Blue is one object of sensation, green another.

6. Consciousness, which sensations of blue and sensations of green have in common, is different from either blue or green.

7. At times the sensation of blue exists in my mind and at times it does not.

8. But if the sensation of blue includes both consciousness and blue, then when the sensation of blue exists in my mind either
   a) consciousness exists alone;
   b) blue exists alone;
   c) consciousness and blue exist.

9. a), b), and c) are different alternatives.

10. Therefore to say b) is to say something different from saying c). To say they are the same is to contradict oneself.

11. To say that the sensation of blue exists and the sensation of green exists is to say that consciousness also exists, for it is consciousness which is common to both sensations. It is consciousness in virtue of which both are sensations.

12. Since consciousness is a necessary element in sensation, b) cannot be the case.

13. Then either a) or c) is the case.

14. Therefore the existence of blue, b), cannot be the same thing as the existence of the sensation of blue. We are left with either a) or c), but not both together.

15. Therefore the object of sensation must be different from the sensation itself. For to claim that blue is the same as consciousness plus blue is to claim that a part is the same as a whole of which it is only part, or else to identify it with something which it is not: namely the other part.

Moore moves to another tack designed to explicate step 15.

16. Steps 11–13 show that when we have a sensation either a) consciousness exists alone or c) consciousness and blue exist together. Which is the case, and if c) is the case, in what sense do consciousness and its object exist *together?*

Those philosophers to whom Moore is opposed hold that when we have a sensation, c) is the case; that is, both consciousness and its object exist together as an inseparable whole, for they hold that what Moore calls the object of the sensation is really something which they call its *content.* In order to show that this is not true, Moore's next step is to continue the argument by asking what it means to say that one thing is the content of another. He argues that in no relevant sense can blue be called the *content* of a sensation. The argument proceeds by *reductio ad absurdum.* Moore assumes what he wishes to deny—that blue *can* be called the content of a blue sensation—and then draws from that assumption an absurd consequence. Consider a blue flower or a blue bead. Here blue is rightly said to be part of the *content* of the *flower* or *bead,* but it cannot in the same sense be said to be part of the *content* of *consciousness.*

17. To say that 'blue' is part of the content of the sensation of blue is then to say that it has the same relation to the other parts of the sensation of blue as it has to the other parts of the blue flower or bead.
18. But consciousness is the other part of the sensation of blue.
19. Therefore blue has the same relation to consciousness in the sensation of blue as it has to the rest of the flower in a blue flower or to the rest of the bead in a blue bead.
20. The relation between blue and a blue flower or bead is the same as the relation between a thing and its qualities: to say the thing exists is just to say that its qualities exist as well.

21. On this view, if you argue that blue is a part of the content of the sensation of blue, then you are saying that a sensation of blue differs from a blue bead in that a blue bead is made of glass and a sensation of blue is made of consciousness.

Although the argument takes some complicated digressions here, the point Moore is driving at is that if all this were true, then just as a bead is blue because it is made of blue glass, so consciousness would be blue when we had a sensation of blue. But Moore concludes (26) that although for all he knows consciousness may actually be blue, there is no reason to think so, for that fact is never revealed in introspection or in any other way. Although c) is the case—consciousness and its object do exist together—they do not do so as an inseparable whole.

He concludes by saying that consciousness ". . . has to blue the simple and unique relation the existence of which alone justifies us in distinguishing knowledge of a thing from the thing known, indeed in distinguishing mind from matter. And this result I may express by saying that what is called the *content* of a sensation is in very truth what I originally called it—the sensation's *object.*" (26) In having a sensation we are outside the circle of our own ideas and thus reach out to something which is independent of our experience of it. There is no reason to think the proposition *esse est percipi* is true and no reason to think all objects depend for their existence upon a mind to think them.

The Relation of Sense Data to Material Bodies

How are the visual sense data we have related to material bodies? There are several possibilities: 1) there are no bodies and hence no problem about such a relation arises; 2) the sense data are the bodies about which we speak and hence no problem arises; 3) they are parts of the surfaces of bodies; 4) they are related to bodies in some unanalyzable way which we do not know.

Moore disregards the first possibility because, as we saw,

he thought he had good reason to think it false—namely, that common sense and the extended argument we have just followed clearly show that not everything is mental. Indeed, Moore takes the argument to show that sense data are not mental. The second possibility is also disregarded because it is obvious that when I look at something, like my hand, the thing which I take to be my hand has many properties that the sense datum has not. The sense datum is not composed of bones, skin, blood, and cartilage, but my hand is. Thus the sense datum cannot be my whole hand. Perhaps the third suggestion is true and the sense datum is part of the surface of the hand—part of the surface because one only sees (has a sense datum) of that part which is turned toward one's eyes. This analysis intrigued Moore and, in spite of very grave objections which he raised to it, he vacillated between it and the fourth suggestion.

Moore begins a very cautious analysis of the relation in his essay, "Some Judgments of Perception" *(PS,* 220–52). When an ordinary opaque material object is visually presented to me and I say something like 'this is a sofa', 'that is an ink-stand', or 'that is a tree', I am not, or ought not to be, saying or thinking that what is presented to me—the sense datum—is a whole sofa, inkstand, or tree, for at most what I am presented with is a part of the surface of the object, if that. Indeed, an inkstand is presented to me in such a way that I cannot get at it directly, but only through the media-tion of the sense datum. Moore says, "it is not given to me, in the sense in which the sense-datum is given. If there be such a thing at all, it is quite certainly only known to me by description, in the sense in which Mr. Russell uses that phrase; and the description by which it is known is that of being *the* thing which stands to this sense-datum in a certain relation." (234) To say 'this is an inkstand' is to say that I am presented with a sense datum referred directly to by *this,* and there is something which has to the sense datum some unknown relation, and that thing is an inkstand.[7]

Let us suppose that the unknown relation in question is the relation of 'being part of the surface of'. Then to say 'this is a door' is to say that the thing referred to by *this*—the sense datum—is a part of the surface of the door. But is it true that the sense datum is a part of the surface of the material object? Moore raises a powerful objection. Consider the case where we say that something, *x*—a sense datum—which I saw before, is the same *x* which I see now and I know that no change has taken place in it. Now look at a book on a desk while seated at the desk, then look at it from across the room. Look at a coin with your line of vision perpendicular to its surface, then turn it slightly. Look at a white wall and then put your sunglasses on. In each case we would be prepared to deny that the surface of the object actually changed; yet in each case something appears to have changed. The book seems smaller, the coin seems elliptical, and the wall seems green or yellow.

But if we are not prepared to admit, as in fact we are not, that the surface of the object did change in each case, then how can the surface be thought identical with the sense datum with which we are presented? A similar problem arises when many different perceivers are presented with a view of the same object. They each see it differently. Can all these different and mutually incompatible sense data really be parts of the identical surface? The answer would certainly seem to be no, and these objections seem fatal to the view that the sense datum is identical with the surface of the material object.

At this point one might say, as Moore on occasion did, that though it was highly unlikely that all these different sense data were parts of identically the same surface, still it just might be the case that they were. This is unsatisfactory because neither Moore nor anybody else, so far as I know, has been able to explain precisely how this could be. Another suggestion that Moore makes is that although it seems to be the case that these sense data presented to different observers at the same time or to the same observer at different times are different sense data, they may not in fact *be* different: that the sense datum corresponding to the book when seen close-up may not really be perceived to *be* larger than the sense datum of the book from a distance, but it is rather perceived to *seem* larger. (245–46) On this view sense data might appear different than they really are and we would have no direct or immediate relation to them. But what could this relation of 'seeming different' be like? One of the reasons for introducing sense data into our epistemology is just that there was a need for something with which we are directly acquainted when we perceive. To adopt the above line of attack seems to destroy that direct relation—immediate apprehension—and with it, the whole point of having sense data in the first place. Moore claimed that if there is such a relation between us and sense data as 'seeming different', it would have to be ultimate and unanalyzable and that he realized that many objections could be raised, among them that it was nonsensical. In his "Visual Sense-Data"[8] which was written much later, Moore, in speaking of this suggestion says charmingly, "I well remember that, at the Aristotelian meeting at which I read that paper, Russell said that the suggestion certainly *was* nonsensical. I now feel sure that he was right. . . ." (136) If it is not adopted, he sees no way left to argue for the position that a sense datum is identical with part of the surface of a material object.

There is one alternative left. The sense datum directly presented to us is related in some way to a material object but not as part of its surface. Moore confesses that he does not know what this relation could be. He suggests that the relation might be one of cause and effect—that the material object may be one of a possible number of causes of the sense datum. If this is denied, then he has only one other suggestion to make: that the relation between material objects and sense data is simply ultimate and unanalyzable. He gives this relation the name 'being a manifestation of' and he has little else to say about it. Other philosophers, less sure of what they *know* to be true, might take other ways out by denying that there are such things as material bodies or sense data. But Moore was not to be persuaded that what he *knew* to be true was false merely because he could not find a satisfactory analysis of it, and he never abandoned his belief in either.

The External World

If Moore truly held these views, how could he justify his belief in the external world of everyday material objects outside himself? Moore's answer is that he *knows* it exists and that's that. Armed with such an answer he attacks views purporting to show that material objects and the external world do not exist or that we cannot know whether or not they exist. Moore argues that certain principles of Hume's have been used to support such views, and in *Some Main Problems of Philosophy* he argues against them (108–44). Let us look at the essential outline of his argument, ignoring certain details and digressions to which only the full text can do justice.

It is clear from everything Moore has said that in his view we are directly acquainted with or directly apprehend only sense data and not material objects. It is important to bear this in mind in thinking about the argument Moore presents. Moore begins by stating Hume's principles which, he is careful to say, Hume may have expressed differently. Hume may have meant more or less than what Moore will state, but that is not important here. What is important is to see first that people have held that if the two rules or principles (which follow in the next paragraph) are correct, then we do not and cannot know that any material objects exist; second, it is important to see how Moore refutes such an argument, at least to his own satisfaction.

After preliminaries giving definitions of certain terms in the rules (108–9), Moore summarizes them: "I will call the first the rule: That nobody can ever know of the existence of anything which he has not directly apprehended, unless he knows that something which he has directly apprehended is *a sign* of its existence. And I will call the second the rule: That nobody can ever know that the existence of any one thing A is a *sign* of the *existence* of another thing B, unless he himself (or, under certain conditions, somebody else) has experienced a *general conjunction* between *things like* A and *things like* B. And the important thing to remember about this second rule is that nobody can be said to have *experienced a conjunction* between any two things, unless he has *directly apprehended* both the things.*" (109–10) These rules say a) that if you are not directly acquainted with something, then you cannot know it exists unless you are directly acquainted with a sign of it; b) you cannot know that one thing is a sign of another unless you know (have experienced) some usual or general connection between one and the other; c) you cannot know of or experience a general connection between two things unless you are directly or immediately acquainted with both of them.

If Hume's rules are true, then we cannot know that material bodies exist because we are not acquainted with them; remember, we are directly acquainted only with sense data. Furthermore, no one can say that sense data are a sign of material bodies unless he has experienced a general connection between sense data and material bodies. No one can experience a general connection between sense data and material bodies unless he is or has been directly acquainted with both sense data and material bodies. But by hypothesis, by the whole sense datum theory, no one can be directly acquainted with material bodies. Since the only two ways the rules allow for one to know of the existence of material bodies are blocked, it follows from these rules that we cannot know that material bodies exist.

Now the argument Moore is concerned to refute can be put this way:

A—If Hume's two rules are true, then we cannot know that material bodies exist.

B—Hume's two rules are true.

Therefore, C—We cannot (do not) know that material bodies exist.

The main thrust of Moore's attack will deny B—that Hume's rules are true (119ff.). It is intuitively obvious that given statements A and B, statement C follows. But A is of the form of an ordinary conditional statement—'if p then q' —where p and q are any two statements you like. By a law of elementary logic called the law of contraposition, if any conditional statement is true, then the new statement formed by replacing the antecedent (in this case *p*) by the denial of the consequent (not-*q*) and replacing the consequent *(q)* by the denial of the antecedent (not-*p*) will also be true. So if it is true to say 'if *p* then *q*', by contraposition, it is also true to say 'if not-*q* then not-*p*'. Applying this law to statement A and letting *p* = 'Hume's rules are true' and *q* = 'we cannot know material bodies exist' we get a new statement A': 'if we can know that material bodies exist, then Hume's rules are not true.' If A is true then A' must also be true.

Now Moore says, *"my* argument is this: I do know that this pencil exists; therefore Hume's principles are false." (120) That is:

A'—If we can know that material bodies exist, then Hume's principles are false.

C —We can (do) know that material bodies exist.

Therefore, *B'*—Hume's principles are false.

Is this a good argument? Moore thinks so. He says that a ". . . conclusive argument is one which enables us to *know* that its conclusion is true." (120) And its conclusion must also follow strictly from the premises. The first argument using *A* as a premise is certainly valid. Its conclusion definitely follows from its premises. The second argument using *A'* as a premise is also valid, for its conclusion follows as well. Both are equally valid but they lead to different conclusions. The arguments are incompatible for if we accept one of them we cannot accept the other. How shall we decide? Moore has stated one condition of a good and conclusive argument— that we should know that the premises are true. Premises *A* and *A'* are equally true or false. If you accept one of them you must accept the other for they are logically equivalent. But given the explanation of Hume's rules it seems obvious that both *A* and *A'* are true: 'if Hume's rules are true then we cannot know that material bodies exist' and 'if we can know that material bodies exist then Hume's rules are false'. Premise *B* states 'Hume's two rules are true' and the equivalent premise in Moore's counterargument is C', 'we can know that material bodies exist'. Which of these is true: B or C'?

Moore holds, with some plausibility, that it is infinitely more certain that I know material bodies exist than that I know Hume's two rules are true. Pragmatically speaking, we live in and operate with a world of material bodies, but it is not at all clear that we live in a world and operate with Hume's two rules. Therefore he holds that argument A', C'/B' is a good and conclusive argument because it has two premises which we know to be true, while the other has only one which we know to be true and one which is dubious.

In a sense we have come full circle. The problem of sense data arose because we asked what we can learn through the senses and appeared to discover that sense data blocked us from the material world. Attempts to analyze propositions about the material world led Moore to sense data, and his analysis could not get beyond them. But to say that Moore could not find the proper analysis of statements about the material world is not to say that he felt that he had to abandon his belief in it, and this last extended argument was an exhibition of his determination not to give up those beliefs of common sense which he knew to be true, merely because he could not solve major puzzles which they raised.

Moore seems to have been led into a position from which he could not extricate himself, for at least two reasons. First, as he stated it was neither science nor the world which interested him in philosophic problems but rather what other men had said about the world.[9] He therefore paid little attention to science. But acquaintance with and interest in psychology and physiology might have opened to Moore a far greater range of cases of perception. What this wider range of cases would have shown is that a theory of sense data is much more difficult to construct and much less neat—though not impossible—if it is to do justice to all types of perceptual phenomena and to all the senses. This notion is worked out with great ingenuity on purely linguistic grounds by J. L. Austin.[10] But an adequate solution to the problems of perception—of which sense data is one—seems to require at least some knowledge of the relevant sciences. To say this is not to argue that scientific advances solve all philosophic problems, for they don't, though many philosophic problems are dissolved by them. Science as it advances raises at least as many new problems of conceptual elucidation and metaphysics as it dissolves. But it does seem true to say that one is better able to handle conceptual problems about certain phenomena if one is thoroughly acquainted with the phenomena; and it is science which makes us acquainted with the phenomena of perception. It does indeed seem curious how often empirically minded philosophers have lacked interest in getting straight the empirical situation.

The second reason was that, in spite of his deep awareness of the subtleties of language, Moore appears not to have seen that the positing of the sorts of objects he called sense data or at least his way of positing them would leave him open to attacks which attempt to show that something is wrong from a purely conceptual or linguistic point of view. Now from this point of view Gilbert Ryle argues that the whole notion of sense data arises from a failure to use our language correctly and will not, therefore, stand scrutiny.[11] The reader will be interested to compare Moore's analysis with Ryle's attack to see how it fits.

There is also a curious linguistic notion which runs through the work of the early analysts—Moore, Russell, and the early Wittgenstein—the idea that the prime function of words, or even of sentences, is to name things. One is to look for the things to which the words refer. So if one can talk about one's ideas or sensa or the content of one's sensations, then it is likely there is some *thing* corresponding to the words. It should not be thought that Moore was so naïve as to think that every word actually referred to some entity, but it is hard to rid oneself of the idea that in coming to the notion of sense data as a residue of his analysis of perception, Moore was half induced to think of them as entities—to reify or substantialize them—because he held some such view of the function of words. This view of the function of words will occupy us at some length in the next chapter.

3

G. E. Moore:
Meaning and Reference

A basic theme that runs through Moore's views on meaning is that words or groups of words most often function as names. They stand for or point to something, and what they stand for or point to is the meaning of that word or group of words. As we shall soon see, in his early work Moore goes further than this, arguing that the basic constituents of the world are certain entities which properly combined form the propositions—the meanings of the groups of words. This meaning is what the words stand for. The entities in turn are what the world is composed of. Such a view can be called Platonism.

Propositions: An Early View

Moore's important early view of propositions is set out in "The Nature of Judgment"[1] where his starting point is F. H. Bradley's Idealistic treatise, *The Principles of Logic*. There he wants to revise Bradley's implicit criticism of philosophers like Locke. He wants to treat Locke's theory of judgment more harshly than he thought Bradley had done, by purging it of certain mental elements which Locke had introduced. In doing this he has a good deal to say, by way of comment, on Kant's work, about which he had written his Fellowship dissertation in the years 1896–98.

In *An Essay concerning Human Understanding* Locke had written that "the faculty which God has given man to supply the want of clear and certain knowledge, in cases where that cannot be had, is *judgment:* whereby the mind takes its ideas to agree or disagree; or, which is the same, any proposition to be true or false. . . ."[2] And in the "Introduction" (8) he said that the word 'idea' is ". . . that term which, I think, serves best to stand for whatsover is the *object* of the understanding when a man thinks. . . . [It] express[es] whatever is meant by *phantasm, notion, species*. . . ." According to Locke, then, ideas are psychic phenomena: whatever one has in the mind, whether little pictures, images or simulacra, concepts, or the like. Judgment consists in a comparison of these with one another or to things which they represent or for which they stand. Moore holds that this view is untenable. Let us state Moore's position.

He begins by quoting some passages from Bradley to the effect that judgment is at least in part about our ideas as mental entities, and whether they do in fact correspond with what is the case or reality. These passages he then proceeds to attack. What he wants to show is that ". . . the 'idea used in judgment' is not a part of the content of our ideas, nor produced by any action of our minds, and that hence truth and falsehood are not dependent on the relations of *our* ideas to reality." ("NJ,"177) Moore introduces the word 'concept' by which he means the same as Bradley's 'universal meaning'. We may understand it as something very like the textbook notion of Plato's Forms or Ideas, which are different from any mental entities. Concepts are not dependent upon any mind to think them and so are neither abstractions nor ideas in the sense of Locke. They are immutable; they can be the objects of mental acts on our part and therefore can be related to the knowing subject by some action on his part; but they are indifferent to our mental acts.

Examples of such concepts would be 'red' or 'white' or 'large' or 'soft' or 'flower' or 'chair'. They are not individuals or particulars. They exist in some eternal way. Their proper conjunction gives rise in some way to more specific concepts and to particular things. For instance the combination of 'red', 'large', 'soft,' and 'flower' gives rise along with further unspecified concepts to the concept 'rose'. These in turn combined with the concepts 'now' and 'this' give us a particular rose. (179) Neither Moore nor Plato before him specified more exactly what this combining or participating of concepts or Forms was. They were also unable to say exactly what concepts there were. Plato brings up many criticisms of his own theory in the *Parmenides* and I believe that Moore is open to similar ones. By 1910 he appears to have abandoned this portion of his theory.

Then a proposition on Moore's view is composed neither of words nor thoughts nor any mental entities, but of concepts related in a certain way. When you say 'this rose is red' you are talking neither about words nor ideas, but, as above, you are ". . . asserting . . . a specific connexion of certain concepts forming the total concept 'rose' with the concepts 'this' and 'now' and 'red'. . . ." (179) Moore calls a proposition a complex concept or a synthesis of concepts which can stand to each other in an infinite number of relations. Propositions are said to be true or false according to the relations which their concepts have to each other, and not according to whether or not they correspond to some existing reality. A proposition like 'the cat is on the mat' is true on this view *not* because there really is a cat on the mat, as one might ordinarily think, but for other reasons. Indeed, here it is not some state of affairs that is the object of belief when someone believes something, but the proposition itself.

Truth or falsity is ascribed to propositions in virtue of the relations among the concepts of which they are composed. One must immediately recognize that a proposition is true or false just as one recognizes whether a rose is red or yellow. One cannot say what yellow is, nor red, nor truth, nor good, because these things are ultimately simple and undefinable.[3] One either recognizes that a rose is red or one doesn't. There is nothing else to say. A red rose is exhibited and if you do not see that it is red no explanation appears possible. Moore holds the same view about true and false.

Although Moore gives a number of short arguments in order to support his views about propositions, it does not seem that these are either conclusive or convincing as they stand. One such argument is that if the truth of a proposition depended on some relation to reality, such as the fact that the particular combination of concepts making up the proposition stood for or referred to something which is really to be found among things in the world, then we could call concepts alone true or false as well. We would not have to have them related as propositions and then call only the proposition true or false. Even aside from Moore's theory, on our own usual view this would be odd, for we tend in many cases to think of words like 'red' or 'fast', which stand for concepts, as referring to or pointing them out: that is, as denoting. We think of the name 'Mr. Jones' as denoting or standing for some real man, Mr. Jones. But we think of propositions or declarative sentences as asserting or denying that something is the case and it is these which we call true or false. Hence, even for us it would be queer to say that red was a *true* concept.

But Moore has an argument against such a view, which is based upon his own theory. If the truth of a proposition depended upon its relation to reality, then, since mere concepts alone and not in combination appeared to stand for or refer to things, mere concepts would appear to have a similar relation to reality. Then these concepts, too, could be said to be true. For concepts like red would seem to be related to whatever red things are in the world. And chimera would be a false concept because there are no chimeras. But the whole notion of correspondence is incorrect for two reasons. First consider the statement '2 + 2 = 4'. It is true ". . . whether there exist two things or not." So some propositions are true without corresponding to any so-called state of affairs. And so it cannot be the case that propositions are true by virtue of such a correspondence. Second, and perhaps more interestingly, Moore doubts whether the concepts of which the proposition consists—the concepts 2 and 4—really do exist. "We should have to stretch our notion of existence beyond intelligibility, to suppose that 2 ever has been, is, or will be an existent." ("NJ," 180) Therefore, concepts like these cannot correspond, to anything and hence they cannot be true by virtue of such a correspondence, and neither, presumably, can the propositions which are made up of them. But this argument hardly seems conclusive, for it is not clear what justification Moore can give for the notion that concepts like the concept of 2 cannot exist.

At this time Moore distinguished between being and existence. Everything seems to have been granted being. If you could mention it, then it *was*. But only those concepts combined in propositions with the concept existence were said to exist. From this it seems to follow that those concepts not in any combination at all could not exist, for *by definition* to exist was to be combined in propositions in a certain way. The way in which you *knew* that tigers existed and chimeras did not was by an elementary intuition much in the way that you knew tigers were striped. Either you saw it or you didn't, and that was that. Thus it seems that to accept on these grounds the notion that 2 could not exist was already to accept Moore's whole theory. But it is just the theory which he is concerned to justify. Hence this argument cannot justify it, for the argument presupposes what is to be shown.

Moreover, although it is certainly true that $2 + 2 = 4$ is true whether or not two things exist, that is so because mathematical propositions are true or false independently of the world. They are analytic. But it remains to be shown that all propositions are like mathematical ones before you can develop an argument from mathematical ones which holds for all of them. Moore did not seem to be aware that he was in danger of blurring the distinction between sentences which we usually think of as true before all experience, like 'all bodies are extended' (how could anything be an unextended body?) and sentences which are true or false according to our experience like 'this rose is red' (it might have been white). On his theory we would be deprived of one important way of discovering whether a proposition is necessarily true or whether it only happens to be the case. For him, at this time we did not compare our sentences with states of affairs, but appeared to discover by some other unspecified means what sentences were true. But we usually think a sentence analytic just when no possible state of affairs could falsify it, and we think of a sentence as not analytic or contingent just in case some possible state of affairs would falsify it. Hence, by denying that the truth of sentences is to be known by comparing them with reality, Moore appears to have made it more difficult to tell analytic ones from contingent ones.

Now, by denying that a proposition is true because it corresponds to reality, Moore reverses the traditional dependence of truth upon existence, which is a result of the correspondence theory of truth. It has often been held that a proposition is true just in case a state of affairs really exists to which it corresponds. Hence the truth of a particular proposition depends upon the existence of that particular state of affairs. But Moore makes it rather the case that existence must be defined in terms of truth, for "when I say 'This paper exists,' I must require that this proposition be true. If it is not true, it is unimportant, and I can have no interest in it. But if it is true, it means only that the concepts, which are combined in specific relations in the concept of this paper, are also combined in a specific manner with the concept of existence. That specific manner is something immediately known, like red or two." (180–81)

Moore goes on to say that the *world* must be seen as formed of concepts which are the only objects of knowledge. This is very much like the view once held by Plato, described above, that real things are congeries or 'intersections' of Forms—Socrates, for him, is a combination of the Forms Whiteness, Manness, Snubnoseness, etc. So Moore says, ". . . an existent is seen to be nothing but a concept or complex of concepts standing in a unique relation to the concept of existence." (183) Thus he argues against the empiricist tradition which holds that concepts are abstractions from either things or ideas. According to Moore, to say that anything is true of things or ideas is just to say first that those things or ideas are composed of concepts; concepts are the stuff of things and ideas, and hence prior to them, not abstractions from them. Truth is properly applied only to propositions, and propositions are composed of related concepts. But how odd all this seems. If one knew anything about analytic philosophers, it was that they were hard-headed empiricists to a man. Thus, much to one's surprise, perhaps, it is necessary to see the early Moore as anti-empiricist, or even as a Platonist.

Some objections to Moore's views might be sketched at this point, without developing any of them. Because this theory is similar in some respects to Plato's theory of Forms it is naturally open to all the objections to that theory which its critics, from Plato himself on,[4] have raised against it. But because the theory is formulated from quite a different point of view than Plato's theory, and because it concerns the nature of judgment, truth, and meaning, it is also open to objections from this quarter as well.* One might easily refuse to accept the arguments which Moore puts forward in support of his view. One might defend a more sophisticated version of the correspondence theory of truth. One might express reservations about "simple unanalyzable properties." One might point out that on this theory *existence* is on the same level as all other concepts, and concepts appear very much like properties or predicates, so all the objections urged against the notion of existence as a predicate might be urged against it, too. The objections which Moore himself raises against his own theory are different from these. In order to appreciate them, let us look at the way Moore develops the same theory ten years later, specifically in order to criticize it.

Propositions: The Early View Attacked

In *Some Main Problems of Philosophy* (258 f.) Moore begins to develop his later theory of propositions from the notion of false belief, a notion which has raised many problems in philosophy ever since Plato tried to analyze it in the *Sophist.* Moore asks what relation ". . . holds between a true belief

---

*Moore himself will develop objections from this point of view. See below.

and the fact to which it refers? The relation which we mean by calling the fact *the* fact to which the belief refers? The relation which we express by saying that the belief does refer to the fact?" (258)

In Moore's example we are asked to consider what it would be like if we were now hearing a brass band. What is actually in question is not what would really be the case if we were actually hearing the band, but rather what would be the case if someone believed that we were in fact hearing the band, whether we were or not. What is the relation of his belief to the fact? The answer he gives to begin with is a re-statement and elaboration of the theory which we examined above, a theory he proceeds to reject. He holds that every belief has two elements: an act of belief and an object of that act. The act is the same in all cases but the objects may differ from case to case and this accounts for different beliefs. The objects of belief he calls 'propositions' meaning something different from mere words. 'Proposition' is a name for what is expressed by sentences; it is what you understand when you understand a sentence. It is what a sentence means. The same meaning may be expressed by many different sentences. 'It is raining', *'es regnet'*, and *'il pleut'* are three different sentences each expressing the same propo-sition, and that proposition is not identical with any of them.

Two different beliefs are, in one sense, the same, for they are both beliefs, but in another sense they are different be-cause they have different objects. One person may believe that bears exist and another that lions exist. The beliefs as beliefs are the same in kind, but they are different beliefs because, according to Moore, one has as its object the propo-sition that bears exist and the other the proposition that lions exist. If this account is correct, we should expect it to cover the case of false belief as well, so that if one person be-lieves that griffins exist and another that centaurs exist, both beliefs are the same considered as acts but they differ in having two different propositions for their objects. The object of the first belief is the false proposition that griffins exist and the object of the second belief is the false proposition

that centaurs exist. Belief, then, is one way of having or entertaining a proposition before the mind.

But, Moore says, one indication—though scarcely a conclusive one—that the theory is false is that it requires us to hold
that whenever a belief is true there are, in some unspecified
sense, two different facts which must be called by the same
name. Whenever something is believed by someone there is
a) one fact, an object of belief, which is the proposition believed; and b) where the belief is true there is something
else which is a fact—the proposition that, e.g., lions exist,
believed together with the property truth—which is in the
world as well. (261) The person who believes that lions
exist is in some way confronted with a) the object of his
belief: the proposition that lions exist, and b) since his belief
is true, the actual fact that lions exist as well. For Moore
holds that the proposition 'lions exist' is true just in case
". . . there is such a thing as 'the existence of lions'. . . ."
(260)

On this theory Moore holds that the relation of a true belief to the fact to which it refers is this: that the proposition
which is the object of the belief has both being and also another simple unanalyzable property—truth. True propositions
have both being and truth, while false propositions have
being but not truth. There are thus two different facts which
both have the same name: a) the proposition, i.e., that 'lions
exist' or that 'chimeras exist'; and b) the possession by one of
those propositions of the property truth, i.e., that 'lions exist
[is true, has truth]'. Naturally the proposition 'chimeras exist'
lacks truth and so 'chimeras exist [is true, has truth]' has no
being. There is no such fact. Remember that according to
the 1899 account, propositions are composed of concepts and
are, or have being, in some sense, whether true or not. They
are indifferent to our believing or knowing them.

The relation which holds between a true belief and the
fact to which it refers is that the fact to which a true belief
refers ". . . *is* the truth of the particular proposition which is
the object of the belief." (261) In the case of Moore's example again, the true belief is the belief that lions exist, the

proposition which is the object of the belief is the proposition 'lions exist', and the fact to which the true belief refers is the proposition 'lions exist' plus the possession by that proposition of the property truth. We might schematically represent it this way:

Someone, *A*, believes that lions exist and that chimeras exist.

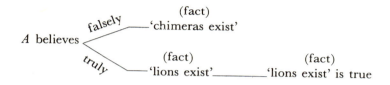

Thus the objects of *A*'s belief are the propositions expressed by the sentences 'lions exist' and 'chimeras exist.' The propositions have being. They are facts. But lions *do* exist, and to say this is just to say that the proposition 'lions exist' also has truth; that, too, is a fact. But chimeras *don't* exist; that is to say the proposition 'chimeras exist' has no truth and hence it is not a fact that chimeras exist.

This explanation leaves us with many of the notions entailed by Plato's theory of Forms as well as the following notions. Things are really propositions. All propositions alike have being, whatever that is. The facts to which true beliefs refer are just the possession by certain propositions of some simple unanalyzable property called 'truth'.

Moore raises two objections to his theory: 1) it just does not (intuitively?) seem to be the case that facts which are referred to by true beliefs consist in the possession of a simple property, truth, by a proposition which *is* or has being independent of whether the belief is true or false, 2) it does not seem to be the case a) that there are such things as propositions in the sense that this theory requires them and b) that belief is just a relation of our minds to anything.

This second objection is a powerful one, for in the case of false belief it does not seem that one's mental attitude is related to something which is, but rather, if we can speak this way, it appears to be related to what is not, or in other words, is not related to anything at all. If, for example, there are no chimeras, then should we happen to believe that there are, there is nothing for our belief to be related to. But if two things are related then, says Moore, ". . . both the two things must certainly be; and how then is it possible for any-one to believe in a thing which simply has no being?" (263) Perhaps, then, belief is not such a relation. The words in a sentence which appear to express a relation between two objects may not always name what they appear to name or, indeed, name anything at all. Moore, as noted, appears to think that words and groups of words forming sentences basically are names and stand for something or appear to stand for something.

Now, Moore argues, on the earlier theory which he has been expounding, it seems that you were committed to saying that your mind was related to something in the case of false belief, and that thing was a proposition. But it seems truer to say that in the case of false belief it is just that there is no fact to which your mind can be related. That is why the belief is false. So that in a true belief your mind is related to a fact, and in a false belief it is not. There appears no need to introduce the proposition as an intermediary having being. By eliminating it we gain an economy in our conceptual structure, which costs us nothing. (Moore had previously designated 'fact' what he now calls 'proposition'. Compare page 52 above.)

Moore goes on to say that there are simply no such things as propositions. But this is a slip which he notes in his "Preface," for he says there that what he really means is that in the sense in which this analysis requires propositions—an analysis which he now rejects—there are none. He does not wish to say that there are no propositions altogether. There are propositions expressed by declarative sentences which are true or false.

What then of truth? Moore now defines it in the following way: "to say that a belief is true is to say that *the fact to which*

it refers is or has being; while to say that a belief is false is to
say that the fact to which it refers is not—that there is no
such fact." (267) But what does the expression 'referring to'
mean? Moore says he cannot analyze it completely, but he
does know perfectly well what it means. He is acquainted
with it. This distinction between knowing what something
means and being able to give an analysis of it is important in
Moore's work. We have already seen how in his "A Defense
of Common Sense," a later work, Moore argued that everyone knows the meaning of countless expressions with which
he is familiar and which he uses daily even though he may
not know the meaning of them in the sense of being able to
give a correct analysis of them. A brief elaboration of this
distinction and of the notion of naming will occupy us shortly. In the meantime what about propositions? Now that he
denies that they are either the constituents of the world or
the objects to which we are related in belief, what does Moore
want to say they are?

Propositions: A Later View

Moore devotes Chapter III of *Some Main Problems of Philosophy* to propositions which he introduces in a discussion of
ways of knowing. He says that propositions *are* and ". . .
that a very large and important part of *our knowledge* of the
universe consists in the knowledge with regard to propositions that they are true." (56) Propositions are not collections
of words but they are: 1) what a collection of words
(sentence) means or expresses; 2) what also may be *expressed*
by single words or gestures of an appropriate sort; 3) what
may be said to be true or false; 4) about something.

When you read or hear or think of a sentence you also
(over and above the reading or hearing) may understand it.
You understand many different sentences. In Moore's example you may understand '2 + 2 = 4' and also
'4 + 4 = 8'—two acts of understanding and two things
understood. As acts of understanding they are the same, but
what is understood is different in each case. This is familiar
from our previous discussion. A proposition is neither a sen-

tence nor the understanding of a sentence, but what it is that is understood: the meaning expressed by each sentence. To comprehend the meaning of a sentence some act over and above the mere hearing or seeing of it is required. This is understanding. One may hear or see a sentence in an unfamiliar foreign language, but not necessarily understand what it means.

There are three things we may do when we understand a proposition:

1) We may believe it.
2) We may disbelieve it.
3) We may neither believe it nor disbelieve it but simply understand it.

All these cases involve understanding, although cases 1) and 2) involve something besides understanding. All of them also involve being confronted with propositions or entertaining them in some way, and this Moore calls 'direct apprehension'.

Moore is careful to note that we directly apprehend other things as well, like sense data, and though he feels that direct apprehension of sense data may be different from direct apprehension of propositions, he is unable to give an analysis of this difference. But once again he will not permit this to make him doubt that there may be some difference; the mere fact he cannot say what the difference is, is no reason for him to doubt its existence. Nevertheless, propositions are different from sense data, which we directly apprehend, for sense data require sensing and no understanding, while propositions require understanding and no sensing.

Another characteristic of propositions is that they are *about* something. For example Moore says that '2 + 2 = 4' is about 2 and 4. Now although our relation to a proposition which we are entertaining is the relation of direct apprehension, we are not necessarily directly apprehending the things that the proposition is about. To be sure, one may also be doing this. One may be directly apprehending a proposition about a sense datum and at the same time directly apprehending the sense datum: e.g., 'this red patch which I now have is the same shade as one I saw before.' In this case we are directly apprehending both the proposition and the sense datum. But most of the propositions which we directly apprehend are about things which we are not, at that moment, directly apprehending. Suppose, for example, I think or say a similar sentence to the one above: 'the sense datum which I had yesterday is similar to one I had two days ago.' I am then directly apprehending the proposition, but not what the proposition is about, although the proposition is still about things which under other circumstances I could directly apprehend. In this case the proposition is about something, and the relation that we have to that thing Moore calls indirect apprehension.

Another characteristic of propositions is that they are the only sorts of things of which it is proper to say that they are either true or false. And Moore still holds that to say a proposition is true or false is to ascribe some simple property to the proposition. But what about other things which we usually call true or false: beliefs, sentences, and images? In the case of beliefs and sentences Moore wants to say that they are called true or false in some derivative sense. A belief is true just in case it is a belief in a true proposition, and false just in case it is a belief in a false proposition. A sentence is true just in case it expresses a true proposition, and false just in case it expresses a false proposition. But an image must be said to be true or false in a still more derivative sense. Suppose I have an image and I apprehend a proposition to the effect that the image has or has not some relation to that of which it is an image. Then I call the image true or false according to whether the proposition is true or false. If I had an image which was a very accurate copy of my desk, yet never thought that it was an accurate copy of my desk, how could my image be said to be true? But if I did think some thought about the image, then this thought could be true or false. Only in such a case could the image be said to be (derivatively) true or false. In fact, Moore holds that "nothing in short can be true or false in the same sense in which propositions are true or false. So that, if we never apprehended any propositions we should not be capable of ever making any mistakes—a mistake, an *error,* would be impossible. Error always consists in believing some proposition which is false. So that if a man merely apprehended something, which was *in fact* like something else, but without believing either that it was like or unlike, or anything else at all about it, he could not possibly be said to make any mistake at all: he would never hold any mistaken or false opinions, because he would never hold any *opinions* at all." (66–67) One way in which propositions are important, then, is that without them informative discourse appears impossible.

This is as far as we shall follow Moore's development of the notion of propositions. He has described them as being in some sense what whole sentences, certain sorts of partial sentences, gestures, or kinds of thoughts stand for or name. Propositions are the meanings of these things. Let us look briefly at what Moore has to say specifically about meaning as the relation of standing for or naming.

Meaning: The Object Named or the Concept Named

Moore repeatedly spoke of words and sentences as naming certain things which were their meanings. Sentences name propositions and certain words name concepts. In his early view concepts are things which *are* in the world, and propositions, whether true or not, are facts in the world—the ultimate references of sentences. *(SMPOP,* chs. III, IV, XIV, XV, XVI.)

In a very famous passage in *Principia Ethica* (secs. 5–14), Moore elaborates his notion of meaning and definition. He begins by asking what the province of ethics is, and he answers that it is undoubtedly concerned with good conduct. But ". . . 'good conduct' is a complex notion: all conduct is not good . . . and . . . other things, beside conduct, may be good. . . ." (2) We must first ask what is good and what is bad, how is 'good' to be defined—and this is squarely in the province of ethics. Good is a simple object of thought. How is it to be defined? He means by this question what is the nature of the object or idea for which 'good' is used to stand?

For this inquiry neither dictionaries nor a survey of customary use will do to supply an answer.

Real definitions, definitions which describe "the real nature of the object or notion denoted by a word" (7) are only possible when that object or notion is complex, for definition, as Moore uses that term here, is a kind of decomposition. Hence, whatever is absolutely simple cannot be defined because what is simple cannot be decomposed. Complexes may be defined but not simples. In this sense neither yellow, nor good, nor true can be defined, for Moore holds them to be absolutely simple notions. One can say how people use the words which stand for these concepts or objects, and one can set up criteria for their correct employment, but what they denote, their meanings, can only be pointed to. If a man does not know what yellow is, we can point to examples of it, but if he still doesn't know, there is nothing else to be done. All definition is by analysis, a sort of inspection and decomposition, although, as we shall shortly see, there is another important sense of 'analysis' in Moore's work. But analysis, as carried on by decomposition, ultimately "refers us to something which is simply different from anything else, and which by that ultimate difference explains the peculiarity of the whole which we are defining. . . ." (10)

Moore presents a detailed example. Suppose we say ". . . the definition of a horse is 'A hoofed quadruped of the genus Equus'. . . ." (8) Three things may be meant: 1) 'I use the word "horse" to mean "hoofed quadruped of the genus Equus" '; 2) 'Most English-speaking people mean by horse "hoofed quadruped of the genus Equus" '; and in either of these cases simples like 'good' and 'yellow' are definable, for surely anyone can say how he intends to use a word or how most people use a word. But in the third sense good would be undefinable. That sense is: 3) 'some object, namely a horse, is composed in a certain manner of: one heart, one liver, four legs, one head, etc., related in definite ways to each other.' In this sense, definition consists in enumerating the parts of an object until you get to parts which themselves have no parts, which are ultimately simple. This is an ancient view which one may see worked out, for example, by Plato in the *Theatetus*. It was shared by Russell and Wittgenstein at one time and, as we shall see, Wittgenstein subjects it to attack in his later work.

In this third sense, then, the definition of horse can be elaborated presumably by setting out all the parts of a horse. The procedure is only illustrated in Moore's example, for in order actually to do it you would have to come to parts which have no parts, which are simple, and livers and legs do not seem to fit the requirement here. But in the case of good, which is what Moore is primarily interested in in this section, there are no parts and further elaboration is not possible. The meaning of good is the object or concept for which it stands; that is, what it names. As we saw, Moore felt—and, as we shall see below, so did Russell—that considerable progress is made when one finally realizes that not every word names or stands for or refers to some thing, that some words only look as if they refer or name, and do not do so. But it is not questioned that in fact some words do name or refer to or stand for something, and that thing is their meaning. The problem is to find out which do and which do not: to set up some criterion by which to know. Russell's solution to this problem will occupy us at length in the next chapter. We shall also see that Wittgenstein in his later work denied that a primary function of words is to name things.

If you hold, as Moore did, that the function of all or most words, or anyway of some words, is to name—an assumption which is natural, for we all try to teach others the meaning of words by pointing to what they name—then when you discover that there are no *things to which to point* in the case of certain words, you may try to argue that the words do not name things but concepts. Unfortunately, as we saw in the section on false belief above, this will not do either. Moore says, "[the] fact that single words and phrases which we use will constantly seem to be names for something, when in fact they are not names for anything at all, is what seems to me to create the whole difficulty." *(SMPOP,* 290) Then meaning cannot be successfully explicated as the naming of some object or concept. There are several other senses of 'meaning' in Moore's work.[5] We turn finally to a brief account of two of these.

Meaning: As the Object of Understanding

In the chapter on sense data we saw that Moore often argued that there are many things which we know in the sense that we are certain of their truth; we understand what is being said or written or expressed. We all know that we exist, that others exist, that there are minds, and that there are bodies. We understand these assertions because we can work with them; we use them in our everyday practical life. If someone says 'there is a table in the next room', Moore wants to insist that from a practical point of view we know what is meant and would rightly be thought insane if we seriously pressed him as to just what he meant. In this sense, if someone wanted to see if you knew the meaning of the German word *'gut'* he might ask you to give its English equivalent or its French equivalent and to make some German sentences with it. If you could do this with some proficiency, then it would be agreed that you knew the meaning of the word.

Again, suppose that someone wishes to know if we understand the meaning of saying something like 'the present age is a scientific age'. Surely he would be satisfied if we said that it meant such things as that science provides ever so many wonderful things now: jet travel, medical advances, flight into space, etc. And we might go on to say that people place faith in scientific method and evidence for various opinions, and that some superstitions are checked by contrary scientific findings. There is an indefinitely long list of such things which might be said, the saying of any few of which would suffice to convince on examination that we knew the meaning of the phrase. But there is another sense of 'meaning' in which, because it is a more exacting sense, such answers as these would not suffice to convince that we did know the meaning of the terms, expressions, or propositions in question. Moore, as we shall see below, tried hard to make this notion of meaning explicit, to elaborate and set out the conditions which, if satisfied, would lead us to say that someone knew the meaning of the word, phrase, or proposition in question in this more exacting sense. In his own view Moore was not successful in this effort.

Meaning: As the Results of Analysis

This sense of meaning as correct analysis is stricter than meaning as understanding, and in this sense Moore despaired of ever knowing the meanings of or understanding many propositions. We may recall that such propositions about material bodies as 'this is a human hand' puzzled Moore greatly. Clearly in one sense he did understand them and know what they meant. But in this other sense he did not. He was unable to give what he called a correct analysis of them. What, then, shall we understand him to mean by a correct analysis? What did he think had to be done that he and others could not do to give such an analysis? Moore admitted that he was far from clear on this.

We turn to his views in his "Reply to My Critics" (Schilpp 660 f.) Moore calls what is to be analyzed 'the analysandum'. This thing which has to be analyzed is an idea or concept or proposition, but definitely not a verbal expression. (661) To define one verbal expression in terms of another is not to say what either one means, but only to say that whatever these verbal expressions do mean, they mean the same thing. Should you doubt this, says Moore, pick up a dictionary in a language with which you are unfamiliar and you will see thousands of verbal expressions related in pairs which have the same meaning but you will hardly know what that meaning is.

Moore lays down very strict requirements for giving a correct analysis. In order to analyze ". . . a given *concept,* which is the *analysandum,* you must mention, as your *analysans,* a *concept* such that (a) nobody can know that the *analysandum* applies to an object without knowing that the *analysans* applies to it, (b) nobody can verify that the *analysandum* applies without verifying that the *analysans* applies, (c) any expression which expresses the *analysandum* must be synonymous with any expression which expresses the *analysans.*" (663)

To these he adds three further criteria: 1) if the analysis is correct, the analysans and the analysandum must in some sense be the same concept; 2) different verbal expressions must be used for the analysans and the analysandum; 3) these different verbal expressions must be such that the analysans must mention concepts not explicitly mentioned by the analysandum.

One sample analysis which Moore holds correct is: 'x is a brother' may be analyzed as 'x is a male sibling'. These expressions do appear to mean the same thing; they are synonymous; they apply to the same concept. The expressions are different satisfying 2), and the concepts referred to explicitly by 'x is a brother' appear to be different from the concepts explicitly referred to by 'x is a male sibling'. Nevertheless, many problems arise.

One might ask if Moore's criteria are not so strict as to preclude the possibility of our ever giving a correct analysis of any difficult proposition or concept. We may ask how two expressions, which express the concept to be analyzed and the concept which is the analysis, respectively, both may have the *same* meaning, yet each refer to concepts not explicitly referred to by the other? If this requirement is strictly observed, it would seem that Moore may have been too hasty in saying that 'x is a brother' can be analyzed as 'x is a male sibling'. For how can 'brother' and 'male sibling' each have the same meaning—presumably stand for the same concept—yet each stand for or refer to different concepts? How can one insure that the analysis convey some information and yet still be an analysis? How can one insure that the analysis does not in every case collapse into an empty tautology?

Other difficulties might be raised. For example, how are we to know when different expressions stand for different concepts and when they do not? If we do not know this, then neither requirements 1) nor 3) can be satisfied. Furthermore, it appears impossible to satisfy requirement a), because it is logically possible in any case you like that someone knows that a certain analysandum applies to an object without knowing that the analysans applies to it, for the state of a given person's knowledge is independent of the logical powers of any expression or concept. Though it may be impossible for *x* to *be* a body and not *be* extended, or to *be* a brother and not *be* a male sibling, it is *not* impossible for me to *know* that *x* is a brother without *knowing* that he is a male sibling, or that *x* is a body without *knowing* that it is extended. I may be ignorant of the subject matter, or the language, or just plain ignorant. Always honest and ingenuous, Moore raises further difficulties by retracting his one example of a perfect analysis: he says "[i]t is obvious, for instance, that, in a sense, the expression '*x* is a brother' is *not* synonymous with, has *not* the same meaning as, '*x* is a male sibling,' since if you were to translate the French word *frère* by the expression 'male sibling,' your translation would be *incorrect*, whereas if you were to translate it by 'brother,' it would not." (667)

These and many other problems are left unsolved by Moore, although that is not to say that they are unsolvable. In succeeding chapters we shall see one of the most interesting things about philosophy: how in the hands of other thinkers the entire conception of a problem changes, requiring different methods of attack. In the work of Russell these problems will be partly restructured and analyzed in a quite different, more formal way. Although Moore was clearly disturbed by his inability to solve the problems which troubled him acutely, he never felt that this was a serious drawback to raising the sorts of questions that he raised throughout his life. His contribution to philosophy was perhaps not to construct a system or offer solutions, but rather to raise questions and make distinctions where no one had seen the necessity to raise or make them before. He exercised enormous influence through teaching, scholarship, and the editorship of the influential journal, *Mind,* which he held for many years. This influence extended to younger and older contemporaries, Russell included, both in England and later in the

United States. Yet in the end it may be the case that his style and philosophical outlook were his greatest contribution.

If we are disappointed by the scattered problems never solved and drawn together in the grand manner of classical philosophy, we cannot do better than to look at Moore's words on the subject: "To search for 'unity' and 'system,' at the expense of truth, is not, I take it, the proper business of philosophy, however universally it may have been the practice of philosophers." *(PE, 222)*

4

Bertrand Russell: Meaning and Reference

Russell moved from philosophic positions where he populated the universe with great numbers of metaphysical entities through a series of worlds where the population was systematically decimated by the use of Occam's famous razor:
do not multiply entities beyond necessity. Behind much of
the work of Russell's early and middle years we shall find the
'one name—one thing' theory lurking, too, although he employs it in a more formal and rigorous manner than Moore
had done. Russell began by believing that many sorts of
things really and truly existed as part of some ultimate reality. Among these were numbers ". . . sitting in a row in a
Platonic heaven,"[1] points of space, instants of time, ultimate
particles of physics, universals, and the like. The principle
popularly known as Occam's razor, after the four-
teenth-century philosopher, is an old and common-sensical
one, although it was neither invented by Occam nor stated
by him in that form. (What he actually said was something
roughly like never postulate a plurality of things if you don't
have to.) And it is doubtful that any philosopher ever did
mean to say that there were more real things than he
thought there were. Nevertheless, one could read the princi-

ple as a guide for reducing one's metaphysical world. Where the metaphysical or epistemological functions of many things can be taken over by or reduced to fewer, one should do so. On the same page of his book, *My Philosophical Development,* we find Russell writing that "As time went on, my universe became less luxuriant. Gradually, Occam's razor gave me a more clean-shaven picture of reality. I do not mean that it could prove the non-reality of entities which it showed to be unnecessary; I mean only that it abolished arguments in favour of their reality. I still think it impossible to disprove the existence of integers or points or instants or the Gods of Olympus. For aught I know these may all be real, but there is not the faintest reason to think so."

Changes of this kind were possible for Russell when he concluded that a certain fundamental belief, originally shared by Moore, was false, or at least was not necessarily true. He says: "as time went on, I ceased to be troubled by such problems. They arose from the belief that, if a word means something, there must be something that it means." (63) Some words, he thought, will point to things as their meanings, and some will not. But which are which and how to find out? Russell's answer is his theory of descriptions, first presented in 1905 and presented many times after.

Fundamental to this theory is the notion that the grammatical structure of a sentence may not actually reveal its logical structure; that the sentence may appear to be about or to assert something when it really is not about or does not assert anything at all. A trivial example: 'I met nobody today'. 'Oh! And how was he feeling?' Linguists occasionally construct sentences which seem to obey the rules of grammar but which are obvious nonsense: 'it smokes down the abstract wall jealously'. In such cases it is clear that nothing is being asserted and nothing referred to. But in sentences like i) 'the Absolute enters into but does not combine with all processes'; ii) 'God is the most perfect being'; iii) 'the present king of France is bald'; it is not clear what, if anything, is being asserted and what, if anything, is being referred to by the grammatical subject. Sentence i) looks to be the same sort as a sentence about catalysts in elementary chemistry books: 'catalysts enter into reactions accelerating them without themselves changing'. Sentence ii) looks to be the same sort as 'the Hope diamond is the most perfect diamond'. And sentence iii) looks to be the same sort as 'the present Secretary of Defense of the U.S.A. is bald'.

But there is an important difference. Under the type of analysis Russell is recommending all in the first set would be shown to be false when properly analyzed, for they all turn out to assert the existence of something which does not, in fact, exist. But under his analysis those in the second set would be true, for their subject terms refer to things which do in fact exist, and do in fact have the properties ascribed to them.

Other problems arise, as Plato noted in the *Sophist,* when you have to ascribe non-being to something; that is, to say that it does not exist. For in the very saying must not what you say be *about* something, i.e., what you are asserting not to exist? But how can your sentence be *about* that thing if there is no such thing? Perhaps after all we must assign some being or reality to it. If I say 'dragons don't exist' then the sentence appears to be about dragons. But if it is true, then there are no dragons for it to be about, for it says they do not exist. But then it is not about anything. How can a sentence about nothing be significant? But surely it is significant, we all know what it means, and what is more, it happens to be true. Therefore the sentence must be about something after all. But the only thing it could be about is dragons. Therefore we must concede that although dragons don't exist they must *be,* somehow.

This is the way Russell interpreted the German philosopher Meinong, with whom he had agreed before 1905. In fact, he had already written highly laudatory articles about Meinong's work, which he later came to feel put him entirely on the wrong track. Let us sketch Meinong's notions briefly.

Meinong's Position

As Russell saw it, Meinong's position was roughly that if

you could mention something in a sentence, even if there was no such thing in our ordinary space-time world, then the sentence referred to whatever you mentioned, and then that thing *was* somehow. Such things will not be said to exist but they do have being. Meinong called them ideal objects. They are objects to which one can direct one's mind in performing certain mental acts—judging, assuming, etc. "It is argued, *e.g.,* by Meinong, that we can speak about 'the golden mountain,' 'the round square,' and so on; we can make true propositions of which these are the subjects; hence they must have some kind of logical being, since otherwise the propositions in which they occur would be meaningless."[2]

We may say true and false things about what does not exist. For example, it is true that Hamlet was the prince of Denmark and false that he was married. Meinong held that how a thing is, its so-being *(Sosein)* is independent of its being *(Sein)* as such—whether it exists or not. He says, "as we know, the figures with which geometry is concerned do not exist. Nevertheless, their properties, and hence their *Sosein,* can be established. . . . [T]he principle applies, not only to Objects which do not exist in fact, but also to Objects which could not exist because they are impossible. Not only is the much heralded gold mountain made of gold, but the round square is as surely round as it is square."[3]

Perhaps stating these things out of the context of Meinong's work gives a wrong interpretation of them, but that is a risk we must take, for it was in this way that Russell understood him, and it was a view like this which Russell himself held, led to it by G. E. Moore.[4] Indeed, Meinong's views bear a striking resemblance to early views of Moore. Now Russell understood Meinong to have populated the universe with entity upon entity, and these he determined to cut away. He said that Meinong's theory lacked a feeling for reality. "Logic, I should maintain, must no more admit a unicorn than zoology can; for logic is concerned with the real world just as truly as zoology, though with its more abstract and general features." *(IMP,* 169) We cannot take up the correctness of Russell's view of Meinong, although there are many who say that Russell is wrong. The interested reader may judge this for himself.[5] Nevertheless, Russell developed his theory of descriptions partly as an answer to this problem which he conceived of as Meinong's, and it is against this background that he may best be understood.

Frege's Position

The German mathematician, philosopher, and logician Gottlob Frege presented a solution to these problems also. Russell was not content with this solution either, though he retained the greatest admiration for Frege's work, especially his logical research. Frege introduces a distinction between the sense of an expression and what it refers to.[6] Roughly, two expressions may differ in sense or meaning while referring to the same object. Frege considers the expressions 'the evening star' and 'the morning star'. The morning star (the physical body) *is* the evening star; yet that discovery was an empirical one made by astronomy. But if they are the same, then to say 'the morning star is the evening star' appears to be saying no more than that 'the morning star is the morning star', and to know this, one need not be an astronomer or ever have heard of astronomy. But the distinction between the sense and the reference of an expression saves us from this conclusion. It helps us to see that though the expressions 'the morning star' and 'the evening star' both refer to the same object (Venus) each does so in a different way because each means something different. One means something like 'star seen in the morning' and the other 'star seen in the evening'; but both refer to, denote, or point out the same object: Venus. Therefore the discovery that the morning star *is* the evening star was the discovery that the star seen in the morning was the same star as seen in the evening, and that discovery could not have been made without careful astronomical observation. 'The morning star is the evening star' therefore may provide us with information that 'the morning star is the morning star' would not.

Frege's theory is open to criticism. For one thing, Russell notes that a problem may arise when some word is used as a name which does not actually refer to or name anything: when it has no denotation. He considers the following example:

'if Ferdinand is not drowned, then Ferdinand is my only son', and he says, "now 'my only son' is a denoting phrase, which, on the face of it, has a denotation when, and only when, I have exactly one son. But the above statement would nevertheless have remained true if Ferdinand had been in fact drowned. Thus we must either provide a denotation in cases in which it is at first sight absent, or we must abandon the view that the denotation is what is concerned in propositions which contain denoting phrases."[7] Meinong had provided denotations by reifying or substantializing concepts: making them into entities. Russell will abandon them.

It should be remarked here that the conditional statement 'if Ferdinand is not drowned, then Ferdinand is my only son' is true even if it happens that Ferdinand *is* drowned, because all conditional statements are true whenever their antecedent clauses are false. It is a property that they have. For example, the statement 'if it rains, then the streets are wet' is certainly true even when it doesn't rain.[8]

Now, if the antecedent of 'if Ferdinand is not drowned, then Ferdinand is my only son' is false, that is, if Ferdinand happened to be drowned, the whole statement happens to be true. But in that case what does the denoting phrase, 'my only son', denote? If Ferdinand is drowned, then the speaker no longer has a son and hence no longer has an only son. But the whole statement is still significant since it is true. But how can a significant statement contain phrases which appear to be about something and which are not about anything at all? One may either provide a denotation as Meinong does, by saying that even if Ferdinand no longer exists he has being, or one may provide a purely *ad hoc* or conventional denotation as Frege does.* But Russell rejects Meinong's overpopulation of the metaphysical universe because it is repugnant to one's sense of reality, and he rejects Frege's conventional denotation because it is purely arbitrary.[9]

---

*In these sorts of cases Frege postulates the null class as referent.

Frege's full theory of sense and reference is complicated and difficult to understand, and various commentators advance various reasons for its unsatisfactoriness which we cannot specify here. It suffices to say that Russell rejected it and provided what he thought was a correct alternative. We shall see in detail later on that Strawson in his turn rejected Russell's theory and reopened the whole question which Russell had regarded as closed.

Russell's Theory: Preliminary Notions

Some preliminary definitions of the notions which Russell uses may help the reader to understand the exposition of his theory of descriptions. We look at six of these.

1—*Proposition.* By 'proposition' Russell means any symbolic form—words, thoughts, symbols, or gestures—which can express what may be said to be true or false. Examples are: 'Socrates is a man' and '2 + 2 = 4'. But sometimes Russell uses 'proposition' to mean not the words which express something, but what it is that the words express. Some writers charge Russell with confusion on this point (e.g., Linsky, p. 7) but it will not concern us here.

2—*Propositional function.* A propositional function is an expression with a blank space or a variable in it, such that when the blank space is filled in with, or the variable substituted for, with the right sort of thing, the result is a true proposition. E.g., '_____ is mortal' becomes a true proposition when a name like 'Socrates' or 'Abraham Lincoln' is filled in for the blank. Whatever can fill in the blank and make the whole expression a true proposition is said to satisfy the propositional function. Russell uses propositional functions with variables instead of blank spaces; that is, he uses them like mathematical functions. 'x is rational' expresses nothing until the proper expression is substituted for x. "A propositional function standing all alone may be taken to be a mere schema, a mere shell, an empty receptacle for meaning, not something already significant." (*IMP,* 157)

3—*Variable.* A variable is a letter, usually x, y, z, used in such a way in a propositional function that by substituting certain expressions for the variable you get a proposition. They are also familiar from elementary mathematics. $'x^2 = 4'$ yields a true statement when either 2 or -2 is substituted for x, and $'x$ is human' yields a true statement whenever the name of a real person is substituted for x. In the first case we say that $'x'$ takes numbers for its values or that it ranges over the domain of numbers. In the second case we say that $'x'$ takes names or, in certain cases, descriptions, for its values, or that it ranges over the domain of names.

4—*Names.* For Russell a name is a symbol which must be, or be treated as, simple. Names are similar to individuals or particulars and stand as the logical subjects of ordinary statements. They designate individuals. Individuals are what the statements are about, or what the predicate or relation asserted in a statement is asserted of. Such individuals can only occur as subjects. Russell says, "we shall define 'proper names' as those terms which can only occur as *subjects* in propositions [he means statements expressing propositions]. . . . We shall further define 'individuals' or 'particulars' as the objects that can be named by proper names. . . ." *(IMP,* 142) 'Scott', 'George IV', and 'Bertrand Russell' are all simple symbols and hence names. Certain things may seem to be individuals but may really be capable of further analysis although we do not know this fact. Because of this, Russell will operate as if the things which appear to be individuals really are individuals and some things which appear to be proper names really are proper names. This problem will concern us in the next chapter.

The individual designated by or named by the name is, for Russell, the meaning of the name. Any word which does not designate or refer to a real individual cannot be a name, although it may look like one. In this case it is not a name but a disguised description. Furthermore, Russell holds that the assertion or denial of existence about a real individual is meaningless, for nothing is a name unless it names some individual and then that individual must exist. To say that it exists is redundant and to deny it is self-contradictory. Finally, if Socrates really existed, then 'Socrates' is a name. But if Socrates, about whom we know only what was written by Plato, Aristotle, Xenophon and Aristophanes, did not exist, then 'Socrates' is not a name but shorthand for 'the person mentioned by Plato, Aristotle, Xenophon and Aristophanes in certain of their works'.

5—*Denoting or Descriptive phrase.* There are two sorts of descriptive phrases: definite and indefinite. An indefinite description is a phrase of the form 'a so-and-so'. A definite description is a phrase of the form 'the so-and-so'. These phrases describe or denote but do not name anything. The use of the word 'the' in the definite description implies the uniqueness of the individual whom the phrase is supposed to describe: e.g., contrast *'a* man' with *'the* author of *Ulysses'.*

6—*Incomplete symbol.* An incomplete symbol is one which has no meaning in isolation but only in some context. Examples of these are things like the connectives of the propositional calculus[10] (or, and, not, if . . . then) and arithmetic operators (the signs for addition, subtraction, multiplication, and division). Definite descriptions (e.g., the so-and-so) are also incomplete symbols. Out of the context of the propositions in which they occur they do not have meaning. In contrast, proper names do have meaning in isolation; their meaning is the individual they denote.

A preliminary look at Russell's analysis may make the analysis easier to follow. He formulated his theory because of some puzzles about certain sorts of statements. One such statement is

'the present king of France is bald'

and the problem in this case is how to understand the apparent subject, 'the present king of France'. Since there is no king of France at present, he can be neither bald nor not bald (have hair). Russell quips that in this case, Hegelians, against whom his theory is also directed and who love a synthesis, will conclude that he wears a wig. But he doesn't do that either, for there is no one upon whose head to place either crown or wig. In this case the sentence appears not to be about anything at all. One way out would be to say with Meinong that although the present king of France does not exist, still as an object of our thought he has some sort of being; or we can say with Frege that the phrase 'the present king of France' denotes a purely arbitrary referent, say, the empty set. But Russell takes neither of these ways. He says instead that although to assert that 'the present king of France is bald' looks grammatically as if one statement is being made, logically the joint conjunction of three statements is what is being asserted:

1) There exists at present at least one person who reigns in France.
2) There exists at present at most one person who reigns in France.
3) Whoever reigns in France is bald.

By paraphrase Russell has eliminated the apparent name 'the present king of France'.

Now it is easily seen that 1) is false, for France is not a monarchy and hence no one reigns in it. The conjunction of three statements, one of which is false, is itself false. Therefore the statement 'the present king of France is bald' is neither meaningless, nor a reference to some entity which has being but does not exist, nor a reference to some manufactured class, but false. Let us turn to the theory in more detail in order to see how Russell arrives at his conclusions.

Russell's Theory

Underlying Russell's theory is the principle that in certain sorts of statements what appears to be a name is not one in fact, but a disguised description. If such statements can be reformulated so that the reformulation says explicitly what the original said implicitly, bringing out all the assumptions and without using the denoting phrase, then it will be clear that there is no entity corresponding to the pseudo-name used in the original. In order to see how Russell thinks he will accomplish this, let us follow the order of his exposition and line of thought as set out in Chapter 16, "Descriptions," of his book *Introduction To Mathematical Philosophy*.[11]

He begins with an analysis of indefinite descriptions: descriptions of the form 'a so-and-so'. Consider the indefinite description 'a man'. What is it that is asserted when someone says truly 'I met a man'? What is *not* asserted is that some particular man was met, e.g., Jones. For if that were asserted, then to say 'I met a man, but not Jones', even when in fact I did meet Jones, is not to contradict oneself, although it is to lie. In fact, there is no actual man who is being referred to. The statement names or is about no one at all. The phrase 'a unicorn' or 'a sea serpent' could be substituted for 'a man' and the statement would still remain significant, though false. In these cases the statement deals with a concept and not with some individual.

Russell moves on to point out what is perhaps *the* major point behind his analysis:

> To say that unicorns have an existence in heraldry, or in literature, or in imagination, is a most pitiful and paltry evasion. What exists in heraldry is not an animal, made of flesh and blood, moving and breathing of its own initiative. What exists is a picture, or a description in words. Similarly, to maintain that Hamlet, for example, exists in his own world, namely, in the world of Shakespeare's imagination, just as truly as (say) Napoleon existed in the ordinary world, is to say something deliberately confusing. . . . There is only one world, the 'real' world. . . . When you have taken account of all the feelings roused by Napoleon in writers and readers of history, you have not touched the actual man; but in the case of Hamlet you have come to the end of him. If no one thought about Hamlet, there would be nothing left of him; if no one had thought about Napoleon, he would have soon seen to it that someone did. *(IMP,* 169–170)

In order to avoid error it is necessary to understand that statements and propositions use symbols and to know which symbols have and which have not got significance. To say 'I met a unicorn' is to make a significant proposition using four words; but the subordinate group of words 'a unicorn' is not the name of anything. Remember that names are names only if they refer to individuals. Where there are no individuals referred to there are no names. 'A unicorn' is an incomplete symbol: "... an indefinite description which describes nothing." (170)

Consider some indefinite description like 'a man' and try to make some statement concerning it. Russell chooses the statement 'I met a man', and he wants to give an analysis which eliminates the indefinite description 'a man'. In this case it is obvious that if someone made the statement 'I met a man', no one would feel compelled to look for the 'a man' who was met or to find him in some metaphysical world, but with unicorns and golden mountains this is not so obvious. Indeed, it is just this which gives rise to the Meinongian universe. Men are certain objects having certain properties (e.g., being human). This may be expressed symbolically by using a variable 'x' and some Greek letter 'ϕ' representing the property of being human, 'ϕx' will then mean 'x is human'. Now what we meant to say about 'a man' is that 'there is someone whom I met.' Russell represents 'I met' by 'ψ'. Then the complete translation of 'I met a man' is: 'the joint assertion of "ϕx" and "ψx" is not always false' (171), that is, 'the joint assertion that "I met x" and "x is human" is not always false' (is sometimes—in at least one case—true). Although this may appear clumsy, it has the decided advantage of eliminating the phrase 'a man' and could also be used to eliminate other potentially troublesome phrases as well. "The important point is that, when rightly analyzed, propositions verbally about 'a so-and-so' are found to contain no constituent represented by this phrase. And that is why such propositions can be significant even when there is no such thing as a so-and-so." (171)

Unicorns, golden mountains and square circles are eliminated in favor of propositional functions which are seen never to be satisfied for any value. Though Russell has tried to be careful not to claim that unicorns, golden mountains and numbers do not exist, but to claim merely that there is no reason to believe that they do, he often appears really to have thought that to show that a symbol was incomplete or that a denoting phrase was not a name, was in fact to show that there was no entity corresponding to the symbol or description. But the most that he shows in his analysis is that by reformulating the statement so as to eliminate the phrase in question, one possible reason for believing that some entity corresponding to it does exist is removed. This does not and cannot by itself show that the entity in fact does not exist, but merely removes temptation from our path.

Russell turns to an analysis of definite descriptions. These also will turn out to have no meaning in isolation, but only in the context of a proposition; they are also incomplete symbols. Definite descriptions are grammatically more misleading than indefinite ones because the use of the word 'the' makes it easier to assume that some definite entity is being named.

For his example here Russell takes the proposition

i) Scott is the author of *Waverley*.

He holds that 'Scott' is a name in the sense elaborated under the preliminary notions above, and that 'the author of *Waverley*' is a description. Proposition i) then asserts that the name and the description apply to the same person. The name ". . . is a simple symbol, directly designating an individual which is its meaning, and having this meaning in its own right. . . ." (174) The description ". . . consists of several words, whose meanings are already fixed, and from which results whatever is to be taken as the 'meaning' of the description." (174)

Names and descriptions are different, and if one is substituted for the other in a proposition you get a different proposition, even though the name and the description apply to the same object. Proposition i), 'Scott is the author of *Waverley*', gives you new information. It expresses a contingent fact of literary history, for someone else might have written *Waverley*, or there might not have been a novel called *Waverley* at all. Replace 'Scott' with 'James Joyce' and the proposition is false. But the proposition

ii) Scott is Scott

is true whether Scott wrote *Waverley* or not, or indeed regardless of whether there ever was such a novel at all. Substitute 'James Joyce' for 'Scott' here and the result is still true. Suppose somebody objects that ii) is the same form of proposition as

iii) Scott is Sir Walter.

To this Russell replies that in iii) the proposition being asserted is really

the person named 'Scott' is the person named 'Sir Walter'

and here the apparent names are disguised descriptions. In the same way he holds that 'Homer' is not a name designating some individual but is a disguised description which, when expanded, means 'whoever was the author of the *Odyssey* and the *Iliad*'. Presumably he says this because no one knows whether or not one individual existed who wrote these works. If such an individual did exist, we have no record of him.

Russell is making use of the distinction between a fact which is asserted and the means by which it is asserted, i.e., the words used to assert it. "When a name is used directly, merely to indicate what we are speaking about, it is no part of the *fact* asserted . . . it is merely part of the symbolism by which we express our thought." (175) A name is a word we use to designate some individual so as to assert a fact about him. But ". . . a proposition about 'the person called Scott', [when] the actual name 'Scott' enters into what we are asserting, and not merely into the language used in making the assertion . . ." (175) is another matter. Here the fact asserted involves not the individual designated—the man Scott—but the name used—the name 'Scott'. When we *use* names as names we designate individuals; but when we are talking *about* names as such we are doing something entirely different. We refer not to individuals but to words.

We have seen that a proposition containing a name does not have the same meaning as a new proposition in which all else remains the same but the description of the individual referred to by the name replaces the name. Hence, although it is true to say that '$x = x$' and, if 'Scott' is a name, that 'Scott = Scott', it is not necessarily true that 'the author of *Waverley* = the author of *Waverley*'. We must first know that 'the author of *Waverley*' describes someone who exists. For as Russell remarks, we should not want to say that 'the round square = the round square' is true because we know that round squares do not exist.

A definite description implies that the entity described, if it exists, is unique; there is only one of them. The proposition 'Scott is the author of *Waverley*' could not be true unless: 1) *Waverley* had actually been written; 2) only one person wrote it; 3) that person was Scott. Similarly, the truth of the proposition 'the author of *Waverley* was Scotch' depends upon the following conditions holding:

1) 'x wrote *Waverley*' is not always false.	i.e. There exists at least one person who wrote *Waverley*.
2) If x and y wrote *Waverley*, then 'x is identical with y' is always true.	i.e. At most one person wrote *Waverley*.
3) If x wrote *Waverley*, 'x is Scotch' is always true.	i.e. Whoever wrote *Waverley* was Scotch.

'The author of *Waverley* was Scotch' implies the conjunction of 1), 2), and 3), and the conjunction of 1), 2), and 3) implies 'the author of *Waverley* was Scotch'. They are logically equivalent.

We may recall that the example given at the beginning of the exposition of Russell's theory was 'the present king of France is bald' and that it really asserted the joint conjunction of:

a) There exists at least one person who reigns in France. ('x reigns in France' is not always false.)

b) There exists at most one person who reigns in France.
(If *x* and *y* reign in France, then *x* = *y*.)

c) Whoever reigns in France is bald.
(x is bald.)

So translated, the constituent 'the present king of France'
disappears replaced by a propositional function which is not
satisfied for any value of *x* and hence is always false. What
the theory of descriptions does is to replace purported names
with the explicit statement that the individual purportedly
referred to by the name really exists in the ordinary sense of
'exists'. Once this is done it should be clear whether or not
there is such an individual and if there isn't, the grammatical form will no longer lead the incautious into postulating
entities to act as the subject being referred to by the sentence.

Russell now proceeds to generalize his conclusions. Statements 1), 2) and 3) above become: "there is a term *c* [some
constant] such that '*x* wrote *Waverley*' is always equivalent
to '*x* is *c*'. [And] . . . '*c* is Scotch'." (178) Generally " 'the
term satisfying ϕx satisfies ψx' is defined as meaning: 'there
is a term *c* such that (1) ϕx is always equivalent to '*x* is
c,' (2) ψc is true'." (178) He says that "this is the definition of propositions in which descriptions occur." (178)
When so analyzed, the problem of reifying the apparent
subject term no longer arises and the significance of the
proposition is saved when the subject term is a disguised description which, in fact, describes nothing; for then the first of
the conjoined assertions—the one asserting the existence of
the entity supposedly described—is seen to be false and therefore the entire proposition is false. But the original proposition is logically equivalent to the proposition formed by its
analysis into three conjoined propositions.[12] If two propositions are logically equivalent, then they both have the same
truth value. Hence when one is false, the other is false, and
hence, the original proposition is seen to be false.

Russell makes one more point. He distinguishes primary

from secondary occurrences of describing or denoting phrases in propositions. Consider the proposition 'the present king of France is bald'. The denoting phrase 'the present king of France' has a primary occurrence and denotes nothing; hence the whole proposition is false. But consider the proposition 'the present king of France is not bald'. This could mean either.

a) it is false that the present king of France is bald, or
b) the present king of France is not bald.

In a) the denoting phrase has a secondary occurrence and the proposition is true. In b) the proposition is false and the denoting phrase has a primary occurrence. In a) the negation applies to the whole statement, and as there is no king of France at present the statement says what is true, i.e., it is false that anyone reigns in France and hence, that he is bald. In b) the negation applies only to being bald and hence the proposition says what is false, i.e., that there is a present king of France. Russell concludes, "every proposition in which a description which describes nothing has a primary occurrence is false." (179)

Russell has used his theory of descriptions to cut away what he thinks is unnecessary metaphysics, not to cut away metaphysics itself. He was never a positivist although the movement claimed him as a spiritual father. We shall see in the next chapter how with the use of the theory of descriptions, which he considered a highly successful logical tool, and a desire for simplicity of initial assumptions, Russell creates his own theory of knowledge and metaphysics, which he learned in part from his pupil Wittgenstein. It should be obvious that the theory of descriptions by itself cannot get rid of unwanted metaphysical entities like golden mountains and present kings of France. In order to do that, one must combine the use of the theory with that lively sense of reality which Russell cherished so deeply.

5

Bertrand Russell:
Sense Data

In that engaging account of his intellectual life, *My Philo-sophical Development* (103 f.), Russell tells us that for some time he had come to feel that the problem of how we have knowledge of the external world was very perplexing. For various reasons, many similar to Moore's, he held that it seems difficult to believe that our senses put us in contact with physical objects or with the external world as we ordinarily think of it. He says in another work "physics started from the common-sense belief in fairly permanent and fairly rigid bodies—tables and chairs, stones, mountains, the earth and moon and sun. This common-sense belief, it should be noticed, is a piece of audacious metaphysical theorizing; objects are not continuously present to sensation, and it may be doubted whether they are there when they are not seen or felt."[1] We will trace part of his attempt to found our knowledge of the external world upon the fact that we ourselves construct it as, in his words, a logical fiction. He thus attempts to eliminate the problem which so plagued Moore: how do we come into contact with the things supposed to be existing outside of ourselves?

In his paper "The Relation of Sense-Data to Physics"[2] he advocates, among other things, the program of attempting to show that physical objects, as we usually think of them, can be exhibited as functions of our sense data, which are the only elements which we actually do experience. He soon, however, abandoned this view for another.

The view which he began to expand and refine from 1914 to 1919 he called 'logical atomism', and it is a view which he says he learned in a great measure from his then friend and pupil, Ludwig Wittgenstein. As developed by Wittgenstein, logical atomism diverged considerably from Russell's view of it. Both of them came to abandon it later.[3]

According to Russell's view, logical atomism is the theory that you can in principle, if not in practice, get down to the ultimate constituents of the world and that you can describe the ways in which these constituents are related by using a language whose structure mirrors their relations. As Mr. Urmson says, "the shortest account of logical atomism that can be given is that the world has the structure of Russell's mathematical logic." *(Philosophical Analysis,* 6) Russell may have thought that in the development of mathematical logic, as he and Whitehead constructed it in their *Principia Mathematica* (3 vols., 1910–14), he had in fact found the logically perfect syntax of the world. If he did think this, then what he thought was a metaphysical hypothesis of the greatest consequence. For to say that one knows how the world is really constructed is to say that one has an answer to the fundamental question raised in the history of philosophy. On the other hand, he may only have tried to account for all that we know or think we know by the use of the fewest basic principles and blocks, out of which the rest may be constructed. This would be a weaker attempt for it merely says that whatever the nature of ultimate reality, we can account for things as we know them (for Russell, principally science) by reasoning in a particular way. The problem of the relation of the reasoning to reality itself is left open.

In "The Philosophy of Logical Atomism" we find him writing of a theory which he was rejecting: "I always wish to get on in philosophy with the smallest possible apparatus, partly because it diminishes the risk of error, because it is not necessary to deny the entities you do not assert, and therefore you run less risk of error the fewer entities you assume. The other reason . . . is that every diminution in the number of entities increases the amount of work for mathematical logic to do in building up things that look like the entities you used to assume."[4] (221–22) Further on, he says about the employment of his second favorite weapon, Occam's razor (the first weapon is mathematical logic), ". . . you go through, if you are analyzing a science like physics, these propositions [of physics] with a view to finding out what is the smallest empirical apparatus—or the smallest apparatus, not necessarily wholly empirical—out of which you can build up these propositions. What is the smallest number of simple undefined things at the start, and the smallest number of undemonstrated premises, out of which you can define the things that need to be defined and prove the things that need to be proved?" (271) And again he writes ". . . one thing that our technique does, is to give us a means of constructing a given body of symbolic propositions with the minimum of apparatus, and every diminution in apparatus diminishes the risk of error." (280)

Whether we understand logical atomism as a metaphysical theory about the way the world is ultimately built as some commentators do, and as some logical positivists did, or merely as a device for constructing the world as we know it with the utmost possible elegance and simplicity, is not important here. What is important is to see that two streams of Russell's thought run together to produce it. One stream was generated through his logical studies, including his theory of descriptions, and the other was generated from his work on the problem of what we can know about the external world. To speak of the first stream it is necessary to say something about truth functional propositions. To speak of the second it is necessary to say something about sense data. A well conceived combination of the two will result in logical atomism. We begin with sense data.

Sense Data: How the Problem Arises

Russell held many different views about sense data, for he changed his ideas often. We shall concern ourselves with parts of the views expressed in *Our Knowledge of the External World* (1914), "The Relation of Sense-Data to Physics" (1914), "The Ultimate Constituents of Matter" (1915), and "The Philosophy of Logical Atomism" (1918). G. E. Moore was led to the various notions that he had of sense data through his attempt to show that the common-sense view of the world was correct and how that was so. But for Russell neither common sense nor ordinary ways of speaking, which he has consistently derided as criteria of philosophic correctness or importance, are to the point at all. It is science and the scientific picture of the world with which he consistently attempts to reconcile philosophy, and, among sciences, physics, psychology, and physiology occupy a central position.

Russell divides our knowledge roughly into two parts: that which is believed or justified on its own account without other evidence, and that which is believed or justified because it is in some way derived from something else. The clearest, though not the only example of the first, is knowledge given through the senses: ". . . the immediate facts perceived by sight or touch or hearing . . ." *(OKEW,* 58) With these we are directly acquainted, and we cannot doubt them. Knowledge of almost everything else is an example of the second kind: science in general and our everyday common-sense knowledge, such as that there is a chair in this place or a table in that. This distinction leads to a distinction between hard and soft data. The hardest data we have are the particular facts of sense and the general truths of logic, some bits of memory and some pieces of introspection. Reflection shows these to be nearly indubitable. "Real doubt in these two cases [Russell refers specifically to sense data and logic] would, I think, be pathological." (60) Its only result could be universal skepticism where nothing at all is believed. Soft data are virtually everything else—that is, whatever is not a particular fact of sense, a general truth of logic, or a result of introspective investigation of some types of memory fact. Soft data are such things as the existence of the pieces of furniture in a room which are not presently being perceived, or indeed the very inside of the room. The belief in these, while probably true, requires some support, whereas the momentary existence of a sensory patch of color or sound is its own proof. For it no further argument is necessary nor could one even be produced.

Russell's problem may then be put as the problem of constructing soft data from hard data. Soft data, like the continuity of what we call material bodies in space and time, are useful hypotheses but eliminable in principle. The belief in their existence depends upon the view that things which are outside us and more or less permanent cause our sensations, and this view in turn seems to be true simply because we are or feel passive when we are having a sensation. When we look at what we come to call a red book we really have a red-patch sensation which, short of closing our eyes or looking away, we cannot avoid seeing. But the arguments against the view that what we see outside ourselves is just like the sensations that we have are both strong and well-known. We reviewed many of them in the discussion of Moore. Changing perspectives, changing light, pressing one eyeball, and magnifying—all change what we actually see or have as a sensation, but they do not give us any reason to believe that what is outside of ourselves, if anything, has itself changed. In fact, if you analyze the situation you will see that what is really known is just that some sensations (e.g., red patch that size) are correlated with other sensations (e.g., feel as if extending an arm). All the rest about what caused the sensations is an inference. You are unable to experience these things directly because in principle they cannot be experienced; they lie, so to speak, beyond all experience. Russell puts it this way: "I think it may be laid down quite generally that, *insofar* as physics or common sense is verifiable, it must be capable of interpretation in terms of actual sense-data alone. The reason for this is simple. Verification consists always in the occurrence of an expected sense-datum." (68)

Strictly speaking, you have no hard data which support the view that when no one is in a certain room all its furniture is still there. The fact that you think of physical objects like tables and chairs as having fairly permanent and continuous existence is not due to the fact that you can verify this, but rather to the fact that it is a convenient hypothesis. You assume it to be true because you have no evidence to the contrary, and life would be very difficult without it. But the only means you have of verifying that something is there is to go and look at it, and you are precluded from doing this by the very terms of the problem when you want to know whether things remain the same if no one is there to observe. Russell asks: "Can the existence of anything other than our hard data be inferred from these data?" (69) Under hard data Russell includes such things as illusions of the senses, hallucinations, and mental images. When and while we are having these they are as real as any other objects known to us. When we have them we cannot doubt that we are having them any more than we can doubt any of our sense data. How could we be sensing something and at the same time doubt that we are sensing that thing? Notice that it is about sense data or patches of sense qualities that Russell is speaking. He is concerned to argue that while we are sensing we cannot doubt either that we are sensing or what we are sensing. He is *not* arguing that what on the naïve view would be thought to exist in some permanent and continuous way, is actually existing. He could not argue this, for it is a hypothesis which he is trying to eliminate from his theory of knowledge. The argument is only that in sensing 'red-patch-now' one cannot doubt that one is sensing it.

In dreams, illusions, and hallucinations, in his view, one is having what he calls a 'wild' sense datum: a sense datum by itself which is not correlated with other sense data as we have come to expect. "Objects of sense are called 'real' when they have the kind of connection with other objects of sense which experience has led us to regard as normal; when they fail in this, they are called 'illusions.' But what is illusory is only the inferences to which they give rise. . . ." (71)

The argument for the unreality of illusions depends upon the view that there is a real substance underlying and causing our sense data, and somehow resembling them. Then, because in certain circumstances we seem to have more sense data than we think can be correlated with their supposed underlying causes, we reason that they cannot be caused by these objects and hence that they are illusory. But Russell wants to insist that nothing is or can be more real than the data of sense. If we look at a table, press one eyeball, and sense two brown-patch sense data, all that we may infer is that at least one of these is not correlated with other sense data in the way in which we have been accustomed to expect. Only one of them will correspond to our field of touch in what we call the normal way. The other will not. Notice that in taking this line Russell has reduced the common-sense world, as he wished to reduce the uncommon world of physics, to systems of sense data. These arguments on strictly empirical grounds are powerful ones, as Berkeley and Hume saw, and because they appeal so heavily to observed fact they are difficult to reject. As we shall see, they exercised considerable charm on the logical positivists but, as we shall also see, they are rejected in principle by Wittgenstein, Austin, and Ryle.

Russell moves on to argue that the assumption of continuous permanent substances underlying our appearances need not be made: that on the basis of our hard data another view may be put forward which explains the facts as we know them, which makes fewer assumptions, and which is hence less open to error. Suppose that ". . . each mind looks out upon the world, as in Leibnitz's monadology, from a point of view peculiar to itself. . . ." (72) No two minds see exactly the same thing; there is always a slight difference in what is called perspective when two minds are said to be seeing the same thing. Given two such minds which are seeing the same thing, it is always possible to interpose some other mind between them so that it would see the same thing from a slightly different perspective from the other two.

What is seen, the sense data, is conditioned by the fact

that what men see depends upon their sense organs, their nerves, and their brains. Therefore, although the world as seen by a particular man would not exist if that man were not there at that time, ". . . we can reasonably suppose that *some* aspect of the universe existed from that point of view, though no one was perceiving it." (72–73) These unperceived aspects he calls 'sensibilia'. They are what would be sensed if a mind and proper sense organs connected to it occupied that point of view. There are infinitely many such points of view.

In *My Philosophical Development* Russell uses the example of a photographic plate, which can reproduce a picture of the night sky, in order to illustrate what he means. Such a plate, correctly exposed, will reveal what a human observer would have seen at that place. And any region in space will do if you wish to photograph the sky from any perspective at all. Similarly, any place will do to provide an aspect for an embodied mind to get a perspective.

Suppose we now think of the collection of all the appearances at one place and one time. Russell calls that 'a perspective'. Each observer has a space private to him in which all his sense data appear and the totality of these data at any time make up the perspective. The history of all perspectives of such an observer is just the history of certain of his mental functionings.

On the other hand, the thing or object in the world is a bundle of all the events which consist of the various appearances of it—the sum of all its actual and possible appearances. Think of the visual sense datum an observer has when, as we would naïvely say, he sees a table. At any moment he has a sensory patch in one particular aspect; it has one shape. If it is the table top which he sees, then his brown-patch sensation will be more or less the shape of a parallelogram. Try it. Look at the top of a rectangular table from a slight distance and angle. The surface of the top will appear as a parallelogram. The sensory patch may have a certain thickness as well because of the apron and legs, but we may ignore this.

What we have here is one perspective of the table top. Now think of several observers in different positions. They would each, if they were doing what we called looking at the table, have a sense datum of a slightly different shape from any other observer's sense datum. Finally, consider all the possible points of view from which, as we would say, some observer could be seeing the table—near and far, top and bottom, one side and the other. The table, or physical object, is now defined as the class or system of all the possible perspectives of it. "Thus an aspect of a 'thing' is a member of the system of aspects which *is* the 'thing' at that moment. . . . All the aspects of the thing are real, whereas the thing is a mere logical construction." *(OKNEW* 73–74) Here Russell is not denying the existence of the thing, but merely pointing out that it can be constructed from our hard data and hence there is no need to affirm its existence.

Now each observer has his own space in which the aspects or data appear. If this view is adopted, it seems to solve one aspect of the problem which so plagued Moore.[5] Many different appearances are seen to be not in one object, but each one is in the different private space of each observer. The appearances are not in the object nor are they parts of its surface. Rather, what we call the object is the sum of all its possible and actual appearances. Once the permanently existing object 'out there' is dispensed with in favor of logical constructions, there is no longer any problem of correlating all our sense data with it, nor is there any problem about how we know that there is an object.

Parenthetically we should remark that this notion of Russell's is, in broad outline, quite similar to notions held by Husserl at about the same time and by Sartre twenty years later. Each of them in his own way reduced the existent object to the series of its appearances. Naturally both Husserl and Sartre make different uses of the notion, and it is not to be inferred that they are Russellians nor that Russell was a Husserlian. But this passing resemblance is worth noting. Both Husserl and Sartre start out from an empirical point of view and ask how we can have certainty. Husserl gets it by ultimately constructing the world out of mind stuff; Sartre leaves it as a fundamental datum; Russell eventually abandons the quest.

Russell postulates a single space in which all the points of view or perspectives are themselves located. There are many actual private spaces, an infinite number of possible ones, but only one public space or perspective space which contains them all. Perspective or public space is defined as the system of private spaces, just as the object was the system of aspects in private space. It, too, is a logical construction, or if you like, a fiction.

A partial, though somewhat misleading, example may make this clearer. Consider a big block of ice in which many air bubbles are frozen. Each air bubble represents a monad, a perspective, or point of view. The block of ice containing them is perspective or public space. Besides the actual air bubbles there are places not occupied by air bubbles but which could be. If, then, you can think of the block of ice as not really existing and the air bubbles as not really being located anywhere, but think of their locations in the block of ice as another convenient fiction, you will have an idea of public space as a logical construction.

Now the object must be located in our block of ice somewhere. How can this be, since the block doesn't exist? Consider a penny. You can form a straight line of its perspectives when it looks circular—that is when, as we say, you are looking at it with your line of vision perpendicular to its surface. You can arrange the various perspectives again according to size, calling the larger ones nearer. Straight lines drawn through each of these perspectives will meet somewhere in the constructed perspective space, and this point we define as the location of the object.

This completes a rough sketch of what Russell called a rough sketch of how the world may be constructed from hard data and ingenuity. The account here is not rigorous, but neither is Russell's account. In order for it to be rigorous it would have to be framed not to appeal to illegitimate concepts, like the place where the object is, before those concepts are constructed from hard data. The whole question of whether or not Russell's theory is adequate to explain not only the ordinary world but also the world of physics depends upon whether or not the required constructions can actually be carried out in detail: not just for sight but for all the senses, taking into account all refinements made necessary by the structures of the special sciences. It is also necessary to show how to account for other people's minds, since these cannot be hard data for us.

For the belief that other minds exist, Russell adduces certain arguments from analogy. We have data which seem to come from other people and are like the data which we have from ourselves. We produce these data as the results of thoughts and feelings, so if the apparent actions of others match our data as actions of sentient beings, then we have some, though not conclusive, reason to believe that other people with minds exist. As Russell says, "the hypothesis that other people have minds must, I think, be allowed to be not susceptible of any strong support from the analogical argument. At the same time, it is a hypothesis which systematizes a vast body of facts and never leads to any consequences which there is reason to think false. . . ." (79) It may, then, be used as a hypothesis on a par with other hypotheses which frame and order the relations of our hard data. According to this view other people's existence cannot be a hard fact for me: a somewhat unhappy conclusion for a social being.

Next we shall have to say something brief about what sense data are in Russell's view, and then go on to detail the nature of the logical atoms out of which logical atomism proposes to construct the world.

Sense Data: What They Are

Sense data are, of course, things of whose existence we can be certain. They are the blocks out of which the world can be constructed with the help of mathematical logic and certain other building blocks of which we shall speak shortly. But *what* are they? Moore denied that they are mental enti-

ties when he distinguished between sensations, which are
mental events, and what the sensations are sensations of,
which are not mental events. He had considerable difficulty
in identifying these objects of sensation, which he called
sense data, with physical objects. But Russell's notion of
private space enables him to make this identification. Section
4 of his paper "The Relation of Sense-Data to Physics" is
called "Sense-Data Are Physical."

His first step is to say that the word 'physical' means just
what is dealt with by the science of physics. ("RSDP" in *ML*,
145) Moore had divided what we may call the sense datum
sequence into a sensation, which a mind had, a sense datum,
which was its object, and the physical body to which the
sense datum was related in some way which he could not
explain. Sensations do not exist without minds but sense
data do. Russell, as we have seen, eliminated the physical
thing as such, reducing it to the class of all its possible and
actual appearances. In his sense datum sequence there is also
a sensibile which is an aspect of a particular thing which may
not now be being experienced, but which could be. It is a
possible appearance. There is a sense datum which is a neural
event in somebody's brain or nervous system and finally there
is a sensation, which is an observer's awareness of the sense
datum. A diagram may make this clearer.

Moore:
Physical object ------ sense datum ------ sensation

{either the sur-
face of a physi-
cal object, or
related in some
way to a physical
object

{subject's
awareness
of sense
datum

Russel:
Physical Object -- sensibilia -- sense datum -- sensation

{logical fiction;
constructed of
the series of all
actual and possi-
ble appearances

{which a
sentenient be-
ing would
sense if he
were in the
right posi-
tion

{neural event

{subject's
awareness
of sense
datum

For Moore sense data exist when they are not data for anybody, but for Russell they may or may not cease to exist when they are not data for anybody. If there is no appropriate nervous system in which they could exist, they cease to do so. Nevertheless, the fact that something does not exist when no one is having it as a datum does not imply, as Berkeley thought, that it is mental. For sense data are not data when the appropriate physical conditions are lacking. Sense data as neural events are in the subject's body and so very likely cease to exist when there is no subject; for when there is no subject it appears that we can say with some degree of certainty that there is no body either. But this can in no way imply that sense data are mental. "What I mean," says Russell, "may perhaps be made plainer by saying that if my body could remain in exactly the same state in which it is, although my mind had ceased to exist, precisely that object which I now see when I see the flash [of lightning] would exist, although of course I should not see it, since my seeing is mental."[6]

The difference in approach to sense data between Moore and Russell might be put this way. Moore *knew* that he saw tables and chairs, and he asked himself what had to be happening when he was sensing them. The result of his analysis was a queer entity called a sense datum, for whose relation to both perceiver and perceived he could not account. On the other hand Russell asked himself what was likely to be the case given that knowledge was possible and science got it. The result of his investigation was the conclusion that something existed immediately in sensation, and he asked, regardless of what that thing was, how you could use it to construct both the world of common sense, in which he had little trust, and the world of science. His solution proceeded by means of a clever use of the logical language of *Principia Mathematica* together with certain sorts of building blocks, among which were sense data.

The emphasis is neither on finding what is metaphysically there nor in analyzing its precise relations to us and the objects in the world (though, to be sure, this is done); but it is rather on making a construct which will yield the core of science with the fewest possible assumptions.

Moore spent most of his time trying to analyze the relations between ourselves, sense data, and physical objects, while Russell spent proportionately less time doing this and more trying to use sense data as the building blocks out of which to construct a world. It is much as if two men were confronted by a pile of bricks, and one, a Moorean, examines each brick carefully, turning it over and picking at it with care and concentration. The other, a Russellian, picks at them awhile, says that he thinks they are clay or mud or composition, and spends the rest of his time building interestingly shaped hollow structures with them, his basic interest being in what you could make with them.

Truth Functional Propositions: A Brief Account

We shall understand the term 'proposition' to refer to whatever is referred to by the words 'what George said' in sentences like 'what George said was true' or by the word 'statement' in 'George's statement was true'. Russell divides propositions into two kinds: atomic and molecular. Roughly speaking, atomic propositions contain just one verb or relational term. Molecular propositions are built up of atomic ones, as their name implies, by means of such links between them as 'and', 'or', 'if then', and 'not'. Atomic propositions may be said to be the smallest units which can be called propositions. Examples of them are 'today is Tuesday', 'we have made a mistake', 'Theatetus sits'. Examples of molecular propositions are: 'either today is Tuesday or we have made a mistake', 'if today is Tuesday then we have made a mistake', and the like.

Now, whatever propositions may be, the logician assumes that they are the sorts of things which are either true or false. Logic does not concern itself with how one finds out the truth or falsity of any proposition, but only with the relations among propositions, given that they are the sorts of things which are true or false. Particular propositions are not used in this sort of examination but variables like *p, q, r, s,*

. . . are. These variables are said to range over propositions as their values, and since propositions can either be true or false, these variables can take on the values true or false.

In the same way, to facilitate matters the logician uses symbols to represent what he calls the logical constants: '·' for 'and'; ' $\lor$ ' for 'or'; ' $\sim$ ' for 'not'; and ' $\supset$ ' for 'if, then'. By using one or more of these constants or connectives and propositional variables, molecular propositions may be constructed. In terms of one of the above examples we might write 'today is Tuesday $\lor$ we made a mistake'; 'today is Tuesday $\supset$ we made a mistake'; $p \lor q$; $p \supset q$.

The connectives '·','$\lor$', ' $\sim$ ', and ' $\supset$' are given a minimum interpretation which corresponds to the weakest possible interpretations of their translations into English. Nevertheless, they are defined purely formally and do not depend upon these translations. The definitions may be given by means of a device called a truth table. The interested reader may refer to any standard elementary logic text for these. A molecular proposition composed of two atomic propositions connected by '·' (and) is true if and only if both atomic propositions are true; it is false in all other cases. A molecular proposition composed of two atomic propositions connected by ' $\lor$ ' (or) is false if and only if both atomic propositions are false; it is true in all other cases. A molecular proposition composed of two atomic propositions connected by ' $\supset$ ' (if, then) is false if and only if the antecedent proposition is true, and the consequent proposition is false; it is true in all other cases. If an atomic proposition is true, then writing it with ' $\sim$ ' (not) in front of it makes it false, and if it is false then ' $\sim$ ' in front of it makes it true. Compounds of more than two atomic propositions may be built up algebraically by repeated use of the connectives in any combination, with punctuation to show how the whole is to be read.

A compound statement is said to be a truth functional statement when its truth or falsity can be determined solely from the truth or falsity of its constituent statements. The truth or falsity of 'today is Tuesday $\lor$ we have made a mistake' is, according to the definition given above of '$\lor$', determined solely by the truth or falsity of 'today is Tuesday' and 'we have made a mistake'. The truth or falsity of $p \lor q$ is determined solely by the truth or falsity of p and q.

Many truth functional statements are true and false in turn depending upon the truth value of their constituent propositions. For example $p \lor q$ is true or false in turn depending upon how values are assigned to p and q respectively. But there are two special sorts of truth functional propositions of interest to the logician: those which are true no matter how the truth values are assigned to their constituent propositions, and those that are false no matter how the truth values are assigned to the constituent propositions. The first are called tautologies and the second are called contradictions. For example, the logician may wish to see how many tautologies (sometimes called laws of logic) he can generate.

The main interest we have in truth functional propositions is that it is from languages built up of such propositions that Russell hoped to construct the world as we know it, for he attempted to analyze that world into atomic bits and pieces which could ultimately be exhibited as being related to each other in accordance with the logically perfect language of *Principia Mathematica*. If this language is not the perfect syntax, Russell thought that it is very close to it. ("PLA," 198) Perhaps this is simply because it is economical in basic principles and structure. But Russell may also have felt that logic could be applied to the world with intelligible and interesting results because in the end logic set out the most general features of the world. *(IMP,* 169) Whatever the reason, Russell determined to found the world upon the structure of logic. Truth functions were taken to be the logical skeleton of language. The notion that all language is truth functional, or could be reduced to truth functional propositions, is called the thesis of extensionality. Unfortunately for the logical atomists, the thesis is false, as we shall see. This raised problems for them.

Logical Atomism

The basic thesis of logical atomism, then, is that if one

could construct an ideal language, that language would be isomorphic to the structure of reality, or, at the very least, we could adequately describe the real structure of the world with it. Two groups are said to be isomorphic to each other when they correspond to each other in form, when each element in one has a counterpart in the other, and when the results of any operation performed in the one group corresponds to the result of that operation performed on the corresponding part of the other group.

The ideal language will not, like ordinary language, be vague, but precise. Each particular will be called by one name. Each atomic sentence will be composed of elements which get their meaning by direct correlation with experience. Sense data will be among the basic building blocks here. The world will be seen to consist in a vast number of separate and independent facts, and knowledge of the world will be seen to depend upon acquaintance with immediate experience.

The sort of analysis which Russell is running in logical atomism can proceed in two directions, both of which have already been discussed. In his theory of descriptions, analysis proceeds by breaking down sentences containing disguised descriptions into sentences containing overt descriptions of things in the world. This is termed by Mr. D. F. Pears 'horizontal analysis'. It starts from the level of things in the world and ends there. "But the analysis of the phrase 'object in the external world' into descriptions of sense data is a deep analysis, because it takes us down to things of an entirely different kind." (Pears, 16) We are now to be concerned with the sorts of things there are on the deep level. A number of things may be sorted out at this point.

Propositions. Propositions for Russell are the sorts of things which are true or false. They are expressed by sentences in the indicative. They assert, but do not command or wish. They symbolize something. They are complex symbols, being symbols whose parts are symbols. Because they are complex they may be understood on first reading or hearing, provided you know the language. But words whose meanings are simple cannot be so understood. These word, like 'red', whose

meanings are simple cannot be understood ". . . except
through seeing red things. There is no other way . . . It is no
use to learn languages, or to look up dictionaries." ("PLA,"
194) All language is symbolic. ". . . [T]he components of
a proposition are the symbols we must understand in order
to understand the proposition. . . ." (196) But to understand
the components you must be, or have been, acquainted
with the things they symbolize.

Now, as we said above, propositions are either atomic or
molecular. An atomic proposition is a proposition none of
whose parts are propositions. But propositions are not real
constituents in the world. An examination of the basic ingredients of the world reveals no propositions, but only facts
and particulars. Russell has changed his early position on
this point, as did Moore.

Proper names. Proper names are words which name particulars. Either they name an individual or it is wrong to call
them names; they would then be empty noises. Propositions
may state or fail to state a fact, but if a word fails to refer to
an individual or particular, then it is no name. Names name
individuals but not facts, nor do propositions name facts.
Facts cannot be named. As Russell says, "the only kind of
word that is theoretically capable of standing for a particular
is a *proper name*. . . ." (200) In the sense of ideal, though not
of normal ordinary language, "Proper names = words for
particulars. Df." (200) Since we are not now, nor have been
acquainted with Socrates, we cannot name him. "When we
use the word 'Socrates', we are really using a description.
Our thought may be rendered by some such phrase as, 'The
Master of Plato', or 'The philosopher who drank the hem-
lock'. . . ." (201) These are descriptions in the now familiar
sense, and so are most names in ordinary language.

Individuals. Individuals or "Particulars = terms of relations
in atomic facts. Df." (199) There are an infinite number of
kinds of individuals or simples: particulars, qualities, relations, etc. These things are, for the atomist, the ultimate entities in the world. The real Socrates may have been thought
to have been a particular, but words purporting to name

particulars often do not do so. Take the word 'Piccadilly' which ". . . on the face of it, is the name for a certain portion of the earth's surface. . . . If you wanted to define it, you would have to define it as a series of classes of material entities. . . . So that you would find that the logical status of Piccadilly is bound up with the logical status of series and classes. . . ." (191) These, we have seen, Russell holds to be logical constructions or elaborate fictions. So Piccadilly is an elaborate fiction. Actual particulars can be thought of as the ultimate subjects of acquaintance. If we can discover what has to be counted as one sense datum, one patch of color, sound, or the like, that sort of thing is an individual. Though we and Russell try to give examples of particulars for the purpose of exposition, it is not necessary to do so. ". . . [T]he definition of a particular is something purely logical. . . . In order to understand the definition it is not necessary to know beforehand 'This is a particular' or 'That is a particular'. . . . The whole question of what particulars you actually find in the real world is a purely empirical one which does not interest the logician as such." (199)

Whatever particulars there are, they are simple things. They cannot be decomposed or defined, but merely pointed to. Simple words and symbols, proper names, can be defined by pointing to the objects for which they stand. In the end 'this' and 'that' are the properest of all names. But objects in themselves are in a fundamental sense indefinable. The important thing to remember is that the doctrine Russell advocates is *logical* atomism. Its ultimate residue will be what is logically required by the analysis. What empirical bits and pieces these turn out to be is not important, although on Russell's view patches of color do turn up among them. Among the more *logical* of the atoms we find predicates and relations. These sorts of things are the ultimate data, and it is out of them that all other data are constructed. (179, 214)

Atomic Facts. There are many sorts of facts that Russell recognized: atomic facts, general facts, negative facts, and 'intensional' facts. Basically, a fact is the sort of thing existing in the world which makes the proposition stating or corresponding to it either true or false. The expression of a fact always involves a sentence. Roughly, an atomic fact is a particular and a relation in combination: 'this is red', 'this is nice', 'that is large' all express atomic facts. The particular may be a sense datum and the component may be a predicate. Russell calls these 'monadic facts' to indicate that one predicate or relation is involved. But there could be atomic facts expressed by 'this is next to that', where there were two particulars or constituents and one relation or component. This is a dyadic fact. One could in principle have triadic, quadratic, and, in general, *n*-adic facts: facts with one component or relation and *n* constituents or particulars. Atomic propositions express or fail to express atomic facts. A proposition is atomic, as we said, if it contains only one relation or predicate, if it cannot be broken down into parts which are propositions, and if its constituents are names. Facts are just there or not there, but propositions expressing them are true or false according as they do or do not state facts. "A man believes that Socrates is dead. What he believes is a proposition on the face of it. . . . There are *two* propositions corresponding to each fact. [But not in the same way as they did on Moore's theory.] Suppose it is a fact that Socrates is dead. You have two propositions: 'Socrates is dead' and 'Socrates is not dead'. . . . [T]here is one fact in the world which makes one true and one false." (187)

Individuals are simples—they are named. Facts are complex—they are described or pictured in propositions. Facts are analyzable into parts which are not facts. Particulars and relations which are the parts or constituents of facts are unanalyzable. Facts are what make propositions true or false; and the parts of a fact are the meanings of the component symbols of the proposition. These symbols are really proper names and hence their meanings are the individuals—the parts of the fact—for which they stand.

General Facts. Russell is forced to admit that ". . . when you have enumerated all the atomic facts in the world, it is a further fact about the world that those are all the atomic facts there are about the world, and that is just as much an objective fact about the world as any of them are." (236) It is clear that general facts of the form 'all x's are y's' cannot be derived by counting up any number of particular facts of the form 'this x is a y'. No matter how many of them you count you will not be saying the same thing as you say when you say 'all x's are y's'. Suppose you are counting crows to see if they are all black. After several days you are up to the 10,956th crow which, like the previous 10,955, is black. You then say 'all crows are black' and by this you do not mean 'all the crows I have seen are black', but rather 'if anything is a crow, then it is black, regardless of whether I have seen it or not'. This is usually what is meant by saying 'all' in such a context.

But if this is what 'all' means, then saying 'all' cannot be the same as saying 10,955 or 10,956 or, indeed, saying any number whatsoever. It is saying something else. It is picturing a new fact. And, unfortunately, propositions of the form 'all x's are y's' cannot be constructed out of any finite number of atomic propositions put together by truth functional connectives. There is, then, this one new kind of proposition picturing one new kind of fact which cannot be called a truth functional proposition. But this shows that the thesis of extensionality is false. It means that the pantheon of facts would have to be enlarged and enlarged not only by more of the same sort of fact, but by facts of a different sort. Continued enlargement will tend to detract from the beauty and simplicity of the theory. But it was just these features that made it interesting to the atomists. So we might say that as more such facts became needed, a good part of the impetus behind the whole enterprise began to slack off.

Negative facts. Negative facts are kinds of particular or atomic facts. Such a fact would be the indubitable fact that 'Socrates is not alive'. Propositions are true or false according as they do or do not say what is the case. One can say 'Socrates is alive' and that would be a false statement because it does not state what is the case or the fact: namely, that Socrates is not alive. Now if you accept a correspondence theory of truth as Russell does, then when a negative proposition is true, as is the proposition 'Socrates is not alive', then there must be something which is the case and which this proposition mirrors or pictures. And what *is* the case is that in fact, as we say, Socrates is not alive. As Russell puts it, "a thing cannot be false except because of a fact, so that you find it extremely difficult to say what exactly happens when you make a positive assertion that is false, unless you are going to admit negative facts." (214)

But Russell is then left with the problem of saying either that the word 'not' named some element in the world, or else that it could be eliminated in principle from discourse. For how else could language be said to mirror the world or picture it? You cannot say this if you are left with too many linguistic pieces which do not stand for real entities. But 'not' was not a popular word, for no one wished to say that it referred to a logical atom and no one could get rid of it.

Intensional facts. Propositions containing verbs such as 'wishes', 'wants', 'believes', and the like are not truth functional propositions. The truth or falsity of propositions such as 'Jones believes that p' or 'Smith believed that p is a q' cannot be determined from the truth or falsity of 'p' or of 'p is a q'. Jones may believe that it is raining whether it is raining or not. The truth or falsity of the whole statement is independent of the truth or falsity of its constituents. But if propositions about intensional facts cannot be treated truth functionally and analyzed into atomic propositions out of which it is built up, then once again the thesis of extensionality is shown to be false. And again, if you hold that language mirrors the world, you must allow this new type of fact into your metaphysics. As Russell says, it becomes a new species for the zoo.

We see already that in its elaboration at a moderately theoretical level, logical atomism began to develop cracks and strains which would eventually lead to its abandonment. The men who developed the theory, and Russell foremost among them, saw its flaws even as they were elaborating it. The beautiful simplicity of a logically perfect language mirroring the relations of a small number of readily describable types of ultimate constituents of the world became progressively more complicated by annoying details which refused to fit in as expected. The result was to burden the theory beyond the point where its beauty and utility were attractive. Parts of it, like the language of *Principia*, remained as permanent monuments, although even here alternative systems and notations were developed by logicians which, had atomism remained viable, might have competed for the position of the logically perfect language. As it was, by showing that equivalent alternative languages were possible, they helped to undermine atomism. But Russell's theory of descriptions, which in 1905 set a foundation stone upon which the rest grew, remained unchallenged until Strawson's attack in 1950. Meanwhile, regardless of its own internal strains, the metaphysics of atomism was attacked by a group of men whose search for logical and epistemological rigor equaled that of the atomists.

6

Logical Positivism: Meaning and Reference

Logical positivism has often been confused with analytic philosophy as a whole. It shares certain ancestors with analysis and the two have some aims in common, but they are not identical. Although the work of Russell and the earlier Wittgenstein influenced the positivists heavily, the positivists set out in different and more radical directions. In the heavily logico-mathematical turns of phrase of the positivists, logical positivism forms a proper subset of analytic philosophy. All logical positivists are analysts, but not all analysts are logical positivists.

Like the names of other philosophic movements, the name 'logical positivism' is used to designate a group of men who share certain aims and common interests, and who perhaps share these to a greater degree than other men in other philosophic groups, but who also differ with each other on major points of doctrine. Despite the fact that their work was so very technical, they became more well known in a popular way than many other philosophic movements because their aims with respect to classical philosophy were so easily popularized, clear, direct, and radical: eliminate all metaphysics—metaphysical statements do not assert anything higher or more fundamental than science. They assert nothing at all. They are neither true nor false, but meaningless. They ought not even to be called statements (i.e., assertions which may properly be called true or false). And out the window with metaphysical statements went the conception of religious, ethical, and aesthetic discourse as assertive in function.

The positivists had the prestige of science on their side, for many of them were scientists or trained in the sciences, and it was a notion of science which they elaborated. Then too, in its popular form, as expounded by A. J. Ayer in *Language, Truth and Logic,*[1] the radical doctrines of logical positivism reached a wide audience because of the forcefulness and clarity of Ayer's exposition. Literary critics like I. A. Richards were moved to respond to the movement (see his *Science and Poetry*[2]), as were intelligent laymen.

The movement itself grew about a group of men who became known as the Vienna Circle. In 1922 the chair of philosophy at the University of Vienna was offered to Moritz Schlick, who attracted a group of men to him. Among these were F. Waismann, O. Neurath, F. Zilsel, H. Feigl, R. Carnap, V. Kraft, H. Hahn, and K. Gödel.[3] This group met frequently to discuss philosophic problems. They were in contact with Wittgenstein, who lived nearby, and with a similar group in Berlin. They founded journals, held congresses, published manifestoes, and, most importantly, produced results difficult to ignore.

If logical positivism is dead today, its death is due to the scrupulous honesty and immense logical powers of the positivists themselves, for it was they who, in attempting to refine their formulations in order to make their key concepts rigorous, finally discovered that some of their main notions were unworkable. In passing, it should be noted that although in their popular work the positivists often attacked classical metaphysics as providing examples of meaningless statements, it was the very handy example of the metaphysics of Moore, Russell, and the early Wittgenstein which as often as not they were interested in attacking.[4] For example, we find Schlick writing that physics is concerned with laws and not with sensations; therefore, bodies cannot be constructed as complexes of sensations. Rather, what should have been said is that propositions concerning bodies are transformable into equivalent propositions about the occurrences of sensations in accordance with laws. The consistent empiricist can neither deny nor affirm the existence of a transcendental world, for to do either of these is to make an equally metaphysical statement and, hence, an equally meaningless one. So much, then, for the problem of the external world and the metaphysics of logical atomism.[5]

One of the main programs of the logical positivists may be understood as the attempt to drive a logical wedge between what was on the one hand verifiable and scientific, and hence meaningful, and what on the other was not verifiable and scientific, and hence not meaningful. In the first instance this can be seen as an attempt to eliminate metaphysics. This attempt is not all that new in the history of philosophy. The skeptics of ancient Greece and the nominalists of the middle ages stand out as examples of anti-metaphysicians in great periods of classical philosophy. Kant himself, at least in one phase of his critical work, attempted to show that metaphysics of a certain sort was impossible and that knowledge must have sensory content. In the early nineteenth century Auguste Comte attempted to show that metaphysics belonged to an intellectually darker period in man's history than science, which superseded it. Even Leibnitz, with his attempt to use logical analysis to solve philosophic disputes, may be counted a forerunner of the positivists, although he was a metaphysician. Empiricists like Mill, and pragmatists like James and Peirce may be counted here as well.[6]

But most of all it was to Hume that the positivists owed a debt, as do all analytic philosophers. His attempt at thoroughgoing empiricism and his rejection of metaphysics is characteristic of the positivists. What they added was a logical rigor which replaced Hume's psychological analyses, and a passion for dealing with formalized languages. In one of the most famous passages in philosophy Hume writes:

"When we run over libraries, persuaded of these principles, what havoc must we make? If we take in our hand any volume; of divinity or school metaphysics, for instance; let us ask, *Does it contain any abstract reasoning concerning quantity or number?* No. *Does it contain any experimental reasoning concerning matter of fact and existence?* No. Commit it then to the flames: for it can contain nothing but sophistry and illusion." *(Enquiry,* sec. XII, III)

Roughly speaking, Hume divides statements into two kinds: what we call analytic and synthetic. He called it the division between relations of ideas and matters of fact. (sec. IV, pt. I) Statements concerning relations of ideas are true merely by virtue of their form. They can be demonstrated by logical or mathematical methods without appealing to sensory experience. In one way or another they are, as Wittgenstein calls them, tautologies: '2 + 2 = 4', 'all bachelors are male,' etc. Their denial makes a contradiction. But statements of matters of fact, such as 'the sun rises in the east' or 'the North won the Civil War' depend upon experience, or, if you like, the way the world is. To deny them may be to say what is false, but it is never to contradict oneself. Statements which fit into neither of these two categories may be called, in Hume's words, 'sophistry and illusion'. If we substitute for this phrase the word 'meaningless' we shall have the positivist doctrine.

The positivists thought that it was comparatively easy to recognize analytic or *a priori* statements, and they concentrated their energies on synthetic or *a posteriori* statements. They asked what characterized such statements, and their answer was roughly that they were verified or falsified by some experience. Then if a statement was such that it was not analytic and could not be verified by some experience, it was felt to be meaningless. For example, Ayer writes:

> The criterion which we use to test the genuineness of apparent statements of fact is the criterion of verifiability. We say that a sentence is factually significant to any given person, if, and only if, he knows how to verify the proposition which it purports to express—that is, if he knows what observations

would lead him, under certain conditions, to accept the propositions as being true, or reject it as being false. If, on the other hand, the putative proposition is of such a character that the assumption of its truth or falsehood, is consistent with any assumptions whatsoever concerning the nature of his future experience, then, as far as he is concerned, it is, if not a tautology, a mere pseudo-proposition. The sentence expressing it may be emotionally significant to him; but it is not literally significant. And with regard to questions the procedure is the same. We inquire in every case what observations would lead us to answer the question, one way or the other; and, if none can be discovered, we must conclude that the sentence under consideration does not, as far as we are concerned, express a genuine question, however strongly its grammatical appearance may suggest that it does. (Ayer, 1936, 1946, p. 35)

And Carnap puts it this way:

Suppose, *e.g.,* he [some scientist] asserts that there is not only a gravitational field having an effect on bodies according to the known laws of gravitation, but also a *levitational field,* and on being asked what sort of effect this levitational field has, according to his theory, he answers that there is no observable effect; in other words, he confesses his inability to give rules according to which we could deduce perceptive propositions from his assertion. In that case our reply is: your assertion is no assertion at all; it does not speak about anything; it is nothing but a series of empty words; it is simply without sense. (1935, 13–14)

It is true that he may have images and even feelings connected with his words. This fact may be of psychological importance; logically it is irrelevant. What gives theoretical meaning to a proposition is not the attendant images and thoughts, but the possibility of deducing from propositions what we can observe—in other words, the possibility of verification.

The Verifiability Principle

The central issue here is how to construe the notion of verification. Can a verifiability principle be set up which states the necessary and sufficient conditions to show that a statement is, in fact, verifiable? What is wanted is a rule or principle which will tell us what sorts of statements have or do not have empirical content, for we cannot examine every individual statement. It is easy to see that '2 + 2 = 4' has no empirical content. But this is an analytic statement and its truth can be shown by purely formal methods. It is easy to see that statements like 'the temperature outside here and now is 81 degrees Fahrenheit' or 'this pot of water will boil at 100 degrees centigrade' have empirical content. You find out that the first is true or false by looking at a standard thermometer, and you find out that the second is true or false by taking the pot of water, heating it, and measuring its temperature when it boils.

But not all statements are so straightforward. Consider statements like 'Saturn is made of green cheese' (at this writing no planetary probes have landed on Saturn) and 'all water is composed of hydrogen and oxygen, two parts to one'. In the first case we cannot get to Saturn to look or taste, and in the second how could we analyze *all* the water there is to see if it is composed of H_2O? What principle will show that all the above are meaningful? What principle will show that they all have empirical content, while showing that statements like 'the Absolute enters into, but is itself incapable of, evolution and progress', 'God is everywhere', and 'light bulbs light up because spirit fulminates in a vacuum' have no empirical content and, hence, are meaningless? Historically there have been several attempts to formulate such a principle. They are conveniently outlined and discussed in Carl Hempel's important paper, "The Empiricist Criteria of Cognitive Significance: Problems and Changes" (1950)[7] We shall follow his order of exposition, outlining his main points.[8]

Complete Verifiability

In his "Positivism and Realism" (Ayer 1959, pp. 82–107), Schlick states that the unique business of philosophy is to ascertain and make clear the meanings of statements and questions. Philosophic analysis cannot say what is or is not real. It deals merely with language. He attributes the chaotic state of philosophy throughout its history—presumably in contrast to the tranquil state of science—to its failure to grasp that certain questions which looked like real questions did not make any sense at all. The meaning of a question is clear when and only when we can state the conditions which would lead us to answer it. These conditions define the meaning of the question. Similarly, to perform the operation he calls verifying a proposition you must know what to do in order to find out whether it is true or false. Failure to know this is failure to know the meaning of the proposition. To state what experience would make a proposition true is to state its meaning.

The requirement in which Schlick is interested is verifiability in principle. We may, for technical reasons, be unable to verify the statement 'Venus supports life' because as yet we have no means of going to Venus and looking or of sending up a probe sufficiently sensitive to gather the information. But the fact that we can state those two empirical conditions whose satisfaction would enable us to verify the proposition is enough to allow us to say that the proposition is verifiable in principle. We know what experiences we must have in order to see if the proposition is true, and it is logically, though not technically, possible that we might have them.

But if someone should say 'God exists everywhere', what possible experience could show the truth or falsity of that statement? Where would we look? What conditions would we describe to discover its truth? There is no place to look and there are no conditions to describe. It is not that we have not got the technical means at our disposal in order to go to see, as in the case of Venus, but that there is just nothing *to* go to see. The impossibility of verification is not technical but logical. In principle we could not verify that statement. It is clear that, if verification were interpreted as 'actual ability to verify', there would be a great many statements which scientists consider they have every right to accept, which would be ruled out as meaningless (such as our statement about Venus, or all statements about the future). For example, the statement made by Mendeleev in his development of the periodic chart of the atoms, that an as yet undiscovered element (germanium) would be found having atomic weight 32 and a greyish white color, which would be unaffected by acids and alkalis, and which would give off a white oxide when burned in air, under this criterion would have been meaningless. Yet it was one of the very important statements of modern chemistry.

The whole tension set up in philosophy by the adoption of a verifiability principle may be thought of in terms of getting a criterion which would keep in all of what were thought of as scientific statements, and rule out all of the so-called metaphysical ones, without ruling out any scientific ones or allowing in any metaphysical ones. From our point of view we should not look at the whole business as a search for a principle which would tell what statements were meaningful. In most cases the positivists thought they already knew which statements were and which were not meaningful. What they wanted was a set of criteria which could be exhibited to show which traits meaningful statements had and which meaningless ones lacked. The problem was really worked backwards, since they knew roughly what types of statements they would admit; they lacked only a precise way of characterizing these statements in the aggregate. Even the criterion was known roughly. The statements had in some way to have empirical content. But how was this to be specified? Surely with a little ingenuity it could be done, for we already have an intuitive grasp of what counts as empirical and what does not. Here, as elsewhere in philosophy, Russell's dictum holds: you find out which conclusions you wish to support and then you work backwards to see what premises you need to buy.

As Hempel states it, the verifiability principle put forward by Schlick in the paper already discussed (Ayer. 1959, p. 87) is that a sentence is significant ". . . if and only if it is not analytic and is capable, at least in principle, of complete verification by observational evidence; i.e., if observational evidence can be described which, if actually obtained, would conclusively establish the truth of the sentence." (Hempel, 1965, p. 103)

Hempel's criticism is first directed to the word 'conclusive.' Consider any universal law or general statement such as

(*S*1) All storks are red-legged.

What observation or finite number of observations will conclusively establish this? The notion of an observation sentence is introduced. It is a sentence—either true or false—which says that some observable object, or group of objects, has or has not got some property which can be seen by direct observation. Hempel now states the requirement of complete verifiability in principle more accurately as the requirement that "a sentence has empirical meaning if and only if it is not analytic and follows logically from some finite and logically consistent class of observation sentences." (104)

Given this criterion, how would we attempt to support (*S*1)? If we begin observing storks and say that stork 1 is red-legged, and stork 2 is red-legged, we will never count enough storks to imply that (*S*1), *all* storks are red-legged. We have already seen this as the reason that Russell was forced to admit general facts. No finite number of singular propositions taken together suffices to imply a universal proposition. We may count 10, 50, 100, 500, 5,000 or 9,000,000, or any number of red-legged storks you like, but we can never count enough to imply that *all* storks are red-legged. 'All' refers not only to all that we happen to see, but to all that there are, were, and will ever be, and these cannot be counted, nor can any number ever be said to equal them, for it is always possible that there will be more.

Thus, we cannot get any finite number of observation statements of the form 'stork 1 is red-legged', 'stork 2 is red-legged', . . . 'stork *n* is red-legged', to imply that they are *all* red-legged. Hence (*S1*) and any other universal statement is not verifiable according to Schlick's criterion. But, unfortunately, many important statements of science are universal generalizations and, since Schlick's criterion would rule them out, it is not acceptable.

Hempel raises three additional objections to this formulation of the verifiability principle, one of which was subsequently withdrawn. (see Hempel p. 120) Let us look at the remaining two. The first is that many statements of science contain both universal and existential quantifiers—that is, the words 'all' and 'some'—and if Schlick's criterion is accepted, some, though not all of these, cannot be verified. (Technicalities are omitted here; see Hempel, 1965, p. 121.) The second is: consider any statement at all. If it is true, then its negation is false; and if it is false, its negation is true. This is just what is meant by negation. And remember that any statement is meaningful, just in case under appropriate circumstances it could be either true or false. Now, under the criterion of complete verifiability a strange thing happens. Our original statement was:

(S1) All storks are red-legged.

Its negation is:

(not-S1) There is at least one stork which is not red-legged.

But (not-S1) is deducible from a finite number of consistent observation statements—namely:

(01) This is a stork

and:

(02) This is not red-legged.

(01) and (02) together imply:

(not-S1) There is at least one stork which is not red-legged.

Therefore, by the criterion of complete verifiability in principle, (not-*S*1) is meaningful. But the denial of (not-*S*1)—[not-(not-*S*1)]—is just (*S*1). Two negatives make a positive, if you like. But (*S*1) is just our old universal:

(*S*1) All storks are red-legged.

And this, as we saw, is not verifiable, hence meaningless.

However, the definition of negation states that if a statement is true, then its negation is false, and if it is false, then its negation is true. Therefore the negation of any meaningful statement is itself meaningful according to the definition of negation; for any statement is meaningful if and only if it is either true or false. In the case we are now considering, however, the denial of (not-*S1*), which we expect to be a meaningful statement, is neither true nor false, but *meaningless*. This violates the definition of negation, and the definition of negation is a foundation stone of logic that we would prefer to keep. If we keep it we must abandon the criterion of complete verifiability in principle. There are, then, in all three reasons for abandoning it: 1) no universal statement can satisfy it; 2) some statements with mixed—universal and existential—quantifiers cannot satisfy it; 3) it destroys the notion of negation.*

Hempel moves on to show that similar objections apply if a principle of complete falsifiability is adopted in place of complete verifiability. He states this as the principle that "a sentence has empirical meaning if and only if its negation is not analytic and follows logically from some finite logically consistent class of observation sentences." (106) In a footnote to a previous edition of the paper (Ayer, 1959, p. 113) Hempel notes that Karl Popper originally proposed a criterion of falsifiability. But he did so as a method of marking off scientific from non-scientific statements, and *not* as a criterion of meaning.[9]

Unfortunately the principle of complete falsifiability de-

---

*Hempel's fourth reason for rejecting complete verifiability (which he later withdrew and which is hence omitted from the discussion here and on p. 115 above) is similar to his reason for rejecting a weaker version of the principle. It is discussed below, pp. 118f.

nies significance to singular statements, which assert the existence of something. Consider the statement:

(A) There exists at least one unicorn.

Now consider its negation:

(not-*A*) There are no unicorns.

(Not-*A*) is a negative existential statement. It says something about the entire class of unicorns, namely that it is empty. But negative existential statements cannot be deduced from any finite class of observation statements. Failure to find a unicorn no matter how long one searches does not imply that there are none at all. Hence, on the criterion of complete falsifiability, *(A)* is meaningless, since its negation cannot be derived from the required class of observation statements.

There are further objections which, as we might expect, are analogous to those against complete verifiability. First, some statements of science containing both universal and existential quantifiers—'all' and 'some'—cannot be falsified. Second, as in the case of complete verifiability, the negation of a meaningful statement becomes meaningless. Consider universal generalizations. Under the criterion of complete falsifiability they are meaningful, for their denials are singular statements, and singular statements are derivable from a finite class of consistent observation statements. For example,

*(S*1) All storks are red-legged

has for its denial

(not-*S*1) There is at least one stork which is not red-legged.

But (not-*S*1) is deducible from a finite class of consistent observation statements, namely,

(01) This is a stork

and:

(02) This is not red-legged.

Therefore *(S1)* is, on this criterion, a meaningful statement.

But now consider the denial of *(S1)*, which is (not-*S1*). That statement is:

(not-*S1*) There is at least one stork which is not red-legged.

It is a singular statement asserting that something exists but lacks a certain property. But by the criterion of complete falsifiability it is meaningless. To test whether it is meaningful or not we apply the criterion in question—we see whether its denial can be deduced from some finite class of consistent observation statements. Its denial is

[not-(not-*S1*)], which is just *(S1)* All storks are red-legged.

But this is a universal generalization, and therefore not deducible from any finite class of consistent observation statements. Hence (not-*S1*) is meaningless. Therefore, the definition of negation is violated again, for the negation (not-*S1*) of an allegedly meaningful statement, *(S1)*, is meaningless, and not either true or false. Thus we see that complete verifiability denies significance to universal statements and complete falsifiability denies significance to singular statements.

All these attempts to found a principle of verifiability foundered because they required too much. They required complete and direct verifiability. We therefore turn to attempts to formulate a weakened version of the principle. Let us look at Ayer's formulation of a weaker principle.

Weak Verifiability

Ayer (1936, 1946) derides Schlick's attempt to avoid these difficulties by denying that universal propositions are, after all, meaningful. Schlick had called them nonsense, but 'important nonsense'. Ayer rightly objects that the word 'important' is a hedge on Schlick's part which does not avoid the problem. And he adds that the requirement of complete verifiability simply excludes the possibility of the significance of statements about the remote past as well. His solution is to weaken the criterion. In Ayer's words, ". . . it is the mark of a genuine or factual proposition, not that it should be equivalent to an experiential proposition, or any finite number of experiential propositions, but simply that some experiential propositions can be deduced from it in conjunction with certain other premises without being deducible from these premises alone." (38–39) That is, a sentence S is meaningful if, in conjunction with some suitable hypotheses Q, R, etc., at least one observation sentence O can be deduced, which could not be deduced from either S, or Q, or R, alone. Hempel remarks that this is usually what scientists usually do to get observational results from a theory. They combine certain initial conditions with a theory in order to deduce some observational result. For example, if you know that 'distance = rate x time' you do not know anything observational until you put in a speed and an amount of time and solve for distance. Unfortunately the criterion is too weak, as Ayer himself remarks in his introduction to the second edition. (18)

Consider the following statement:

The Absolute is lazy.

For the subsidiary hypothesis let us take:

If the Absolute is lazy, then this is white.

By the law of classical logic known as *modus ponens*, if you have 'A' and also 'if A, then B', you can infer 'B'. Applying this law to the above we get the observation statement:

This is white.

This statement does not follow from either of the above two

statements alone, but only from them when they are taken together. Hence Ayer's criterion is satisfied by the statement:

The Absolute is lazy.

But since this is the very paradigm of what the positivists wish to call a meaningless statement, it is a very unfortunate result. Consequently, Ayer proposes another version of the principle:

> I propose to say that a statement is directly verifiable if it is either itself an observation-statement, or is such that in conjunction with one or more observation-statements it entails at least one observation-statement which is not deducible from these other premises alone; and I propose to say that a statement is indirectly verifiable if it satisfies the following conditions: first, that in conjunction with certain other premises it entails one or more directly verifiable statements which are not deducible from these other premises alone; and secondly, that these other premises do not include any statement that is not either analytic, or directly verifiable, or capable of being independently established as indirectly verifiable. And I can now reformulate the principle of verification as requiring of a literally meaningful statement, which is not analytic, that it should be either directly or indirectly verifiable, in the foregoing sense. (13)

It is easy to see that this proposal rules out subsidiary hypotheses like 'if the Absolute is lazy, then this is white', which caused the trouble last time. Such a hypothesis is neither analytic, nor an observation statement. But unfortunately, it will still not do. There is a rule of logic called 'simplification', which says that from a conjunction, either of the conjuncts may be inferred: from *'S* and *N' ('S·N'* in logical notation) we may deduce *'S'.* Therefore anything which can be deduced from a sentence *'S'* which has empirical significance, can also be deduced from *'S* and *N',* where *'N'* may be a metaphysical statement which we are trying to exclude. Consider the following: supposing that *'P'* and *'Q'* are observation statements.

$$\text{either P or } \begin{array}{ll} \text{Not-P} & (\sim P \\ \text{Not-Q} & (P \lor \sim Q) \end{array}$$

$$\text{therefore, } \quad \text{Not-Q} \quad (\sim Q)$$

By Ayer's criterion 'not-*P*' is meaningful, since together with 'either *P* or not-*Q*', which is an observation statement, it implies:

'not-*Q*', which is also an observation statement.

But, because of the rule of simplification we could do the entire deduction by conjoining some nonsense statement, '*N*' to 'not-*P*'. We then simplify for 'not-*P*' and go through the same steps. Concretely it is as follows:
Let the statement whose meaningfulness we wish to test be

1) It is not raining now (not-*P*) and the Absolute is crazy (*N*).

2) Either it is raining now or the streets are not wet (either *P* or not-*Q*).

From 1) by simplification we get:

3) It is not raining now (not-*P*).

But 3) taken together with 2) yields:

4) the streets are not wet (not-*Q*).

2) is an observation statement, and so is 4). But this satisfies Ayer's criterion and hence the original statement:

It is not raining now and the Absolute is crazy

is meaningful. But statements about the Absolute are the sorts of statements that Ayer wished to exclude. Hence his criterion fails in its main purpose.

In addition, Alonzo Church, in his review of Ayer (1936, 1946) in *The Jl. of Symbolic Logic*, 1949, has shown that given Ayer's criterion, if there are any three observation statements, none of which entail any of the others, then any sentence *S*, whatsoever, or its negation, has empirical content.

Hempel comments that there is little hope for formulating a verifiability principle and that empiricists must look in other directions for an adequate characterization of science. The direction he proposes is to attempt to specify some artificial empiricist language which could be restricted in certain ways. Significance or meaningfulness would then be characterized as translatability into that language. But so far this is a mere program and it has difficulties similar to those elaborated in this chapter. In the next chapter we shall follow some of Carnap's attempts to provide an entirely empirical basis for the structure of science. He begins from the notion of sense data, which he will take as primitive.

7

Logical Positivism: Sense Data—The Basis of Knowledge

We have seen how the verifiability principle in any attempted formulation rests upon the possibility of having sensory experience. The question now before the positivists is how to construe such experience. We have also seen that the problem of the external world could not be a problem for the positivists if they adhered strictly to their principles. To speak of some thing in itself, some physical object from which we are forever barred contact, as Moore appeared to speak, was to speak metaphysically, and this is forbidden. Even to speak of sensory experience as the 'given', as Schlick remarked ("Positivism and Realism" in Ayer, 1959, pp. 83–84), implies both a giver—beyond experience—and those to whom it is given—other persons, also beyond experience. But for the positivists, as we have seen, to say that there is something beyond all possible experience is to say what is meaningless. Unfortunately, the positivists themselves did not always avoid doing the first and could not always avoid doing the second. In any case, the problems of the nature and the status of sense data in their classical form are problems which could not arise for the positivists. In this form, they arise in connection with the problem of the external world, a problem ruled out of bounds because for the positivists it is no problem at all. For them, following Russell's lead, the problem of sense data becomes, instead, the problem of how to use sense experience to construct our scientific knowledge. It is no longer the problem of whether to use it—for they took things a step further than Russell—or of how sense data are related to the external world.

At one point in his distinguished career, Carnap wished to confine philosophy to the logical analysis of science, and to that end he concerned himself with the construction of sets of formal language systems in which science might be imbedded. But since science does find uses in the world and does not exist in a vacuum, and since this world is represented to us by the experience or data we have, the formal language systems must concern themselves with the ordering of our sensory data or experience. Because the positivists could not, in their critical moments, talk about the external world or other minds, they were driven to ingenious extremes to provide the basic data for science and to make the whole enterprise intersubjective, while they avoided saying what they thought could not be said.

Let us look at what Schlick has to say in 1932 about the problem of the external world, and then move backward in time to Carnap's views of 1928 on logical construction, which we will follow in outline up to 1936–37, when they change their emphasis. Schlick argued that the consistent positivist cannot use the words 'the given' without qualification, lest he give rise to the belief that he shares the views of the metaphysician. For the positivist 'the given' merely means what is most simple or what can no longer be questioned. It is simply what one uses as fundamental data, beyond which one cannot go. If the positivist rejects a transcendent reality, as he must, then it might be held that he calls only the given 'real'. Schlick puns on the German *'es gibt nur das Gegebene'* which means 'there is only the given' or 'only the given exists'. But in German, 'there is' is expressed by the verb *'geben'*, which means literally 'to give'. One might then express the force of the statement, doing violence to the English, as 'only the given is given' which, Schlick remarks dryly, appears to be the most self-evident of truths.

But his, too, is a metaphysical assertion. How could it be verified? To assert or deny the existence of the external world is to make a metaphysical statement. To assert it is to be a Realist; to deny it, Schlick argues, is to be an Idealist: either a solipsist or a Berkeleyan. To speak of the existence of the external world is to make a distinction between what is in our consciousness and what is outside of it. What is given then becomes a mental thing. To say that only the given is real would be, on this view, to say that nothing outside of consciousness is real, and this is Idealism—solipsistic, if it is argued that one can only speak of what is given to oneself; and Berkeleyan, if one argues that the given is given to others as well. But this is surely an untenable result, a result which no positivist would accept for a minute. If this sort of thinking about the given leads to either Realism or to Idealism, the positivist must abandon it. And the way to abandon it is to show that the problem of the external world, taken as a problem about some ultimate entity beyond experience, is a meaningless pseudo-problem, an apparent problem which is no problem at all.

When is a proposition understood? Only, Schlick argues, when the meanings of the words in it are understood. And when are these understood? When they are shown, or indicated, or pointed at. What is pointed at must be given. But beyond this, one cannot go. We recall that Schlick said, "The criterion of the truth or falsity of the proposition then lies in the fact that under definite conditions . . . certain data are present, or not present. . . . The *meaning* of every proposition is finally to be determined by the given, and nothing else." ("Positivism and Realism" in Ayer, 1959, p. 87)

Schlick considers an important example. Observe two pieces of paper and judge that they are the same color. That judgment is verified by the two experiences of the different sheets of paper, by the fact that the judgment describes what is given. Now show one piece of paper to someone else. Is his experience of the color like that of the first person? No answer to this question could possibly be verified. The second may use the same words as the first person to describe his experience, and he may use them no matter how close a color description we demand of him. But no matter how closely the statements of the two agree, says Schlick, we cannot infer that the same experience is happening to both. We are barred forever from having identical experiences with others. What one sees as green, the other may see as red, but if they used the same words to describe their experiences we could never know. Philosophers have often taken this as a reason for saying that although we could not *know* that the two were having similar experiences, since their judgments are expressed in the same way, we can say that it is *very likely* that their experiences are similar (in color quality). But such a statement could not be verified in principle, and hence is meaningless. The only verifiable statement to be found here is the statement that their behavior is the same. The sole agreement between the two subjects is their behavior, including speech. Schlick calls this occupying the same space in the order of the system. Only the structure of their behavior may be compared. Their 'inner' experiences cannot. To speak of them is meaningless.

To say meaningfully, according to Schlick, that something exists, is just to say that under the right circumstances one will have the requisite sensations. To say that mountains exist on the moon is just to say that under the right circumstances one would have certain visual and tactual perceptions. One would see the mountains and be able to climb them.

What about the external world? In ordinary life and in science 'the external world' is just a phrase denoting all the things about us: trees, houses, flowers, clouds, stars, people, cities, etc., and even such scientifically abstruse and subtle things as atoms and fields—for these latter, according to Schlick, are only the constituents of houses and trees and the like. Their existence is known in the same way. One knows that they exist because under the right circumstances one has a sensory experience which is relevant to the verification of the propositions stating that they exist. But, Schlick says, when scientists stop being scientists and plain men stop being plain men, and take to being philosophers, they forget all this, and when they ask whether or not the *external world* exists, they want to know whether or not there is something above and beyond what they usually call the external world; something which is behind that world, and which may cause it to exist; something which cannot be known to exist in the usual way that trees and horses and houses are known to exist.

The metaphysician grants a higher or different reality to the things which he thinks underlie the given. But he makes a mistake, Schlick argues, for "our [the positivist] principle that the truth and falsity of all statements, including those concerning the reality of a physical object, can be tested only in the 'given,' and that *therefore* the meaning of all propositions can be formulated and understood only with the help of the given—this principle is mistakenly conceived as if it asserted or presupposed that only the given is real. Therefore the 'realist' [metaphysician] feels impelled to contradict this principle and to establish the contrary: that the meaning of an existential proposition is in no sense exhausted by mere propositions of the form 'under these definite conditions that definite experience will occur' . . . but that their meaning lies *beyond* all this in something else, which is to be designated, say, as 'independent existence,' as 'transcendent being,' or similarly, and to which our principle fails to do justice." in Ayer, 1959 (104)

The metaphysician thinks that the positivist denies the transcendent reality, but he is wrong. The positivist does not deny the existence of some ultimate being, but merely says that either to affirm or to deny it is to make a meaningless statement. The metaphysician expresses his feelings or his emotions or his very profound seriousness, but no proposition. If the meaning of a proposition is bound up with the conditions which make it true or false, and if those conditions are just what Schlick calls the given, then if a string of words is uttered which in principle cannot be compared with any given because they make the claim that something lies beyond the given, that string of words says nothing either true or false, for it says nothing at all.

And this is the position of the metaphysician when he asserts or denies the existence of a transcendent world. His disagreement with the positivist is more profound than he thinks it is, for it is not the sort of disagreement where one asserts and the other denies. When the metaphysician asks his metaphysical question, the positivist simply claims that there is no question at all. Therefore, for the positivist there can be no problem of the external world, for those words have no meaning. You may translate them as transcendent reality, but all you can mean is the ordinary world about us, and science deals with that quite respectably.

Rudolf Carnap: The Stream of Experience

If all this is granted and the problem of sense data does not arise in the way that it did for Moore and those before him, just how does the consistent positivist construct his scientific language so that at some point it relates to experience? In his preface to the second edition of *The Logical Structure of the World*,[1] Carnap tells us that the system he builds up has, as basic elements, certain things which he calls elementary experiences. Out of these, with one basic concept—similarity—all other concepts are constructed in a step-by-step process with the aid of mathematical logic. These elementary experiences are distinguished from sense data, but further on in the same preface Carnap tells us that were he now writing the book he would choose sense data as his basic elements and enlarge his stock of primitive notions by the use of other relations.

The point of his procedure is to exhibit the fact that all the concepts of social and natural science may be defined in terms of these elementary experiences. All scientific statements will then be reducible to some relations of these elementary experiences and will be checked against them. Statements not so reducible will fall outside the realm of the meaningful.

In the introduction to his book Carnap writes, "we choose as basic elements of the system 'my experiences' (more precisely, entities which initially have neither names nor properties, and which can be called terms of relations only after certain constructions have been carried out). Thus we choose a system form with an 'autopsychological basis'." (12–13) He refrains from calling these entities 'sense data' and they are not defined or specified by reference to the external world, as indeed they could not be without our doing metaphysics and hence being inconsistent with positivism.

The elementary experiences which Carnap chooses as the basic elements of his system are chosen from a group of possible objects ('object' is here being used to denote anything that can be mentioned or talked about) within what he calls the domain of the autopsychological. 'Autopsychological' means what is unique to or pertains to one individual. 'Solipsistic' also describes this position, but Carnap wishes to avoid the problems usually associated with solipsism. For him the problem of solipsism is a pseudo-problem, if taken literally, and if seriously held would make science and all communication impossible. Hence he calls his 'autopsychological' base 'methodological solipsism' in order to indicate that he adopts it not as a metaphysical position, but as a starting point. His reasons for doing so will appear shortly.

Within what, speaking very loosely, is a system based upon ". . . the acts of consciousness or experiences of the self. . . ." (107), there are many possible entities which could serve as basic elements upon which the system is to be built. Among these are sense data—which Carnap understands as elementary parts of sensations—'red-here-now', 'square-shape-there', and the like. He rejects these in favor of what he calls 'the given', which he is careful to disassociate from its usual metaphysical connotations. The given for him is what one gets in a total perception before analysis and abstraction set in. In other words, he believes that the Gestalt psychologists are right and what we get in perception of all kinds is not the atomized sensations of the British empiricists from Locke to Russell, but objects presented in a field with background.

When one looks at a wooden desk, one does not see a brown parallelogram but a desk standing in a room, some of whose objects appear more or less distinctly with the desk as a fore-ground and background for it. In Carnap's example, a musi-cal chord is perceived first and analyzed into its component notes later. We may put this view by saying that chords and desks are epistemologically prior with respect to notes and sense data. We come to know or be acquainted with them first. These elementary experiences are not found discrete and separate from each other and everything else, as sense data allegedly are, but in clumps and fields, and even these expressions are abstractions. For Carnap it is only necessary to ". . . presuppose that statements can be made about cer-tain places in the stream of experience, to the effect that one such place stands in a certain relation to another place, etc. But we do not assert that the stream of experience can be uniquely analyzed into such places." (109) Their choice is arbitrary.

From the point of view adopted in Carnap's system these elementary experiences are unanalyzable. He does not wish to argue that they are absolutely unanalyzable, for that would make no sense. It is only relative to the system which Carnap is proposing to construct that they are unanalyzable, for they are taken as the basic stuff out of which the system is to be built. But another system could be easily devised, as Carnap pointed out, which took sense data rather than ele-mentary experiences as basic. In that system the elementary experiences would be analyzable into sense data, but the sense data would not themselves be analyzable.

For Carnap, in a sense, any basic elements would do to build up a system, so long as they could conveniently be used. Russell had appeared to waver in his view of logical atomism: sometimes he spoke as if those atoms were the real ultimate constituents of the world, and sometimes as if they were just one simple and convenient type of element out of which he attempts to construct things, merely because those atoms are easy to work with. For Carnap there is no such wavering. He attempts to construct his system in a specific way for a specific purpose, and should another purpose present itself, then perhaps another system constructed in another way would do the job better. One purpose which Carnap has in mind is to exhibit what he calls *epistemological priority*—the order in which we come to know things.

He defines this notion by saying ". . . an object . . . is called *epistemologically primary* relative to another one, which we call *epistemologically secondary,* if the second one is recognized through the mediation of the first and thus presupposes, for its recognition, the recognition of the first." (88–89) What his formal system will represent is a schema or outline of this epistemic primacy.[2] We have already seen an argument for the epistemic primacy of elementary experiences within the autopsychological domain. They are known first, and sense data are known through them by analysis. Carnap lists what he calls a ". . . stratified epistemological system of the four most important object types [or domains or groups]. . . ." ("Pseudo-problems" in *LSW* 321)

4) Cultural objects
3) Heteropsychological objects
2) Physical objects
1) Autopsychological objects

Any of the four, he thinks, could, in turn, be reduced to the first three as a base, and one could construct a system with any of the first three as a base in terms of which the others could be defined. But 1) is epistemologically prior to the others because they are, in fact, known through the mediation of it. Physical objects are identified and known only because the individual perceives them or has sense experience of them and in no other way. They are given. Heteropsychological objects, other persons or psyches, are known through their psychological manifestations or behavior, and hence depend upon knowledge of the physical, which is epistemically prior to them. Cultural objects, products of society and civilization, are known through manifestations of other persons, and hence the heteropsychological is epistemically prior to it.

Carnap sketches his system in this way:

> The objects within each of these levels can in turn be orga
> nized according to their epistemological reducibility. The final
> result is a system of scientific objects or concepts which, from a
> few 'basic concepts', leads in a step-by-step construction to all
> the remaining concepts. In this system each concept which can
> become the object of a scientific statement has a definite place.
> The organization of concepts in this system has a twofold
> significance. To begin with, each concept is epistemologically
> secondary relative to the concept which stands below it. . . .
> Furthermore, each concept can be defined, that is, a definite
> description of it can be given by referring only to concepts
> which stand below it. Hence the system is also a derivational
> system, that is, a 'genealogy of concepts.' ("Pseudo-problems"
> in *LSW* 321-22)

It should be noted that Carnap's aim is a completely rigorous construction, and that therefore many of the terms used
in the description of his work are, strictly speaking, illegitimate. The various elements of the system and the structures
into which they are built only become the sorts of objects we
have been calling them *after* the system has been built. Only
then are the 'streams of experience' really streams of experience, and the various domains—cultural, heteropsychological,
physical, and autopsychological—really those specific domains. This is because the systematic structure defines those
things by their relations in it, and without it they can mean
nothing. In an analogous way, a diamond-shaped pattern
with sides ninety feet long laid out onto a field is constituted
as a baseball field only after the rules and the institution of
the game have been developed. If there were no such rules and
no such institution, it would make no sense to use the words
'baseball diamond' to characterize that particular pattern.
But in a heuristic non-formal exposition of the kind which
Carnap gives prior to the development of the system, it is not
possible to proceed in any other way.

Rudolf Carnap: Physical Language

For various reasons it began to seem that there was something wrong in constructing a public world of scientific knowledge from bits of intrinsically private experience. To call a program *methodological* solipsism is perhaps to indicate one's good intentions, but it is not the way to get around the problems of private experience which it raises. Carnap therefore replaced his basic elements, streams of experience, with basic sentences, which referred to recognizable and public physical objects.

In "The Physical Language as the Universal Language of Science" (in Alston and Nakhnikian, 1963) Carnap argues that ". . . science is a unity, that all empirical statements can be expressed in a single language, all states of affairs are one kind, and known by the same method." (397) These are the language and method of physics. Carnap calls science in general a system of statements which is based upon direct experience. It needs, therefore, to be shown that the statements of physical language can be intersubjective, even though they are based upon the experience of the individual. In order to do this he needs first to argue that all basic or protocol sentences which are expressions of experiences can be adequately expressed as, or translated into, a statement about a human body. Otherwise they will be subjective, incommunicable, and unverifiable.

For instance, the direct experiential protocol statement 'pain now' is translated into something like 'the body at space-time coordinates w, x, y, z, has pain', and this can be verified by observing that body's behavior. The basis of the system is thus at the same time a record of direct experience and also publicly verifiable. It therefore satisfies the criterion that it provide an intersubjective basis for science.

Carnap gives an elementary exposition of his position in his *Philosophy and Logical Syntax 3*. There he contrasts empirical science and philosophy by dividing sentences into three kinds (58ff: 1) real-object sentences of empirical science such as (1a) 'the rose is red'; 2) pseudo-object sentences in what he calls the material mode of speech, such as (1b) 'the rose is a thing'; 3) syntactical sentences, in what he calls the formal mode of speech, such as (1c) 'the word "rose" is a thing word'. When done badly, philosophy consists of pseudo-object sentences, for they are misleading; and when done correctly, of syntactical sentences, for philosophy is really talking about the logical syntax of language.

Sentence (1a) 'the rose is red' contains a rose as its object, for the sentence speaks of that object which we call 'a rose'; (1c) 'the word "rose" is a thing word', is a syntactical sentence which refers not to a rose but to the word 'rose'. However (1b) is a pseudo-object sentence, for it looks as if it talks about a rose as (1a) does, but it really does not talk about it at all. According to Carnap, (1a) is synthetic because it asserts some new information about the rose. But (1b) tells us nothing at all about the rose, though it appears to. Carnap calls it analytic, for we learn its truth without observing any roses, at all. It merely tells us about the way in which words are used, asserting in a misleading way what (1c) asserts clearly. Sentences like (1b) in the material mode are misleading and, to avoid error, should be translated into the formal mode. He says "here we find again that deceptive character of the material mode as to the subject-matter of its sentences. Most of the sentences of *philosophy* deceive us in this way, because, as we shall see, most of them are formulated in the material mode of speech." (67)

The translation of sentences into the formal mode serves two purposes. First, it shows that these sentences can be handled by consideration of syntax alone; second, it avoids the misleading problems of content, which give rise to philosophic controversy. Carnap gives an example from the foundations of mathematics. What he wishes to show about certain kinds of philosophic controversies is that they arise through what he calls an incompleteness of theses. "This incompleteness is concealed by the usual formulation in the material mode. When translated into the formal mode, the want of reference to language is noticed at once. Then by adding such a reference the theses are made complete, and thereby the controversy becomes clear and exact. . . . *The relativity of all philosophical theses in regard to language,* that is, the need of reference to one or several particular language-systems, is a very essential point to keep in mind." (77–8)

Consider the apparent controversy between proponents of the Russell-Whitehead view that numbers are classes of classes, and the proponents of the Peano-Hilbert view that numbers are primitive objects. They appear to be asserting two incompatible theses about a basic element. But this is seen not to be the case if they translate their theses into the formal mode. The Russellian says 'numerical expressions are class expressions of the second order' and the Hilbertian says 'numerical expressions are not class expressions but elementary expressions'. However, to complete their translations it is necessary for them to make reference to a particular language structure, a particular set of rules, primitive expressions, and primitive elements. When this is done it will be seen that their disagreement is dissolved, for each of them is taking a different primitive base and constructing a different system on that base. But as Carnap stated before, what base you choose and what system you construct upon it is a matter of indifference, so long as each one does the job. Either elementary experiences or sense data would have served his system of 1928; they cannot be compared with each other, for they both determine different systems. Hence the argument between the Russellian and the Hilbertian is a little like two men arguing which of the words, *'pain'* or *'Brot'*, is the proper one to use to refer to what they are eating. The proper reply is that the question is decided upon the basis of whether you want to speak French or German. Neither can be called correct or incorrect in the abstract. They both serve a purpose. Hence the full statement of the disagreement between the Russellian and the Hilbertian should be expressed in this way. In a certain language system L_1, numerical expressions are class expressions of the second order. In another language system L_2, numerical expressions are elementary expressions. It is then seen that, like the Frenchman and the German, they have no substantive disagreement, but are stating compatible theses.

If it is true, as Carnap argues, that any meaningful expression can be translated into the language of physics, then he must answer objections based upon the view that psychological states, for example, cannot be reduced to sets of physical states. After giving an extended example of how such a translation might proceed in a non-controversial case (89ff), Carnap replies by saying that any psychological predicate expressed in the material mode, if it has a meaning, implies that any sentence containing it must be empirically examinable. Suppose that there is a psychological state or quality Q_1, which has no effect upon behavior whatsoever. How could anyone know that some subject A, is in state Q_1? Suppose, then, it is replied that although Q_1 has no observable effect such as shame or anger have—blushing, rapid pulse, trembling—still we could know that A was in state Q_1 because he told us so. He knows it and communicates it to us.

Carnap replies that his telling us is a behavior pattern which is empirically examinable. "If there is in the psychological language a predicate which is originally used only in describing one's *own* mental state, experienced by introspection, then the mere using of this predicate in speaking or writing *is* in fact an expression of that state. Thus the psychological language can contain no predicate which designates a kind of state for which no expression exists." (93–4)

The position sketched here is a uniting of the logic of Russell and Whitehead with physics and psychological behaviorism. It has several defects which must be mentioned briefly. First it is not clear that all the translations we wish to make from the material mode to the formal mode can successfully be made. Carnap's own examples are not particularly felicitous. He translates 'this book treats of Africa' into 'this book contains the word "Africa"'. But surely a book may contain the word 'Africa' without treating of Africa. For Carnap's own book contains the word 'Africa' and does not treat of it, that is, do what history or geography or economics or sociology books do when we say that they treat of Africa.

Second, it is not clear that the logical constructions which Carnap needs can actually be carried out in detail. Third, as a philosophic position radical behaviorism has many defects and has had to be amended several times. It has been argued that behavior is simply not enough to explain all that needs explanation about human psychical states.[4] An epistemological theory based upon it is liable to the same defects.

Finally, Carnap was bound to try to reconcile the generous conventionalistic view he held, that everybody was free to build his own system upon his own base, with the fact that scientists work with particular systems, and not just any system. They accept some things as evidence and reject others. How could this be the case, if one is free to develop one's own system as one wishes? Why is it that the scientific community accepts Einstein's version of relativity theory, but rejects both Whitehead's and Milne's formulations of it? The early positivist answer comes as a shock to those who identify analysts with Realists, for it is a turn back to what looks very much like a version of the coherence theory of truth which the Idealists first formulated, and which Moore and Russell attacked so harshly. This is the theory that truth is not the isolated correspondence of ideas or sentences with some sensory reality or content, but a whole, systematic, coherent structure. Otto Neurath, a positivistic social scientist and important member of the Vienna Circle, gives the following characterization of how the positivist should judge the truth of a statement: "When a new sentence is presented to us we compare it with the system at our disposal, and determine whether or not it conflicts with that system. If the sentence does conflict with the system, we may discard it as useless (or false). . . . One may, on the other hand, *accept* the sentence and so change the system that it remains consistent even after the adjunction of the new sentence. The sentence would then be called 'true.' " ("Protocol Sentences" in Ayer, 1959, p. 203) Here the reference to each protocol sentence is not to anything in the world, not to experience, but to an already developed system in which we cannot say either that parts of it do, or do not, correspond to some outside reality. But science would seem to have to touch the world somewhere and to use, at least in a way, that touch-point as a basis upon which to construct the rest. How will the scientist decide whether or not to accept or reject a new sentence should that sentence conflict with the body of sentences of his already-developed discipline? If the answer is that he accepts it or rejects it in terms of his own convenience, one must then ask: convenience for what? It cannot be *mere* convenience, for the most convenient system would be one that contained no statements; it would be the easiest to master. No, one at least must say: convenience for prediction, and then at the least one means: prediction of future sensory experiences. A system which did not allow for this would in the end be an empty shell, of no use at all. But if this is admitted, the entire project falls and another tack must be developed.

Rudolf Carnap: An Empiricist Language

The problem of meaning and verification is now to be construed as the problem of constructing a language such that all its predicates are either derived from primitive experiential predicates, reducible to such predicates, or are such predicates themselves. All statements of empirical science will either be in such a language or translatable into it. Carnap says, "As empiricists, we require the language of science to be restricted in a certain way; we require that descriptive predicates, and hence synthetic sentences, are not to be admitted unless they have some connection with possible observations, a connection which has to be characterized in a suitable way."[5] Complete verification is abandoned in favor of ". . . gradually increasing *confirmation*" of the law. (134)

There were problems, however, in constructing the empiricist language. How, for example, shall we construe and write out the definitions of dispositional predicates like fragile, soluble, visible, malleable, and the like? These are used in everyday construction of scientific statements. We return to Hempel and follow his outline a little way. (Hempel, 1965, pp. 109 f.) Suppose you want to say that an object ". . . is fragile if and only if it satisfies the following condition: if at any time *t* the object is sharply struck, then it breaks at that time." (109) Now the whole point of the procedure is to use these definitions in a logical language, i.e., to express them formally. In that case, unfortunately, some of the properties of the formal language will intervene, and we must be careful to see that they do not destroy the usefulness of the definition. By this time logicians had learned that formal languages had properties of their own, and that different systems might have different properties. The days were disappearing when it was possible to think that such a formal language would do whatever one wanted it to do.

The definition of fragility just given is expressed formally by Hempel as

$$(D) \; Fx \equiv (t) \; (Sxt \supset Bxt)$$

That is: an object, *x*, is fragile, *Fx*, if and only if, $\equiv$, at any time at all, *(t)*, *x* is sharply struck, *Sxt*, then, $\supset$, *x* will break at that time, *Bxt.* Now two expressions are united by the equivalence sign, $\equiv$, just in case they always have the same truth value. Hempel considers the case where some object, *x*, which we know is *not* fragile—a rubber band or a drop of water—is never struck at all throughout its whole existence. Then the statement *Sxt*, '*x* is struck at time *t*' is always false; its truth value is *f.* We saw in the chapter on logical atomism that a conditional statement (one containing $\supset$) is true when its antecedent condition is false. (Recall the statement 'if it rains then the streets are wet' which is true whether it is raining or not.)

But in this case by hypothesis the antecedent statement, *Sxt*, is false. Hence the whole expression to the right of $\equiv$ is true, regardless of whether the consequent, *Bxt*, is true or not. The value of *Bxt*, '*x* breaks at time *t*' is in this case irrelevant to the truth value of the whole expression,

$$Sxt \supset Bxt.$$

That value is true. Hence our definition allows that any object would be called fragile if it should happen that it was never struck, since *Fx* in the definition has whatever truth value *Sxt* $\supset$ *Bxt* has. Hence, by the definition, rubber bands, drops of water, and anything else which are never struck are fragile, whether we usually think of them as fragile or not. Clearly this is unsatisfactory.

Carnap has suggested an alternative which Hempel outlines. Construct a reduction sentence. Reduction sentences are unlike definitions in that they do not attempt to specify the meaning of a term in all cases, but only partially. The reduction sentence for 'fragile' is: For any object at any time, if that object is struck sharply at some time, then it is fragile if and only if it breaks. In symbols:

$$(R) \ (x) \ (t) \ [Sxt \supset (Fx \equiv Bxt)]$$

Incidentally, it is easy to see why symbolic languages are so highly regarded, for with a little practice they are far easier to read than their English equivalents. If you don't believe it, try writing out quadratic or differential equations in ordinary English, and then solving them.

This reduction avoids the difficulty, for if rubber bands and drops of water are not struck, then even though the entire expression $(x) \ (t) \ [Sxt \supset (Fx \equiv Bxt)]$ would be true because nothing satisfies Sxt, the expression does not say that x is fragile. It only says that if an object is struck, then *if it breaks* it is fragile, and if it doesn't break then it is not fragile. But it does not allow that objects never struck are fragile. It doesn't say anything about them at all. Hence it is a partial definition.

On the basis of reduction sentences or partial definitions, a new requirement can be stated for a term to have empirical significance. It ". . . must be capable of introduction, on the basis of observation terms, through chains of reduction sentences." (110) This aids the strict empiricist partly, if he will liberalize his criteria this far. Unfortunately other methods must be developed, if he is to include theoretical terms of advanced scientific theories. We can say no more about these problems here.[6]

8

Ludwig Wittgenstein: Meaning and Reference

The last four chapters have been occupied with an account of philosophers whose concerns with science, logic, and formal methods took them into areas of technical philosophy where few seemed willing or able to follow. Much of this concern was generated by the logicizing of Russell; but it was also to the *Tractatus Logico-Philosophicus* of Wittgenstein that the positivists turned and out of which they began to build their conception of philosophy. But even while logical positivism was being elaborated, Wittgenstein had begun a fundamental rethinking which was to lead him far from the notions of his early years. Eventually he was to repudiate these notions. His new doctrine of philosophy will be recounted in this chapter and the next. It had deep repercussions on philosophy in England, causing philosophers to think in a less formal or scientific direction, resulting in what came to be called 'ordinary language philosophy'. It caused Russell to write angrily that, "[t]he later Wittgenstein, on the contrary, seems to have grown tired of serious thinking and to have invented a doctrine which would make such an activity unnecessary. I do not for one moment believe the doctrine which has these lazy consequences is true." *(MPD,* 216–17)

Commentators on Wittgenstein usually divide his work into an earlier and a later period. The earlier period is said to be the period during which he worked out the ideas which he published in his *Tractatus Logico-Philosophicus.*[1] The theory put forward there may be called logical atomism. Recall that Russell, in putting forward his own version of logical atomism, gave generous credit to Wittgenstein for having given him many of the ideas. But Wittgenstein's version of the theory, though it is basically like Russell's, is far more rigorous in drawing out all the consequences of the position.[2]

When he wrote the *Tractatus* Wittgenstein conceived of philosophy as a discipline which was amenable to scientific procedures. There were problems to solve and he had solved them. In the preface to that work he wrote, "On the other hand the *truth* of the thoughts communicated here seems to me unassailable and definitive. I am, therefore, of the opinion that the problems have in essentials been finally solved." And he adds modestly, ". . . if I am not mistaken in this, then the value of this work secondly consists in the fact that it shows how little has been done when these problems have been solved." (29)

In his later period, which for our purposes may be confined to the period of the *Philosophical Investigations,*[3] Wittgenstein set out to show that most of what he had done in the *Tractatus* was incorrect. He had left philosophy shortly after completing that work. But he became gradually less and less sure that what he had done was correct, at least as it stood, and so he returned to philosophy in order to begin again. In this book I have let Russell's work stand as the representative of logical atomism, and Wittgenstein's criticisms in his later work may be seen, of course, as directed against Russell as well as against himself.

Nevertheless, it will be useful to summarize briefly some of Wittgenstein's earlier conclusions. It might be noted in passing that not all commentators make such a distinction between Wittgenstein's earlier and later work, and some profess to find at least the germ of his late work in the *Tractatus,* or at least some continuity between them.

In the preface to *Philosophical Investigations* Wittgenstein had stated, "It suddenly seemed to me that I should publish those old thoughts [from the *Tractatus*] and the new ones together: that the latter could be seen in the right light only by contrast with and against the background of my old way of thinking." (x^c) His old way of thinking may be summarized by the following points. 1) There is one and only one correct way of thinking about the world. 2) The ultimate constituents of the world are a unique set of atomic facts whose combinations are pictured or mirrored in the relations among symbols in a logically perfect language. 3) A proposition may be analyzed in one and only one way into a set of simple atomic propositions, of which the original proposition is a truth function. This is familiar from our account of Russell's work. 4) This third point means, of course, that every proposition has one and only one sense. 5) That sense will be the state of affairs pictured or mirrored in the proposition. 6) This means that the world can be described completely by knowing all these atomic propositions and their truth functions. 7) There is one basic use of language: to convey information. 8) Information is conveyed just in case something is expressed exactly and determinately. 9) Thus, all language which conveys information is exact and determinate. 10) Certain words are genuine proper names whose meaning is the object denoted by them, and the only genuine proper names are the names of simple objects. This is a view Wittgenstein held along with Russell. 11) If you have a proposition with names which are not really genuine proper names, it can always be analyzed into a conjunction of propositions with genuine proper names referring to absolutely simple objects by the use of some device like Russell's theory of descriptions. 12) Since genuine proper names always have meaning and their meaning is just what they refer to, those objects must be indestructible, for if they were destructible, then the words which denoted them might someday lose their meaning.

The *Philosophical Investigations* is a book which presents more than the usual difficulties of philosophic works, which are formidable enough. It is not a connected treatise in the

manner of Aristotle or Kant, nor a series of deductively ordered propositions like Spinoza's *Ethics,* but a group of apho-
ristic sets of statements of paragraph or occasionally page
length. They are numbered but not always grouped so that
they follow in sequence or all pertain to a central topic or
theme. Wittgenstein himself wrote that he was unable to
bring his remarks into a continuous whole: ". . . my
thoughts were soon crippled if I tried to force them on in
any single direction against their natural inclination.—And
this was, of course, connected with the very nature of the
investigation. For this compels us to travel over a wide field
of thought criss-cross in every direction.—The philosophical
remarks in this book are, as it were, a number of sketches of
landscapes which were made in the course of these long and
involved journeyings." *(PI,* Preface ix^e)

As a philosophical style this presentation has ancestors.
One might look at the collection of Plato's dialogues as a series of very extended sketches now illustrating this, now that
aspect of a problem. Of course, Plato's dialogues, while interconnected, contain fully developed arguments and positions,
and each may stand alone more readily than Wittgenstein's
short remarks. Others whose work comes readily to mind
here are Nietzsche, Pascal, and the fragments of the
pre-Socratics, though it is difficult to tell whether in all cases
these appear as they do because they were meant to, or because intervening bits have been lost. Wittgenstein's style
also has a literary connection with the style of such authors
as Sartre in his novel *Nausea,* and Rilke in his *Notebook of
Malte Laurids Brigge.* No sustained narrative is presented.
Illustrations of the narrator's point of view are given in scattered pieces which the reader must connect himself. This is
not to suggest that any or all of these writers influenced
Wittgenstein, but merely to note that his style has near relations. Following out the workings of his thought, Wittgenstein often illustrates his points with questions or commands
addressed to the reader to do something or to say what some
view actually comes to. One must often construct one's own
arguments to support or see what Wittgenstein is driving at.

One reason for this style of exposition is suggested by Professor Warnock.[4] He says that it is surely true that both Russell and Wittgenstein were not less but more acute than most men. Yet they both held theories which Wittgenstein came to feel could not explain the way things are. Moreover, there are decisive arguments against their theories, and it would have been strange if two such men had been unable to see the efficacy of them. But Wittgenstein's point is not that they couldn't see that these arguments were good, but that they didn't see them at all. They were spellbound by the picture of reality that they had painted and scarcely looked for any arguments against their views. If this is true, then presenting arguments will not convince proponents of such a view that they are wrong. They will not go to the root of the problem, which is a false picture of the way things have to be. A prejudiced man thinks that he already knows the truth, and arguments do not convince the superstitious. No one gives up his belief in astrology because he has its ambiguities pointed out to him; he merely incorporates them as part of the belief. What is necessary is not some sustained argument or dialectical ingenuities, but a change of world-view, and this is what Wittgenstein attempted to provide in sets of short, pungent descriptions, sayings, questions, and commands. With these jabs and jolts striking at one topic and then another he attempts to get the reader to think out for himself the implications of his picture of reality and to see that it cannot be the way he thinks it is.

The problems of interpretation of such a work are enormous. Even to state a theme or several themes and then to illustrate them is to destroy the structure of the work. But this is the only way to convey something of what Wittgenstein had to say without merely reprinting his words verbatim, and so it will be attempted here.

One basic theme of *Philosophical Investigations* is that philosophers have been trapped by a false picture or paradigm of the world. They search for certainty, unity, and the essential properties of things and, because they have predetermined their goal, because they require in advance that things show this order and unity, they either ignore whatever they find which fails to fit the pattern, or they bend and twist what is recalcitrant until it does fit. This is what was wrong with his and Russell's early work. It is what is wrong with searching for an ideal language and finding that ideal in mathematical logic.

We may turn to specific comments. To say that language has one and only one basic function is wrong because there are

> . . . *countless* kinds: countless different kinds of use of what we call "symbols", "words", "sentences". And this multiplicity is not something fixed, given once for all; but new types of language, new language-games, as we may say, come into existence, and others become obsolete and get forgotten. . . .
> Here the term "language-*game*" is meant to bring into prominence the fact that the *speaking* of language is part of an activity, or of a form of life.
> Review the multiplicity of language-games in the following examples and in others:
> Giving orders, and obeying them—
> Describing the appearance of an object, or giving its measurements—
> Constructing an object from a description (a drawing)—
> Reporting an event—
> Speculating about an event—
> Forming and testing a hypothesis—
> Presenting the results of an experiment in tables and diagrams—
> Making up a story; and reading it—
> Play-acting—
> Singing catches—
> Guessing riddles—
> Making a joke; telling it—
> Solving a problem in practical arithmetic—
> Translating from one language into another—
> Asking, thanking, cursing, greeting, praying.[5]

Language has countless functions. The number of them is indefinite because we always invent new ways of using it; but if one has one's eyes steadily fixed on any one of these functions as *the* function of language, then one will ignore the others. What results from this is a theory of descriptions, a theory of the *real* structure of language, a theory which holds that some uses of language are important but others are not fruitful and do not matter: a theory which assimilates the countless uses of language to just one use which is really important.

Similarly, to assume that the world divides up into 'ultimate' constituents which language mirrors embodies several mistakes. It is, first of all, to be a prisoner of one idea: that there is just one way things are divided. But it is we who divide them according to particular purposes which we have at particular times, and these change.

> But what are the simple constituent parts of which reality is composed?—What are the simple constituent parts of a chair?—The bits of wood of which it is made? Or the molecules, or the atoms?—"Simple" means: not composite. And here the point is: in what sense 'composite'? It makes no sense at all to speak absolutely of the 'simple parts of a chair'.
>
> . . . .
>
> We use the word "composite" (and therefore the word "simple") in an enormous number of different and differently related ways. (Is the colour of a square on a chessboard simple, or does it consist of pure white and pure yellow? And is white simple or does it consist of the colours of the rainbow?—Is this length of 2 cm. simple, or does it consist of two parts, each 1 cm. long? But why not of one bit 3 cm. long, and one bit 1 cm. long measured in the opposite direction?) (47)

The search for absolute simples, like the search for absolutes in general, is the wrong kind of search because we could not know what to look for, what counts as a simple. Why this rather than that? Why persons or facts or sense data, rather than chairs, wood, colors, or form? We don't know, and the reason that we don't know is that what we count as simple depends upon what purpose we have in mind or how we are using the word 'simple'. In Wittgenstein's phrase, it depends upon what language game we are playing. And we are always forced to play one.

In the same way, what does it mean to say that language is used to convey exact and definite information? What can the words 'exact' and 'definite' mean? Are they to be opposed to 'inexact' and 'indefinite'? But what do these words mean?

> If I tell someone "Stand roughly here"—may not this explanation work perfectly? And cannot every other one fail too?
> But isn't it an inexact explanation?—Yes; why shouldn't we call it "inexact"? Only let us understand what "inexact" means. For it does not mean "unusable".
> . . . .
> We understand what it means to set a pocket watch to the exact time or to regulate it to be exact. But what if we were asked: is this exactness ideal exactness, or how nearly does it approach the ideal?
> . . . .
> . . . Am I inexact when I do not give our distance from the sun to the nearest foot, or tell a joiner the width of a table to the nearest thousandth of an inch?
> No *single* ideal of exactness has been laid down; we do not know what we should be supposed to imagine under this head. . . . (88)

Then it cannot be the function of language to convey ideas exactly, first, because there is no *one* function of language which can be called *the* function and, second, because standards of exactness change with changing requirements, situations, or language employed. What counts as being exact in carpentry does not count as being exact in solid state physics; what counts as being exact in diplomacy does not count as being exact in writing a poem. There is no one essential 'exactness' which is the ideal to be striven for. There is no one essential feature of anything, and to attempt to search for it is a prime error in philosophy.

What of the doctrine that the meaning of a proper name is the object it stands for?

> Let us first discuss *this* point of the argument: that a word has no meaning if nothing corresponds to it.—It is important to note that the word "meaning" is being used illicitly if it is used to signify the thing 'corresponds' to the word. That is to confound the meaning of a name with the *bearer* of the name. When Mr. N. N. dies one says that the bearer of the name dies, not that the meaning dies. And it would be nonsensical to say that, for if the name ceased to have meaning it would make no sense to say "Mr. N. N. is dead." (40)

So then, if names retain their meaning when their bearer,

the object to which they refer, no longer exists, if after these objects are destroyed it is not nonsense to use their names, then the individuals or objects named cannot be the meanings of the names. And it is a fact that the names must retain whatever meaning they have after their bearer dies, for otherwise we could not use the names to say that the bearers had been destroyed. For the names would be meaningless and, if they were meaningless, we could not make a significant sentence using them. But to say 'Jones died' is not to say anything meaningless, but to say something significant.

The doctrine that words get their meanings ultimately by referring to objects comes from an oversimplified view of language and how we learn it and how we teach it to foreigners. It is the view that one points to an object and calls out its name in order to teach it. This is an ancient view as illustrated by the quotation which Wittgenstein adduces from Augustine's *Confessions*.[6] But this is not how things are at all. In order to understand what someone is doing when he points to an object and utters its name—gives an *ostensive* definition, as we say—you already need to know something about that language or about some language. How else could you know what he was doing?

> When one shews someone the king in chess and says: "This is the king", this does not tell him the use of this piece—unless he already knows the rules of the game up to this last point. . . .
> . . . .
> We may say: only someone who already knows how to do something with it can significantly ask a name. (31)
> Suppose, however, someone were to object: "It is not true that you must already be master of a language in order to understand an ostensive definition: all you need—of course!—is to know or guess what the person giving the explanation is pointing to. That is, whether for example to the shape of the object, or to its colour, or to its number, and so on."—And what does 'pointing to the shape', 'pointing to the colour' consist in? Point to a piece of paper.—And now point to its shape—now to its colour—now to its number (that sounds queer).—How did you do it? —You will say that you 'meant' a different thing each time you pointed. And if I ask how that is done, you will say you concentrated your attention on the colour, the shape, etc. But I ask again: how is *that* done? (33)

Travelers in a foreign country whose language they do not know well will often rely on learning new words by having someone point out various things and name them. It is obvious that this works best in simple situations. One goes to a hotel and stumbles through the business of getting a room. The proprietor proudly points to the bed and says *'bon lit'*, to the sink and says *'de l'eau courrant'*, and you understand that he means to indicate that the bed is a good one and that there is running water. But suppose the situation were not that explicit. Suppose you were in Finland and not in France; suppose you had not taken three years of college Finnish as you did college French. Suppose you meet a man on the road in the countryside who stops you and begins speaking and gesticulating, pointing now up, now to the sides, now to the ground. Is he:

1) Showing you the landscape?
2) Preaching and saying that God made the heavens and the earth?
3) Claiming that God is everywhere?
4) Denying that God is anywhere?
5) Denying that God made any of the things he is pointing to?
6) Denying that God exists?
7) Urging the patriotic glories of Finland?
8) Pointing out the possible Russian invasion routes?
9) Warning you of an approaching storm?
10) Saying that the weather is nice for this time of year?
11) Declaiming Finland's greatest epic?
12) Mad?

Try understanding what the waiter in a Russian or Chinese restaurant is saying when he is speaking his own language, if you don't understand those languages. To know what is going on in such situations is both already to know some language and to know something about that particular language. Where there is no shared background or implied context there is no understanding. This is one of the points behind Wittgenstein's cryptic remark, "If a lion could talk, we could not understand him."[7]

Parrots and mynah birds 'talk' as we say. But what they really do is to imitate sounds, some of which are the sounds we make in speaking. What they utter is pure gibberish. Suppose a lion really could speak, and not just utter sounds like human speech. Wittgenstein seems to mean that we still could not understand what he is saying because there is no shared background or context of behavior and associations. Suppose we witnessed a Wittgensteinian lion attacking an antelope (to change Professor Pitcher's example),[8] and as he tears open its throat he says in a gentle and cultivated voice, 'my, the meat is perfectly aged and the sauce is delicious. We must dine at this inn more often'. We simply would not know what to make of this. Our understanding would be put out of joint because the familiar words went with such an unfamiliar creature perpetrating such an unfamiliar act. They don't belong together. We should wonder what the lion could mean and whether he meant anything at all, much as we often wonder whether people who do us a bad turn, while preserving and professing all the outward manifestations of warm friendship, are *really* doing us in. Their words and actions don't go together; we fail to understand.

How then do we usually understand language? How do we know what people mean to say? Wittgenstein says, "For a *large* class of cases—though not for all—in which we employ the word 'meaning' it can be defined thus: the meaning of a word is its use in the language." (43) Again he says: "You say: the point isn't the word, but its meaning, and you think of the meaning as a thing of the same kind as the word, though also different from the word. Here the word, there the meaning. The money, and the cow that you can buy with it. (But contrast: money, and its use.)" (120) Compare with Moore and Russell and the naming theory of meaning on this point.

Consider the ways in which one could use the word 'know' in a sentence, or the various contexts in which it might appear:

1) I know her (have heard of her).
2) I know her (have met or seen her).

3) I know her (am well acquainted with her).

4) I know her (watch out, she's a nasty thing).

5) I know her (recommend her).

6) I know her (you can count on her).

7) I know her (you can't count on her).

8) I know her (she's liable to do anything).

9) I know her (in the carnal sense).

10) I know arithmetic (can add, can teach it, can adduce theorems).

11) I know Paris (have been there, get around well there).

12) I know Russell (am acquainted with him, know his work, can predict what he'll do).

13) I know baseball (can play, can play well, know the rules, know the statistics, am a connoisseur).

What is *the* meaning of 'know'? If you look about you, says Wittgenstein, you will not search for answers to questions like that. You will reject the questions. This is not a novel or especially new viewpoint. We often get the various meanings of a word by considering examples of its use. Strict definitions of unfamiliar words are little help to our understanding until we see them in action. This is one reason that dictionaries often give an example or two in addition to the abstract definition, and they usually give more than one abstract definition. The *Oxford English Dictionary* lists dozens of contexts for some words in order to establish different, as well as changing meanings.

"Every sign *by itself* seems dead. *What* gives it life?—In use it is *alive*. Is life breathed into it there?—Or is the *use* its life?" (432) Think of walking in a strange countryside. Someone has given you instructions that at a blackened, split oak tree you turn left, cross the field, and you will come to his house. The tree is a sign that you can use to get where you are going. Was it always a sign? No, it becomes a sign when you use it as a sign.

I said that all these things are obvious to us when we are not in our philosophic moments. But apparently it was not obvious to Russell and the younger Wittgenstein. They were frozen into a kind of philosophic rigor mortis; hypnotized by a picture, force-marched by a requirement of the world, seduced by the ideal of unity. They abandoned what Moore would call their common sense (although Moore himself abandoned it on occasion) when they did their philosophy. Now the purpose of philosophy is not to explain the hidden or the recondite.

> Philosophy simply puts everything before us, and neither explains nor deduces anything.—Since everything lies open to view there is nothing to explain. For what is hidden, for example, is of no interest to us. (126)
>
> . . . The problems are solved, not by giving new information, but by arranging what we have always known. (109)

If we play all these language games we might be tempted to ask what is common to them all; what is the essence of language games; why are they called 'language games'? But this is just to be hypnotized by the picture of unity again. All searchings after essences are like this. We remember how Plato in the Dialogues was often dissatisfied with the answers given to Socrates when he asked what is temperance, justice, wisdom, virtue, etc. The answers given would probably be regarded by Wittgenstein as correct, though Plato did not think they were. Plato is given examples of different acts which we might call just, or temperate, or courageous, or acts of knowing.[9] But what he is after is the essential property of the thing: that which makes it what it is; for after all, if two different acts are just, there must be some common element to them in virtue of which we call them both 'just'.

But *must* there? If you will look about you, you will see that it is not so.

> . . . Instead of producing something common to all that we call language, I am saying that these phenomena have no one thing in common which makes us use the same word for all,—but that they are *related* to one another in many different ways. (65)
>
> Consider for example the proceedings that we call "games". I mean board-games, card-games, ball-games, Olympic games, and so on. What is common to them all?—Don't say: "There *must* be something common, or they would not be called 'games' " but *look and see* whether there is anything common to

all.—For if you look at them you will not see something that is common to *all*, but similarities, relationships, and a whole series of them at that. To repeat: don't think, but look!—Look for example at board-games, with their multifarious relationships. Now pass to card-games; here you find many correspondences with the first group, but many common features drop out, and others appear. When we pass next to ball-games, much that is common is retained, but much is lost.—Are they all 'amusing'? Compare chess with noughts and crosses. Or is there always winning and losing, or competition between players? Think of patience. In ball games there is winning and losing; but when a child throws his ball at the wall and catches it again, this feature has disappeared. Look at the parts played by skill and luck; and at the difference between skill in chess and skill in tennis. Think now of games like ring-a-ring-a-roses; here is the element of amusement, but how many other characteristic features have disappeared! . . .

And the result of this examination is: we see a complicated network of similarities overlapping and criss-crossing: sometimes overall similarities, sometimes similarities of detail. (66)

I can think of no better expression to characterize these similarities than "family resemblances"; for the various resemblances between members of a family: build, features, colour of eyes, gait, temperament, etc. etc. overlap and criss-cross in the same way.—And I shall say: 'games' form a family. (67)

The concept involved in language does not have a single essence or characteristic in virtue of which all are called by the name of the concept. To the objection that if what he says is true, then no one would know what was meant by 'game', Wittgenstein replies that the objection is based on the assumption that in the use of any given general description, you only understand that description when you have a strict definition of the terms in the description; and that assumption is absurd. (70)

One major job of the philosopher is just to bring words back from their metaphysical flights: to stop and ask whenever an essence is discovered or a word is restricted to one essential meaning, whether in fact we do use words only like that after all. And if we do not so use them ordinarily, that is a sign that something has gone wrong. (116) When we assimilate grasping a meaning to grasping a railing, the stream of time to the stream of a river, location in space to location inside a container, or feeling pains to seeing color, and begin to ask what is common to each member of these pairs, or to each operation, we have ceased to look at how language ordinarily operates. Guided by the false picture that each member of this pair means what the other means, we ask the wrong questions: What are meanings like, if I can get hold of them? How fast does the stream of time flow? What is outside of space? Had we stopped to consider that we made different uses of the terms, hence different meanings from the ordinary ones, we might better have asked can we play this language game with 'time', 'space', etc.?

But we do need to be cautious as to what counts as different use, as Mr. Strawson points out.[10] If we are not then we may end by making each occurrence of a word a different use, and thus say that the word has a different meaning each time. This would be absurd. Perhaps the various occurrences should be grouped into sets of uses such that each member would count as having the same meaning as the others. But there is a problem of how this could be accomplished; and if it is not accomplished, how to decide what does and what does not count as a different use. I can, to adopt Strawson's example, use the sentence 'once upon a time there was a prince who lived in a castle' to tell a story, to make up a story, to write down a story, to translate a story, to hold a child's attention, or to put Grandpa to sleep. Do all of these count as different uses?

With these examples of Wittgenstein's analysis in mind, what was his view of philosophy? One of his most famous statements is the following: "What is your aim in philosophy?—To shew the fly the way out of the fly-bottle." (309) The fly is the philosopher and the fly-bottle is some convoluted problem into which he has wandered and out of which he cannot find his way, even though the entrance stands open. It is too close to be seen, too obvious to be made anything of. Philosophy does not begin in wonder, as the ancients thought, but in a mental cramp. "A philo-

sophical problem has the form: 'I don't know my way
about'." (123) And what is it that we don't know our way
about? "A main source of our failure to understand is that
we do not *command a clear view* of the use of our words." (122)

Philosophic puzzles are like diseases. One doesn't so much
solve them as cure them. They dissolve upon proper
application of the correct medicines. The first step is to see
that you are indeed ill and in the grip of a confusion. "My
aim is: to teach you to pass from a piece of disguised
nonsense to something that is patent nonsense," (464) says
Wittgenstein. Compare Russell: ". . . the point of
philosophy is to start with something so simple as not to
seem worth stating, and to end with something so
paradoxical that no one will believe it." ("PLA" in Marsh,
193) As we have seen, Wittgenstein hopes to accomplish his
end by a careful examination of language. "The results of
philosophy are the uncovering of one or another piece of
plain nonsense and of bumps that the understanding has got
by running its head up against the limits of language." (119)

Puzzles like Kant's antinomies of space and time or
Moore's problem of sense data arise because we do not see
clearly what can and what cannot be said. We attribute
different meanings to our words than the ones they have,
and go off arguing about things which a clear understanding
of the ways language functions would show ought not to be
argued about at all.

In doing philosophy we must mind what we say. We must
be on guard against a rigid view of language and the simple
false picture which we preconceive of reality. As Moore
pointed out, we all know what we mean by countless
expressions that we employ every day. But when we come to
think hard about them, to prod and poke them into giving
up their hidden secrets, we make all sorts of complications
and end in hopeless confusion. "Language," says Wittgenstein,
"is a labyrinth of paths. You approach from *one* side and know
your way about; you approach the same place from another
side and no longer know your way about." (203) "When we
do philosophy we are like savages, primitive people, who

hear the expressions of civilized men, put a false interpretation on them, and then draw the queerest conclusions from it." (194)

The completely successful philosopher will come to see at the end of his investigations that the problems disappear; it is not, as traditionally supposed, that each succeeding generation offers different solutions to the problems that beset its philosophic ancestors. The philosopher is a man driven by the problems of philosophy; the solutions will at the same time dissolve them and ease his torment, make him able to stop doing philosophy—able to want to stop doing philosophy. (133)

The fact that philosophic problems disappear when the knots into which language has tied us are unraveled distinguishes philosophy from scientific endeavor. Scientific problems reappear in new guises and may profitably be reformulated and reworked in succeeding generations when a new scientific framework has arisen which shows the problems in a new light. But philosophic problems are not scientific ones.

> It is the business of philosophy, not to resolve a contradiction by means of a mathematical or logico-mathematical discovery, but to make it possible for us to get a clear view of the state of mathematics that troubles us: the state of affairs *before* the contradication is resolved. (125)

> One might also give the name 'philosophy' to what is possible *before* all new discoveries and inventions. (126)

In the final analysis, philosophers like Russell and the young Wittgenstein had to be wrong, as were the positivists. They tried to assimilate philosophy to something like the natural sciences, complete with mathematical apparatus and with statements of acceptable problems and solutions formed in terms of the requirements of empirical science—with the same standard of rigor and the same notions of how to make progress in discovery. But philosophy, unlike the sciences, discovers nothing hidden. (129)

> It was true to say that our considerations could not be

scientific ones. It was not of any possible interest to us to find out empirically 'that, contrary to our preconceived ideas, it is possible to think such-and-such'—whatever that may mean. (The conception of thought as a gaseous medium.) And we may not advance any kind of theory. There must not be anything hypothetical in our considerations. We must do away with all *explanation,* and description alone must take its place. And this description gets its light, that is to say its purpose, from the philosophical problems. These are, of course, not empirical problems; they are solved, rather, by looking into the workings of our language, and that in such a way as to make us recognize those workings: *in despite of* an urge to misunderstand them. The problems are solved, not by giving new information, but by arranging what we have always known. Philosophy is a battle against the bewitchment of our intelligence by means of language. (109)

In the next chapter some problems of sensations and mental activities are outlined using Wittgenstein's methods to show wherein lies their nature and how they can be dissolved.

9

Ludwig Wittgenstein:
Sensations and Mental Acts

Wittgenstein will handle the problems of sensation in a different way from Moore and Russell. Russell had asked himself what were the least number of assumptions required to be able to construct the world which appears to us, and what is the nature of these assumptions. He had a theory which put forward the view that if the world seems to be such and such, then it would be simple and more elegant to construct it out of these materials rather than others. Moore, on the other hand, struggled with the problems of sensation, which led him to the notion of sense data. By looking at the world about him, Moore analyzed what it meant to perceive. The result of the analysis was sense data. He then asked what the nature of those things had to be, if they did the job of mediating between our non-material selves (minds) and the material world (bodies).

As we have seen, philosophy for Wittgenstein is not a science or a theory, but an activity which is prior to them. It advances no theses (125, 123, 128). If this is true, then both Russell's and Moore's approaches must be wrong, for the former advances a theory like a scientific theory, and the latter makes an empirical investigation of phenomena. But

Wittgenstein says, "It shews a fundamental misunderstanding, if I am inclined to study the headache I have now in order to get clear about the philosophical problem of sensation." (314) In the first instance we should study the language in which we speak of the phenomena, not the phenomena themselves.

What Wittgenstein has to say about sensations and mental processes is complicated and wide-ranging. It will aid the discussion if we first say something about his notions of meaning and understanding as activities going on in us. We shall then go on to outline one interpretation of Wittgenstein's views on pains and private sensations. These writings have attracted tremendous attention and can only be dealt with briefly here.[1]

Meaning: As in 'I Mean That'

One might easily look at the whole of Wittgenstein's work as a set of mottoes to be adopted which would be their own best introduction to his thought. They would not, of course, be the best exposition or interpretation of it. He says: "Where our language suggests a body and there is none: there, we should like to say, is a *spirit.*" (36) Because we deal with physical things in what is such an open and intuitively uncomplex way, we come to feel at home with them. Often, the paradigm interpretation of 'real thing' is commonly taken to be 'physical thing'. But, confronted with things which do not appear to be physical things—minds, sensations—though we half speak of them as if they are, we make sorts of negative bodies out of them. We speak of them as if they were bodies, only not solid and substantial. We attribute to them properties which should be attributed to bodies, but at the last minute modify the properties so that we may say they apply to unsubstantial things.

Consider the notion of 'meaning something'. How do we know when someone says something seriously and when he says something as a joke? What is the difference between uttering 'I am not going to promote Rodzinsky because I don't like his face' as a joke to a colleague and uttering it seriously? Well, perhaps it's just that in the first case you don't mean it, while in the second case you do. And in what does 'meaning it' consist? The obvious answer is that it is a mental act of some sort. What sort of mental act might it be? A man may be involved in thinking of something and inadvertently hurt his wife by uttering offhandedly, 'for heaven's sake, not liver again' or, 'not that dress again'—things which he did not mean to say; things which, having said, he did not mean. What goes on in a person's mind when he says something and *means* it that does not go on when he says something and does not *mean* it? We see speaking and running as bodily activities, so in a parallel way we try to see meaning as a mental activity. It's like a bodily activity, only a bit different, though it's hard to put one's finger on the difference, as we say.

But this is just the old assimilationist mistake again:

> How does the philosophical problem about mental processes and states and about behaviourism arise?—The first step is the one that altogether escapes notice. We talk of processes and states and leave their nature undecided. Sometime perhaps we shall know more about them—we think. But that is just what commits us to a particular way of looking at the matter. For we have a definite concept of what it means to learn to know a process better. (The decisive movement in the conjuring trick has been made, and it was the very one that we thought quite innocent.) (308)

But saying something and meaning it is not at all like saying something and scratching or saying something and sitting down. What could possibly go on in one's mind that would count as 'meaning it'? Does one think as he says that he is dropping out of medical school, or renouncing the family fortune, or declaring his intention to become a polar explorer, 'and I mean it'? Does he have a positive image of himself walking out of the door, or spurning money, or standing amid icebergs? And if he reported any of these phenomena would that convince us that he *meant* what he was saying, if we doubted it before? Surely not. No more than we would want to declare that he didn't mean what he said if he reported a lack of any of these things.

The search for unity or for the essential qualities of a person's saying something and 'meaning it' is a hopeless search in just the same way that it is a hopeless search everywhere else. It is a philosopher's stone: an ideal which we strive for when we stop acting as ordinary men using ordinary language in the world and begin to philosophize in the abstract. One clue that this is the wrong way to search is given in the fact that if 'meaning it' were a mental process occurring privately in one's mind—a thought, an emphasis, an image—then no one could ever know when someone else was meaning something and when he wasn't. The private mental process of another cannot be shared publicly. But we do usually know when someone is 'meaning it' when he says something, hence 'meaning it' cannot be simply a mental process.

How do we know, in many cases, that someone means what he says? Well, we might know that he is a serious type not given to joking, or we might know that he takes most, though not all, things seriously. But how do we know *that?* One way in which we might know it is to watch his behavior. Suppose a man threatens someone with a gun, or that after a disastrous evening in a restaurant the head waiter gathers his staff and screams, 'I'll fire the lot of you'. But if the gun were a water pistol, or if the man laughs and puts it away, then he did not mean what he said. If on the next day the staff is still in the restaurant, then the head waiter did not mean what *he* said. These simplifications exemplify one of a complicated number of ways in which we can come to know whether or not someone meant what he said. The context of the situation and people's actions in it ordinarily guide us.

Similarly, suppose someone said 'I mean this, not that'—"when I said 'I know the best-looking girl in town', I meant Alice, not Peggy"; "when I said 'Chicago was beautiful' I meant the lake-shore, not the rest of it". His meaning one thing rather than another cannot, again, be some hidden mental process. Suppose you thought that meaning *this* rather than *that* was a matter of concentrating your attention *here* rather than *there?* First, if this is what it meant, how could anyone be expected to know the fact that you concentrated your attention here rather than there? Concentrating one's attention is not a publicly observable act. Second, Wittgenstein can present counterexamples to this view:

> Imagine someone simulating pain, and then saying "It'll get better soon". Can't someone say he means the pain? and yet he is not concentrating his attention on any pain.—And what about when I finally say "It's stopped now"? (667)

In both these cases, the one where pain is being counterfeited and the one where pain has ceased, there is, by hypothesis, no pain upon which to concentrate one's attention; but one can say that the speaker *meant* pain when he spoke. Hence meaning something cannot consist in concentrating one's attention on that thing. There is another difficulty for this view, which is analogous to the difficulty of pointing to certain kinds of things. We recall that Wittgenstein argued that there is no way to point to an object's shape *qua* pointing that was different from pointing to its color, its position, etc. Similarly, one says ". . . 'I mean that this *piece* is called the 'king', not this particular bit of wood I am pointing to'." (35) But how could you concentrate your attention on the piece as a king in chess without concentrating on it as a block of wood, marble, plastic, or ivory? And if you cannot do this, but still wish to say that you *mean it as the king,* then how can 'meaning it as . . .' be concentrating one's attention? In fact, we usually do know what a person means, whether he means this or that, because we know the situation and its context. We see his surroundings, what he said and did before he said that he *meant that,* and what he does afterward. It will be the same with understanding. There is no way to get at someone's occult private processes; no way of looking inward to his mind.

Understanding

Suppose someone says 'now I understand'. Here, too, if we think that he is reporting some private mental occurrence, we are mistaken. We would be mistaken because there is, in fact, no single thing or act or essence common to all the 'understandings' which I may have on different occasions; and also we would be mistaken because if there were such a unique mental act *it* would not be what we mean by understanding. These points have already been made regarding meaning. Let us see how Wittgenstein develops them in connection with understanding. What happens when we search for that elusive act of understanding?

> We are trying to get hold of the mental process of understanding which seems to be hidden behind those coarser and therefore more readily visible accompaniments. But we do not succeed; or, rather, it does not get as far as a real attempt. For even supposing I had found something that happened in all those cases of understanding,—why should *it* be the understanding? And how can the process of understanding have been hidden, when I said "Now I understand" *because* I understood?! And if I say it is hidden—then how do I know what I have to look for? I am in a muddle. (153)

Consider concrete cases of understanding. One man gives another an order to write out the series of natural numbers. (143) How do we get him to understand what to do? Well, we write out the numbers 0–9 for him and get him to copy them. "[B]ut then the *possibility of getting him to understand* will depend on his going on to write it down independently." (143) Understanding will consist here, at least partly, in a certain performance by the subject: his doing what was required; his making the appropriate comments, his answering questions correctly.

Consider someone who says ". . . 'Now I know!'—and similarly 'Now I can do it!' and 'Now I understand!' " (151) Someone writes a series of numbers out and someone else tries to find the structure of the series. Suddenly he says 'now I can go on'. What is happening? The first person ". . . has written down the numbers 1, 5, 11, 19, 29; at this point B [the second person] says he knows how to go on." (151) Wittgenstein considers four possibilities. B may have: 1) tried various formulae and seen that $n^2 + n - 1$ would do; 2) watched ". . . A writing his numbers down with a certain feeling of tension, and all sorts of vague thoughts go through his head."

(151) But then he sees that the difference between the numbers increases by two and says that he can go on. 3) He may just say that he knows that particular series and continue it at some arbitrary point. 4) "—Or he says nothing at all and simply continues the series." (151) He may have been startled upon recognizing that he could continue.

What is involved in 'understanding' in this case? None of these four possibilities can be identified with B's understanding how to go on. All or none of them may have happened. For example, the occurrence of the formula $a^n = n^2 + n - 1$ cannot be what is meant by the mental process of understanding, for that formula might have occurred to B without B's knowing that it was the formula for the series in question. *B* certainly might have continued the series without having thought of the formula, in which case we would certainly want to say that he understood how to go on. In neither case can the occurrence of the formula be identified with B's knowing how to go on. By analogous argument, the understanding of how to go on cannot be identified with any of the other possibilities in the example. It is a mistake to think of understanding as a mental occurrence at all.

> Try not to think of understanding as a 'mental process' at all.—For *that* is the expression which confuses you. But ask yourself: in what sort of case, in what kind of circumstances, do we say, "Now I know how to go on," . . .
>
> In the sense in which there are processes (including mental) processes) which are characteristic of understanding, understanding is not a mental process.
>
> (A pain's growing more or less; the hearing of a tune or a sentence: these are mental processes.) (154)

The fact that some mental process accompanies our understanding does not indicate that our understanding consists in having that process—that flash, image, formula—before our minds. Note particularly that Wittgenstein does *not* deny that there are mental processes in the sense of inner non-physical or non-behavioristic ones. This is important in understanding what he has to say about sensations, which are discussed below. In the sense in which he does allow them it is, I believe, true to say that Ryle, whose *The Concept of Mind* we will discuss briefly in the next chapter, does deny inner mental processes. He attempts to assimilate them to dispositions to behave in certain ways.

In closing this section we may let Wittgenstein speak for himself once again:

> But did "Now I can go on" in case (151) mean the same as "Now the formula has occurred to me" or something different? We may say that, in those circumstances, the two sentences have the same sense, achieve the same thing. But also that *in general* these two sentences do not have the same sense. We do say: "Now I can go on, I mean I know the formula", as we say "I can walk, I mean I have time"; but also "I can walk, I mean I am already strong enough"; or: "I can walk, as far as the state of my legs is concerned", that is, when we are contrasting *this* condition for walking with others. But here we must be on our guard against thinking that there is some *totality* of conditions corresponding to the nature of each case (e.g. for a person's walking) so that, as it were, he *could not but* walk if they were all fulfilled. (183)

Sensations

Two opposite and extreme views of sensations may be held. These are usually called Cartesianism and behaviorism, although Cartesianism was both ingrained in our language long before there were philosophers, and formulated philosophically long before Descartes. Similarly, behaviorism was a theory before the work of the American psychologist, J. B. Watson, with whom it is associated. It is also clear that, in the forms to be presented here, neither Descartes nor Watson might have accepted these theses. In spite of this, the names have stuck and are convenient to use. No serious errors result if the foregoing provisos are understood.

Cartesianism is the view that we and only we have direct access to our own minds. What goes on in them is open to inspection and thus to certainty only to and by us, and to no one else. Therefore, for example, only I can *know* that I am in pain, though others may infer it. They may be mistaken about me, but I can never be. If this view is true, then I can never learn to use pain language from another, but only from my own experience, for I cannot know what another is feeling when he says he has a toothache, but only what I am feeling when I have one.

The complete denial of Cartesianism leads one to embrace its direct opposite: philosophical behaviorism. As a program in psychology, behaviorism states that only human behavior can be studied fruitfully by psychologists because only behavior is observable. Philosophic behaviorism goes farther because it denies that there is or could be anything inner, hence unobservable, going on in a person's psyche. It is a stronger thesis. The possibility of inner psychical process is left open by psychological behaviorism, but denied in principle by its philosophical namesake.

According to philosophic behaviorism, to say that someone is in pain is just to say that he behaves in certain ways. Moreover, since my privileged access to my own mind is denied, it follows that anyone can have as good a knowledge of the fact that I am in pain as I have myself, and also that just as the other learns of my pain from my behavior, so I learn of it in that way, too. On this view, when Jones says that Gronsky is in pain, he is asserting that Gronsky is acting in a certain way and nothing else. Similarly, when Gronsky says 'I am in pain' he is saying the same thing—that he is acting or behaving in a certain way.

Both of these extreme positions are false: Cartesianism because it appears to deny that I can know that others are in pain, and because if it were true, as Wittgenstein argues, then no one could learn to use sensation and pain words. Behaviorism is false because to say that x is in pain is in fact to say more than that he is acting in a certain way, and because Gronsky does not learn of his pain in the same way that Jones learns of it. Gronsky cannot be said to *learn* of his pain at all, for one doesn't learn of one's own pain, one simply has it.

One way of looking at the problem of pain and sensations is to see it as the problem of gliding between these two views: Cartesianism and behaviorism. How can one do justice to the phenomena in question without running into the absurdities of either view? In what follows, I shall try to outline Wittgenstein's approach, as usual, allowing him to speak for himself as often as possible. We may look first at the attack upon Cartesianism.

One consequence that follows from Cartesianism is that if to say someone is in pain is to say that he has a sensation privately before his consciousness, then I could never know whether or not it is true that he is in pain. I may *infer* that he is from his actions, but I can *never know.*

But this is surely absurd. Other people often know that I am in pain and I often know that they are in pain. Wittgenstein says:

> "I can only *believe* that someone else is in pain, but I *know* it if I am."—Yes: one can make the decision to say "I believe he is in pain" instead of "He is in pain". But that is all.—What looks like an explanation here, or like a statement about a mental process, is in truth an exchange of one expression for another which, while we are doing philosophy, seems the more appropriate one.
> Just try—in a real case—to doubt someone else's fear or pain. (303)

Certainly there are borderline cases where we might be puzzled as to whether or not someone was in pain. But there is a point beyond which to doubt is absurd. It is just conceivable that a man with a gunshot wound in the abdomen or a knife wound in the side may be shamming, but it is no more than conceivable. We may be able to conceive it but we can scarcely believe it. There is no basis for the doubt beyond a perverse will to conceive the possibility that it is not true: that he actually feels no pain. One may doubt each time he steps out of the front door that the earth will support him, but he goes out anyway, for his doubt is just a ritual; it is not real. More is involved in doubting than merely saying 'I doubt'. Real doubt consists in acting in certain ways and doing certain things. If someone uses a concept as we use it, but we are supposed to imagine his not meaning it as we do, we become, in a way, unhinged; something has gone wrong. The mechanism of language fails to function. We grind out meaningless doubt. To say 'I doubt' without connecting this up with the rest of one's actions and outlook is, in Wittgenstein's phrase, something like turning a wheel which turns nothing with it. It is not part of any mechanism. (271) It does not belong to the same language game.

Another absurdity which follows from the Cartesian view is that I could not know what anyone else meant when he said that he had a pain. By the Cartesian hypothesis 'pain' means only 'what is before my consciousness' and if this is what it means, how can I understand what someone else means when he says that he has a pain, for his pain cannot be before *my* consciousness.

> Yet we go on wanting to say: "Pain is pain—whether *he* has it, or *I* have it; and however I come to know whether he has a pain or not."—I might agree.—And when you ask me "Don't you know, then, what I mean when I say that the stove is in pain?"—I can reply: These words may lead me to have all sorts of images; but their usefulness goes no further. And I can also imagine something in connexion with the words: "It was just 5 o'clock in the afternoon on the sun"—such as a grandfather clock which points to 5.—But a still better example would be that of the application of "above" and "below" to the earth. Here we all have a quite clear idea of what "above" and "below" mean. I see well enough that I am on top; the earth is surely beneath me! (And don't smile at this example. We are indeed all taught at school that it is stupid to talk like that. But it is much easier to bury a problem than to solve it.) And it is only reflection that shews us that in this case "above" and "below" cannot be used in the ordinary way. (That we might, for instance, say that the people at the antipodes are "below" our part of the earth, but it must also be recognized as right for them to use the same expression about us.) (351)

Just as 'It's five o'clock in the afternoon' has no use which fits conditions on the sun, just as 'above' and 'below' have no use in talking about the whole earth (are not defined for so doing, if you like), so on the Cartesian view 'pain' cannot be used in such a way that I know what it is for others to have pain. The other's pain description may involve images or pity in me, but I cannot know what his pain is like without myself feeling it, and I am barred from doing this in principle.

> The essential thing about private experience is really not that each person possesses his own exemplar, but that nobody

knows whether other people also have *this* or something else.
The assumption would thus be possible—though unverifiable—
that one section of mankind had one sensation of red and
another section another. (272)

A further absurd consequence of the Cartesian view is that
if 'pain' or other 'sensation words' named items in one's own
consciousness, worked, that is, like seeing something and then
naming what that thing is ('That was a golden-throated
warbler'. 'No, you are mistaken, that was a rabbit moving
quickly'.), then we must be able to make errors about our
pains. We should be able to say 'I thought I was in pain, but
I must have been mistaken', and other similar things. But
isn't that nonsense? How could one be mistaken about one's
own pains? Not only is it nonsense, but if accepted, it would
undercut a major point of the Cartesian hypothesis. That
point was just that *I* cannot be mistaken about *my* pains,
though another may be mistaken about them. The Cartesian
hypothesis was supposed to give one the direct access to one's
own mind that is denied to others. But if I can be mistaken
about the occurrences in my mind, then the distinction between the knowledge which I can have of them and the
knowledge which another can have breaks down. Think
what it would be like to be mistaken about one's own pain.
"But I can't be in error here; it means nothing to doubt
whether I am in pain!" (288)

Consider another point. Unless there were some behavior
connected with pain, no one could ever learn to use a
vocabulary about pain. I cannot know from my own case
how to use pain words because if I merely judged each time
that I had a twinge that it was, say, a toothache, how could
I possibly know that the word 'toothache' is generally used
by people in this way?

"What would it be like if human beings shewed no outward
signs of pain (did not groan, grimace, etc.)? Then it would be
impossible   to   teach   a   child   the   use   of   the   word
'tooth-ache'."—Well, let's assume the child is a genius and itself
invents a name for the sensation!—But then, of course, he
couldn't make himself understood when he used the word.—So

does he understand the name, without being able to explain its meaning to anyone?—But what does it mean to say that he has named his pain'?—How has he done this naming of pain?! And whatever he did, what was its purpose?—When one says "He gave a name to his sensation" one forgets that a great deal of stage-setting in the language is presupposed if the mere act of naming is to make sense. And when we speak of someone's having given a name to pain, what is presupposed is the existence of the grammar of the word "pain"; it shews the post where the new word is stationed. (257)

And if you try to teach someone what pain is by jabbing his finger with a needle or burning it with a match, how would you know that he felt anything if he stood there naturally, smiling at you while you did it, just as if nothing was going on? We never think of inanimate things as having painful sensations.

> And can one say of the stone that it has a soul and *that* is what has the pain? What has a soul, or pain, to do with a stone?
> Only of what behaves like a human being can one say that it *has* pains. (283)
> Look at a stone and imagine it having sensations.—One says to oneself: How could one so much as get the idea of ascribing a *sensation* to a *thing?* One might as well ascribe it to a number!—And now look at a wriggling fly and at once these difficulties vanish and pain seems able to get a foothold here, where before everything was, so to speak, too smooth for it. (284)

Suppose it were granted that pain is connected in some way with behavior. It still might be the case that 'pain' is the name of some private sensation which accompanies the behavior, either necessarily or merely in fact. But once we understand how names are ascribed, we shall see that 'pain' cannot be the name of a private sensation. We name publicly observable objects—trees, houses, etc.—by pointing them out, building them, chopping them down, climbing them, describing them, and being mistaken about them. 'That is a eucalyptus tree'. 'No, it's a northern spruce'. 'That's Jones' house'. 'No, it's just a pile of rubbish, but you can't make it out clearly at this distance'. In the case of one's pain or other private sensations, however, these things are not possible. No one else can point them out, or use them, or include them in his activities.

But surely one could reply that though one might not be able to point out one's own pains to others, or have others include them in their activities, surely one can point them out to oneself. Would this show that we can name our pains? Wittgenstein claims that it would not.

> Let us imagine the following case. I want to keep a diary about the recurrence of a certain sensation. To this end I associate it with the sign "S" and write this sign in a calendar for every day on which I have the sensation.—I will remark first of all that a definition of the sign cannot be formulated.—But still I can give myself a kind of ostensive definition.—How? Can I point to the sensation? Not in the ordinary sense. But I speak, or write the sign down, and at the same time I concentrate my attention on the sensation—and so, as it were, point to it inwardly.—But what is this ceremony for? for that is all it seems to be! A definition surely serves to establish the meaning of a sign.—Well, that is done precisely by the concentrating of my attention; for in this way I impress on myself the connexion between the sign and the sensation.—But "I impress it on myself" can only mean: this process brings it about that I remember the connexion *right* in the future. But in the present case I have no criterion of correctness. One would like to say: whatever is going to seem right to me is right. And that only means that here we can't talk about 'right'. (258)

> What reason have we for calling "S" the sign for a *sensation?* For "sensation" is a word of our common language, not of one intelligible to me alone. So the use of this word stands in need of a justification which everybody understands.—And it would not help either to say that it need not be a *sensation;* that when he writes "S", he has *something*—and that is all that can be said. "Has" and "something" also belong to our common language. —So in the end when one is doing philosophy one gets to the point where one would like just to emit an inarticulate sound.—But such a sound is an expression only as it occurs in a particular language-game. . . . (261)

In this case one is merely going through certain motions which have no significance. They are not connected to the rest of the mechanism in principle. There are no practical consequences. It is like my right hand giving my left hand money. It looks as if something is being done, but when you think about it you see that nothing has changed, nothing has gone on at all. (268) What is more, there is no possible way to judge whether in assigning "S" to my sensation I am assigning it to the same sensation each time, for there can be no standard of correctness in this case.

. . . But justification consists in appealing to something independent.—"But surely I can appeal from one memory to another. . . ." No; for this process has got to produce a memory which is actually *correct*. . . . ([It is a]s if someone were to buy several copies of the morning paper to assure himself that what it said was true.) (265)

If someone writes down his sign "S" each time he thinks that he has the same sensation, how will he know whether he is correct each time? He may write "S" for a twinge and, misremembering, write it for a tickle the next. Without some external standard it is impossible for him to know that he is correct. Not only is it true that he merely *would* not know whether he was right in using "S" for a particular sensation, but he *could* not know whether he was right or wrong, because in principle there is no standard which could be employed. It makes no sense to say that you have set your watch if you don't know what time it is (266) and, presumably, it makes no sense to ask if "S" refers to the same sensation on two separate occasions if you cannot know whether you are right or not. (258) It makes sense to ask if the town you are passing through is Roxbury or Danbury, or if Mark Twain was really Samuel Clemens, because there is an objective standard to which all who are in doubt may appeal. Thus it is possible to use the names 'Danbury' and 'Mark Twain' correctly. But if one were to make up new names calling 'Twain' 'xbzchl' and 'Roxbury' 'gdabmlm', and keep this information to oneself, it would be odd to ask if the names 'xbzchl' and 'gdabmlm' were being used correctly, because in fact no one but you knows what those names stand for. But if this is odd, how much odder to ask if the mark "S" denotes one's sensation when no one, not even you yourself, could in principle know whether it did or not. In the first case it happens that there is no way of telling the correctness of the application of the names, though there might have been; in the second case there could be no such way. One cannot summon back one's sensations and compare them with each other. The best one could hope to do is to try to remember to what sensation one applied the name "S", and here there can be no standard of correctness.

Sensations, then, cannot be named, for no rules or criteria exist, or could exist, for naming them. This is not to say that we cannot talk of sensations at all, but to say that there are some ways in which we cannot talk about them: we cannot name them. We cannot name them because the implicit rules for the language game of naming cannot apply in the case of sensations. Sensations are not like the kinds of 'somethings' that can be named, but that is not to say that they are 'nothings'. (304)[2]

> If I say of myself that it is only from my own case that I know what the word "pain" means—must I not say the same of other people too? And how can I generalize the *one* case so irresponsibly?
>
> Now someone tells me that *he* knows what pain is only from his own case!—Suppose everyone had a box with something in it: we call it a "beetle". No one can look into anyone else's box, and everyone says he knows what a beetle is only by looking at *his* beetle.—Here it would be quite possible for everyone to have something different in his box. One might even imagine such a thing constantly changing.—But suppose the word "beetle" had a use in these people's language?—If so it would not be used as the name of a thing. The thing in the box has no place in the language-game at all; not even as a *something:* for the box might even be empty.—No, one can 'divide through' by the thing in the box; it cancels out, whatever it is.
>
> That is to say: if we construe the grammar of the expression of sensation on the model of 'object and designation' the object drops out of consideration as irrelevant. (293)

When we cannot look into the other's beetle box to see what is there, we cannot use a word as the name of what is in the box. From this it follows that we cannot name whatever is in the box, for the way in which we use words as names does not apply in such a case. But it does not follow from this that there is nothing in the box.

When one has what one says is a pain, there is something going on, something which is personal, terrifying, and frightful. Wittgenstein is not denying this. What he is denying is that this personal, terrible, frightful 'going on' can be referred to or talked about in certain ways: that it can be named, described, looked at, held up, and the like.

> "But you will surely admit that there is a difference between pain-behaviour accompanied by pain and pain-behaviour without any pain?"—Admit it? What greater difference could there be?—"And yet you again and again reach the conclusion that the sensation itself is a *nothing.*"—Not at all. It is not a *something,* but not a *nothing* either! The conclusion was only that a nothing would serve just as well as a something about which nothing could be said. We have only rejected the grammar which tries to force itself on us here.
>
> The paradox disappears only if we make a radical break with the idea that language always functions in one way, always serves the same purpose: to convey thoughts—which may be about houses, pains, good and evil, or anything else you please. (304)

> "Are you not really a behaviourist in disguise? Aren't you at bottom really saying that everything except human behaviour is a fiction?"—If I do speak of a fiction, then it is of a *grammatical fiction.* (307)

But we surely do speak of pains and inner sensations. If Wittgenstein's position is granted, what is this kind of talk? Wittgenstein has denied being a behaviorist. He argues that something more is involved in having a pain than mere behavior, for what would be more ridiculous than for someone to say 'I have a toothache. Oh! how I wish I could stop clapping my hand to my jaw', or 'Oh! I burned my finger, won't anything make me stop shaking it'? This is absurd. What one wants is for the pain to cease, not the behavior.

Wittgenstein thinks it instructive to look to see how pain expressions are used in various language games. What function do they perform?

How do words *refer* to sensations?—There doesn't seem to be
any problem here; don't we talk about sensations every day,
and give them names? But how is the connexion between the
name and the thing named set up? This question is the same
as: how does a human being learn the meaning of the names of
sensations?—of the word "pain" for example. Here is one possibility: words are connected with the primitive, the natural,
expressions of the sensation and used in their place. A child has
hurt himself and cries; and then adults talk to him and teach
him exclamations and, later, sentences. They teach the child
new pain-behaviour.
   "So you are saying that the word 'pain' really means
crying?"—On the contrary: the verbal expression of pain replaces crying and does not describe it. (244)

The last sentence of this quotation explains how Wittgenstein thought pain and pain expressions were related. The
pain expression is not descriptive; it does not name pain, but
it is expressive. It is part of the response to pain. The baby's
wail becomes the child's 'Mommy, it hurts', which becomes
the adult's involuntary grimace, or 'Oh!' And, of course, in
the appropriate language game an involuntary 'ouch!' is
neither right nor wrong. It is just there. It requires no criterion for its correct employment for it has no *correct* employment. Indeed, to speak of one employment of pain reports is
to make again the same mistake as looking for an essence or
the correct usage in language. There are many uses of pain
words. One central use is as expression. Wittgenstein gives
the following example of grief and mourning. "When it is
said in a funeral oration 'We mourn our. . . .' this is surely
supposed to be an expression of mourning; not to tell anything to those who are present. But in a prayer at the grave
these words would in a way be used to tell someone something." (p. 189) In the first instance the words 'we mourn
. . .' are expressing the mourners' anguish, but in the second
case they would be used to tell someone something. They are
presumably addressed to God, informing him that people
feel strongly about the death they are mourning. In the same
way, pain expressions may be complaints, or a request for
aid, for sympathy, for companionship, for peace and quiet,
for release, for death and so on. "So the words 'I am in pain'

may be a cry of complaint, and may be something else." (p. 189) Pain expressions might even be descriptions of a sort: 'it hurts here, doctor', 'there is a pressure when I breathe'. Such description-expressions are an important part of the pain behavior of the patient. Witness the doctor's difficulty with young children and foreigners. Doctors need to know where it hurts and what sort of pain it is. One must differentiate between the pressure of asthma and angina.

But all descriptions do not name things. Some do and some do not. "Think how many different kinds of thing are called 'description': description of a body's position by means of its co-ordinates; description of a facial expression; description of a sensation of touch; of a mood." (24) "What we call *'descriptions'* are instruments for particular uses." (291) They are not all the same sorts of things. (609, 610) I can describe a famous château by naming the objects to be found in the various rooms: paintings, tapestries, rugs, tables, chairs, beds, mirrors, sconces; but I can also describe it by giving its situation, the shape of the grounds, the layout, the construction, etc. I can also describe it by describing its atmosphere. This is well known to writers of fiction: compare Melville to Conrad on the South Seas. Thus Wittgenstein holds that it can be maintained that pain language is something descriptive, without denying that pain words fail to name sensations.

At this point we might raise an objection. Isn't it the case that we use descriptions in much the same ways as names? Must it not be possible to be correct or incorrect in describing something? And if this is true oughtn't we to say that Wittgenstein's reasons for denying that we can *name* our pains hold for *describing* them as well? But we do describe our pains to the doctor and to people we know. Indeed, this appears to be one language game we have to play. So if we can describe our pains why can't we name them?

One reply to this objection might be that names are right or wrong—'that's a cow; no, it's an elk'. But descriptions are merely a matter of appropriateness—'that's a gloomy house; no, not gloomy, just dark'. But surely there comes a point beyond which a description is not merely inappropriate, but just plain wrong. Suppose someone says, 'that's a sleek new car', and his companion replies, 'my God, it's a battered old undistinguished 1938 Gulpmobile'. Or again, 'that's an English suit he has on', and the reply is, 'that's hardly an English suit, it was made in Toledo'. In these cases wouldn't we say that 'sleek', 'new', and 'English' were just wrong? And don't these words describe? But Wittgenstein has said that to use names one must have a criterion of correctness. One must be able to know when one is right. One can't *name* one's sensations because such a criterion would be lacking. But what is the criterion for a correct *description* of one's sensations? Description would seem to be in the same logical bind as names.

So it appears that we ought to say either that we *cannot describe* our pains, or that we *can name* them. But we certainly do describe them. One might easily say 'last year I had a queer shooting pain around my heart'. We would have to accept this as description, for the only other alternative on Wittgenstein's view is that it is an expression of my pain, and at a year's remove this would be odd, indeed. Hence, either we can name our pains after all and Wittgenstein's criterion for the use of names is wrong, or if we cannot name them, there must be another criterion for naming them than for describing them. But what is it?

Leaving these objections aside, if the bulk of what Wittgenstein says about philosophy is true, then philosophers of the past as well as the present have made enormous errors. They have proceeded as if the point of philosophy was to construct a theory which was at once deeper and more powerful than scientific theories, because it was more fundamental. It was to get behind what scientists said, and question basics where they had merely assumed them. But philosophers got into muddles because they would always think that in the end they had come up with essential reality, the unity of things: *the* difference between mind and body, *the* correct notion of morality, *the* cause of generation and corruption, *the* nature of justice. And so it went. Against this unconscious urge for unity Wittgenstein urges, shows, describes the multiplicity of language games. Through the examination of countless and indefinite forms of expression, the philosopher will come to see his puzzlement vanish as his problems dissolve.

Finally, we may raise the question whether in fact Wittgenstein had not himself, once he broke the grip in which the superstition of logical atomism had held him, become bewitched by his own picture, put on spectacles of whose existence he was unaware. Is Wittgenstein, for all his ingenuity in diagnosing the problems of others in philosophy, still a victim of the paradigm case, a picture which holds him captive? Is he trapped by a view of philosophy which makes it analogous to types of problems and puzzles like jigsaw puzzles, anagrams, and Chinese boxes, where there is a definite solution which is just the dissolving of the problem?

However we think these questions are to be answered, it should be borne in mind that Wittgenstein set philosophy on a different track by moving it far from the concerns of the positivists with their formal logical methods, and that in England it has largely stayed on this track. Three of the four philosophers we shall consider in the next chapter share many, though not all, of Wittgenstein's views. They do ordinary language analysis. It is also interesting to note that these three are Englishmen. The fourth is an American, and he seems more in line with Russell's tradition, though with a new pragmatic twist, and this is appropriate, for he is a well-known logician.

10

Other Directions

1. Gilbert Ryle: Sense Data

The publication of Professor Ryle's book *The Concept of Mind* has been called one of the major events of postwar philosophy.[1] It was the first large-scale attack on one sort of problem—the mind-body problem—which used the methods of ordinary language philosophy, and its importance has not diminished.

The book was published before Wittgenstein's *Philosophical Investigations* but is generally in harmony with Wittgenstein's views, though there are large differences of detail and emphasis. In one major respect, however, one may read Ryle differently from Wittgenstein and differently from the way in which Ryle himself says that he ought to be read. In this reading one would not be alone. (See Hampshire and Warnock.)

Ryle has claimed to be doing no more than rectifying the logical geography of the concepts we employ in thinking about minds. Doing this will rid us of certain confusions. For him, as well as for Wittgenstein, philosophy is a way of solving perplexities. He says: "This book offers what may with reservations be described as a theory of the mind. But it does not give new information about minds. We possess al-

180

ready a wealth of information about minds, information which is neither derived from, nor upset by, the arguments of philosophers. The philosophical arguments which constitute this book are intended not to increase what we know about minds, but to rectify the logical geography of the knowledge which we already possess."[2] He has also denied that he was advocating a form of philosophical behaviorism, the view that there are no inner occurrences at all. A great deal of his analysis depends upon his being able to show that what philosophers used to say about these inner occurrences—intelligence, grief, vanity, and the like—can be said much more correctly by confining ourselves to statements about bodily behavior or dispositions to behave in certain ways. In this he is only partly successful, first, because he cannot reduce all statements about inner occurrences to states about behavior or dispositions, and second, because much of his analysis depends upon three notions which are themselves in need of further analysis: categories, dispositions, and counterfactual statements. Although all these notions appear to be well enough understood on the surface, each presents special problems and has been the subject of a considerable literature. In what follows I shall say something brief about Ryle's notion of category, less about his notion of disposition, and then go on to outline his attempt to solve the problem of sense data.

Categories

According to Ryle, philosophers have made a great many mistakes in speaking about minds because they spoke of things which belonged in one category as if they belonged in another entirely different one. They are not mistakes in fact, but mistakes in principle. "To determine the logical geography of concepts is to reveal the logic of the propositions in which they are wielded, that is to say, to show with what other propositions they are consistent and inconsistent, what propositions follow from them and from what propositions they follow. The logical type or category to which a concept belongs is the set of ways in which it is logically legitimate to operate with it." (8) But an explicit definition of 'category' is not possible and Ryle resorts to setting out examples. In his earlier article "Categories"[3] he gave the following example: " 'So and so is in bed' grammatically requires for complements to the gap indicated by 'so and so' nouns, pronouns, or substantive phrases such as descriptive phrases. So 'Saturday is in bed' breaks no rule of grammar. Yet the sentence is absurd." (Flew, 70) This is enough to show that 'Saturday' belongs to a different category from anything that could be said to be in bed. One criterion of whether or not two words belong to the same category is whether or not they could be used in the same sentence without creating absurdity.

Critics have argued that this is neither a necessary nor a sufficient condition for showing that two words belong to the same category since one could, in principle, specify a sentence such that given any two words one would fit meaningfully and the other would be absurd. One might exhibit the sentence 'so-and-so is used for storing clothes', into which 'dresser' and 'chest' fit, but 'bed' and 'cushion' do not. But 'bed' and 'cushion' belong to the same category to which 'chest' and 'dresser' belong.[4] At the end of his article "Categories" Ryle himself asked: "But what are the tests of absurdity?" (Flew, 81) For it is clear that to know that two words or concepts belong to different categories one must exhibit a context in which one fits normally and the other is absurd, and in the crucial cases, which are the interesting ones, the argument will turn upon just what uses of the word or concept are or are not absurd. If we do not know this, we shall not know when a 'category mistake' has been made.

In spite of this, Ryle holds that there are clear-cut cases of category mistakes and in *The Concept of Mind* he outlines some. (16–17) Suppose you are visiting a university for the first time and are shown the field house, the library, the dormitories, the administration building, the laboratories, and all the rest. If then you say 'I have seen all the major buildings and installations and have noted them with great interest, but when are you going to show me the university?', you have made what Ryle calls a category mistake, for you have assumed that a university is the same sort of entity as any building which is a building *of* a university. But, "The University is just the way in which all that [you have] . . . already seen is organized." (16) It is not another part of the whole but the whole itself, including all its functions and what it is used for. The university does not belong to the same category as its buildings do.

Similarly, suppose a child watched a parade of an army division. You point out to him the various battalions, batteries, squadrons, and the like. He then says 'yes, I see them all right, but where is the division?' Clearly he has assimilated the division, which is just the sum of the parts enumerated, to being one such part. Divisions are made up of battalions, batteries, squadrons, and the like.

These are theoretically uninteresting category mistakes because they are made by persons ignorant of the correct use of certain words or concepts. More theoretically interesting ones occur when someone who knows how to use certain concepts correctly in situations where they are normally applied misuses them in novel situations because he extends their use. Such a category mistake is, what Ryle calls, 'Descartes' Myth'.

According to Ryle, Descartes took the mechanical theories of Galileo which applied to bodies in space and denied that they applied to human nature and minds. "Since mental-conduct words are not to be construed as signifying the occurrence of mechanical processes, they must be construed as signifying the occurrence of non-mechanical processes; since mechanical laws explain movements in space as the effects of other movements in space, other laws must explain some of the non-spatial workings of minds. . . ." (19) Minds and bodies are connected together, although bodies and bodily actions are publicly observable, while minds and mental acts are private, open only to the purview of their owners. Thus the world is divided in two: one part is the domain of the physical, the other the domain of the mental.

But if this is true, there arises the major problem of how non-material minds are attached to and work on material bodies and cause them to do or refrain from doing something. These and many other problems appear unsolvable when we believe the dogma of the ghost in the machine: that bodies and minds are, as it were, negative counterparts of each other. Ryle says, "I shall argue that these and other analogous conjunctions are absurd. . . . I am not, for example, denying that there occur mental processes. Doing long division is a mental process and so is making a joke. But I am saying that the phrase 'there occur mental processes' does not mean the same sort of thing as 'there occur physical processes', and, therefore, that it makes no sense to conjoin or disjoin the two." (22)[5] One can talk about each of these, but in different ways. One cannot apply the same concepts to them.

Ryle's program, then, is to analyze the most important of our mental concepts, showing in detail how in each case a correct analysis can eliminate the two dichotomies, the mental and the physical, and the private and the public. Let us turn briefly to intelligence, which requires the notion of disposition for its explanation.

What do we mean when we say that Jones is intelligent? What we don't mean, says Ryle, is that there is some non-physical private occurrence going on 'in his head' which, if it is good enough, we call an intelligent act. Ryle thinks that we should look for our answer in how we go about discovering that Jones is intelligent. If we do this, we will see that his intelligence consists in a series of a certain kind of acts and dispositions to act. He knows how to *do* things. He speaks well, solves various sorts of problems, reads and gives a good account of his reading, etc. His intelligence does not consist in his doing or having done any one act or particular set of acts, but in his generally being able to perform in certain ways.

The belief that intelligence is some private mental phenomenon hidden inside a person comes from the notion that the function of intelligence is ". . . finding the answers to questions and that there other occupations are merely applications of considered truths or even regrettable distractions from their consideration." (26) But if it were the case ". . . that the operation which is characterized as intelligent must be preceded by an intellectual acknowledgment of these rules or criteria . . . [if] the agent must first go through the internal process of avowing to himself certain propositions about what is to be done," (29) then in fact no intelligent operation could ever be performed. For Ryle argues that the thinking of a rule or maxim, according to which we should perform a certain act, is itself an intelligent act. Hence one would, on this view, have to think of a rule or maxim for doing *that;* but this in turn is an intellectual act, and so a rule or maxim would have to be thought of for doing *it,* and so on. If each act requires a prior act of rule-making or theorizing before it can be performed, and if each act of theorizing or rule-making is an intellectual act, there would be an infinite number of acts of theorizing or rule-making required before any intelligent act could be performed. And that is impossible. Hence the view that intelligence is some private non-physical occurrence cannot be correct.

Intelligence is manifested in a great many ways, which consist in performing some overt action. Doing logic, being witty, writing well, composing music, and playing chess are all, if done well, evidences of intelligence. A man is intelligent if he knows how to do things well, not if he has a ghostly occurrence in his head. Being intelligent is being able to do certain sorts of things; it is a dispositional property of the agent, much as being brittle is a dispositional property of glass. Under certain circumstances glass breaks. So under certain circumstances the intelligent man performs well.

Sense Data

What about sense data? Ryle begins his destruction of them by observing that verbs like 'see', 'hear', and 'taste'—verbs which are commonly used in speaking about sense data—do not, as he puts it, designate sensations 'neat'. (210) They make what he calls an extended or sophisticated use of sensation talk. "We ordinarily use these words ['sensation' and 'feel'] for a special family of perceptions, namely, tactual and kinesthetic perceptions and perceptions of temperatures, as well as for localizable pains and discomforts." (200)

When someone says that he has a burning, throbbing, or driving sensation we are not usually tempted to speak of this painful type of sensation as something existing apart from his feeling of it. But when we talk about perception and use 'sensation' as a name for it, or use 'sensation' to refer to one of many ingredients in the act of perceiving, and when we begin to puzzle about certain properties that our acts of perception seem to have—then, like Moore, we may be tempted to distinguish the sensation from what it is a sensation of. We erect objects to mediate between us and the world 'outside us', and so create sense data.

My pain stops when I stop feeling it. But, says Ryle, when I stop seeing horse races or tasting wines, the race goes on and the wine is still there. But *something* did stop, and a convenient name for it is my view or my tasting. These sorts of things are made into sense data and it is argued that when we say that we see a material body we are really seeing a sense datum. We no longer see things, but we have visual sensations. This should be familiar from our discussion of Moore and Russell. "[W]hile laymen speak of observing a robin and scanning a page of *The Times*, this theory speaks instead of intuiting colour patches and having immediate acquaintanceship with smells." (212)

Ryle says further, "I shall try to prove that this whole theory rests upon a logical howler, the howler, namely, of assimilating the concept of sensation to the concept of observation. . . ." (213) He puts forward a number of interesting arguments in defense of his assertion. The first is the type of infinite-regress argument which he used against the view that intelligence consists in theorizing. It is a favorite of his, and he employs it often in the book.

According to the sense datum theory, having a visual sensation of, say, a horse race, consists in intuiting a patchwork of color. So getting a glimpse of a horse race is analyzed as getting a glimpse of what we *really* see, namely a patchwork of color. But Ryle argues that if getting a look or glimpse of *X* means you have one sensation, then getting a look or glimpse of that sensation involves having another, call it *Y;* but getting a glimpse of *that* involves still another, and there you go, on to infinity. If each having of a sensation consists in observing or seeing something, then having the sensation of *that* involves a further observing or seeing of something else, and so on. (213)

Again, it is contradictory to say that someone is observing something but having no sensations. You cannot have one without the other. Similarly, "If all clothes are concatenations of stitches, absurdity results from saying that all stitches are themselves very tiny clothes." (214) Observing consists in having sensations, so sensations cannot be like observing. Universities consist of buildings, but no building can itself be a university, though it may be a place that houses one.

Other differences between observation and sensation are the following. Someone · may look or observe patiently, skillfully, or craftily, but it makes little sense to say that he is having sensations skillfully, patiently, or craftily. They don't belong in the same category, and absurdity results from putting them together in one category. In Wittgenstein's phrase, they belong to different language games. Conversely, we can say things about sensation which are not applicable to observation. But if this is true, then having a sensation is not to be in the relation of observer to observed thing, and hence there is no need to postulate the existence of sense data.

Again, suppose someone was looking at a round plate tilted away from him. He might be tempted to say one of two things. In one sense of 'look' the plate certainly does look round and not elliptical, for everyone knows that round plates look round when tilted away from them. Elliptical plates tilted away from you look elliptical. Try it with a round dinner plate and an elliptical serving platter. You would never think that a round plate tilted away from you was elliptical any more than you would think that a penny so tilted was elliptical.

But in another sense the round plate tilted away from you might be said to look elliptical. It might look as an elliptical plate would look if held perpendicular to your line of vision. But to go from saying that the round plate looks elliptical to saying that one is seeing an elliptical look or sense datum is going too far. One does not usually talk about the look of a thing and mean an entity different from the thing itself. This, says Ryle, is like talking about biscuits and nibbles of biscuits. One eats them and takes nibbles of them. So one sees things and things have a certain look or appearance, but one doesn't see their look or their appearance any more than he eats the nibbles of biscuits. Though there is an entirely different use of appearance: the appearance that a celebrity makes on a TV show, in which one can say that he saw the appearance of *X*. But these uses are not connected. ". . . [One] cannot talk of 'seeing looks', since 'look' is already a noun of seeing." (217)

And again, we divide an object's qualities as Locke did, into two sorts: primary and secondary. We then note that the secondary qualities seem different when our sensory apparatus or the intervening medium is disturbed. But this in no way entails that the sensory quality involved in some way belongs to the observer and not the objects observed. Objects are blue or square, not sensations. Alum tastes bitter, but not my taste sensation of alum, for I do not taste the taste sensation of alum any more than I see the look of a stick in the water. I taste alum and see sticks.

If the arguments sketched here are sound, then there are no such things as sense data or sensibilia; for there could be no such things. Every attempt to erect them between us and the physical object results in a category mistake of one sort or another. One might still try to make a case for them in cases of hallucinations, dreams, and mental images. Ryle devoted a section of the book to the analysis of these cases, but the arguments appear less successful there. These things are more difficult to analyze away, and turn up an amazing variety of forms in the literature of psychology. But it is in language and concepts, not science, that Ryle finds the proper sphere of philosophy, and it is with these, and solving problems caused by their misuse, that Ryle prefers to deal.

2. *John Austin: Sense Data*

Austin's work, along with that of Ryle and the later Wittgenstein, may be called 'ordinary language philosophy', for that term is broad enough to cover several different sorts of philosophy. But he stands in opposition to both Ryle and Wittgenstein in that he does not conceive of philosophical analysis as merely or primarily a puzzle-solving activity. It is not so much problems to solve, or dissolve (though he does this, too), but distinctions in language themselves that he is interested in. In his paper "A Plea for Excuses"[6] he says, ". . . I shall illustrate, in more congenial but desultory detail, some of the methods to be used, together with their limitations, and some of the unexpected results to be expected and lessons to be learned. Much, of course, of the amusement, and of the instruction, comes in drawing the coverts of the microglot, and hounding down the minutiae. . . ." (123) For Austin, but not for Ryle or Wittgenstein, the study, analysis, and cataloguing of the tremendous variety of language, as it is ordinarily used, is an end in itself. It is a kind of knowledge which may be sought for its own sake, rather than for the sake of ridding ourselves of conceptual muddles, though it is of great use in this respect. But where Wittgenstein, and Ryle too, are content to show in the large what sorts of errors we make philosophizing—Wittgenstein with his vague notion of language games and Ryle with his notion of categories—Austin feels the real job is to indicate the precise way in which various formulations and meanings are related to different concepts, and not merely different ways of talking about the same concepts. We shall see this in several of Austin's analyses which will be set out below.[7]

For Austin, ordinary language analysis was one way of doing philosophy among others, not the only way of doing it (as logical construction was for Russell, as the realistic analysis was for Moore, and as showing the fly the way out of the fly-bottle was for Wittgenstein). As such, it could be justified by the results it produced, results which "illuminated the terrain" and therefore had intrinsic interest. In the same article, while speaking of the study of the notion of excuses, Austin writes:

> But there are also reasons why it is an attractive subject methodologically, at least if we are to proceed from 'ordinary language', that is, by examining *what we should say when,* and so why and what we should mean by it. Perhaps this method, at least as *one* philosophical method, scarcely requires justification at present—too evidently, there is gold in them thar hills: more opportune would be a warning about the care and thoroughness needed if it is not to fall into disrepute. I will, however, justify it very briefly.
>
> First, words are our tools, and, as a minimum, we should use clean tools: we should know what we mean and what we do not, and we must forearm ourselves against the traps that language sets us. Secondly, words are not (except in their own little corner) facts or things: we need therefore to prise them off the world, to hold them apart from and against it, so that we can realize their inadequacies and arbitrariness, and can relook at the world without blinkers. Thirdly, and more hopefully, our common stock of words embodies all the distinctions men have found worth drawing, and the connexions they have found worth marking, in the lifetimes of many generations: these surely are likely to be more numerous, more sound, since they have stood up to the long test of the survival of the fittest, and more subtle, *at least in all ordinary and reasonably practical matters* [italics mine], than any you or I are likely to think up in our arm-chairs of an afternoon—the most favored alternative method.
>
> In view of the prevalence of the slogan 'ordinary language', and of such names as 'linguistic' or 'analytic' philosophy or 'the analysis of language', one thing needs specially emphasizing to counter misunderstandings. When we examine what we should say when, what words we should use in what situations, we are looking again not *merely* at words (or 'meanings', whatever they may be) but also at the realities we use the words to talk about: we are using a sharpened awareness of words to sharpen our perception of, *though not as the final arbiter of* [italics mine], the phenomena. For this reason I think it might be better to use, for this way of doing philosophy, some less misleading name than those given above—for instance, 'linguistic phenomenology', only that is rather a mouthful. (129–30)

This quotation shows in a short space what Austin is

about and, in the end, what the best sort of linguistic analysis is about. It is clear that appeal to ordinary language is no
court of last resort but, to change an Austinian phrase, a
court of first resort. It settles no recondite disputes but puts a
starting point to one sort of philosophic investigation. It is *a*
place to begin. It is of interest when the topics under investigation are widespread and to be found embedded in the
structure of our everyday thought. It is clearly not of interest
in thinking about solid state or nuclear physics, biochemis-
try, or physiology. But it may be of use in attempting to
transplant results in recondite disciplines into philosophy.
Moreover, certain topics, though they may be examined
from a recondite point of view, are also topics about which
we speak ordinarily. Such a topic is the topic of perception,
which may be examined by physiologists and psychologists,
but about which ordinary men make countless correct statements during their lives. When we speak as theoreticians,
however, things seem to go badly wrong with our talk about
perception, and one of the reasons that they do is that as
theoreticians we forget about what as plain men we seem
instinctively to know quite well. A look at Austin's work in
this area will serve both to point out some conceptual
muddles and to exhibit some of the intrinsically interesting
distinctions to be found in our language about perception.

Austin's *Sense and Sensibilia* is a reconstruction from his
manuscript notes (by J. G. Warnock).[8] The view that Austin
is concerned to attack is the view that we never directly perceive material objects, that we only perceive sense data or
sense perceptions. (2) Although as sources for these views
Austin uses Ayer, *The Foundations of Empirical Knowledge,* Price,
Perception, and Warnock, *Berkeley,* it is almost a precise re-
statement of the views of G. E. Moore, Austin believes that
people hold such views because they are obsessed with a few
words or facts which have not been carefully studied, understood, or described. The words used to describe these facts
are far more subtle than the proponents of these views allow,
and a wider range of examples would disabuse us of the notion that things must be the way the sense datum theorists

say they are. Realism, the opposite view, is also an oversimplified doctrine. "One of the most important points to grasp is that these two terms, 'sense-data' and 'material thing', live by taking in each other's washing—what is spurious is not one term of the pair, but the antithesis itself. There is no *one* kind of thing that we 'perceive' but many *different* kinds, the number being reducible if at all by scientific investigation and not by philosophy. . . ." (4)

The sense datum theorist first sets up a foil for sense data by arguing that the ordinary man would say that he perceives material objects. But Austin says this is not true. Ordinary people do not ordinarily use terms like 'material object'. Suppose that this term is a class designation for such things as tables, chairs, cats, and rocks. But the 'ordinary man' would under the heading 'things he perceived' include things like ". . . people's voices, rivers, mountains, flames, rainbows, shadows, pictures on the screen at the cinema, pictures in books or hung on walls, vapours, gases. . . ." (8) But these are surely not all material things. The first step into the sense datum abyss is taken when you claim that there is one and only one sort of thing you can perceive. (Compare Moore on this.)

Second, the sense datum theorist implies 1) that if you think you are perceiving something but not perceiving a material object, then you think your senses deceive you; 2) descriptions of one's sensory occurrences lead one to think that one is not perceiving a material thing, but a sense datum. This is nonsense. One sees non-material rainbows (what would a material one look like?) and ships which appear nearer than they actually are. Does anyone think that his senses deceive him in the case of the rainbow and that he is seeing a non-material ship which *is* nearer than the material one?

3. The sense datum theorist implies that generally the ordinary man's belief in material objects needs justification in *every* case. If he were a more reflective person he would think that in at least some cases it does need justification; but he does not even see this much.

4. Perhaps there is room for doubt about what we see. Perhaps we get enough certainty from the perceptual world for practical purposes, but we may not really get absolute certainty. The sense datum theorist, however, having prised in this part of the wedge, wants to go further. He suggests that not only is it never absolutely certain that we see material objects, that the senses can be trusted in the main, but that they can never be trusted at all, for we never do in fact see what we think we see. We always perceive sense data, and never anything else. The sense datum theorist's doubt is not just a little doubt in borderline cases, but really is unmasked to reveal total doubt.

5. The sense datum theorist introduces the notion of sense perceptions which stand between us and what is 'out there', and which inform us of the 'outside world'. They are like a television broadcast between the studio and the plain man's living room, but the plain man, along with the philosopher, is trapped in the room. The only way he can find out what is going on outside is to watch the set. And the philosopher is always there to tell him that the transmission may be imperfect.

And, if you go on to wonder how often your sense perceptions deceive you, you are half-way down the slope toward the abyss. But Austin claims that we do not say we are deceived by our senses half so often as the sense datum theorist makes it appear that we do. And even in those cases where we would be prepared to say that the senses deceived us, we must discuss many sorts of deception. Roughly, there are the cases of deception where 1) the sense organ is deranged, 2) the medium or conditions of perception are abnormal, and 3) where a wrong inference is made from what one perceives. Neat dichotomies are not possible.

But if you allow that people usually have reason to think themselves deceived, that there is one sort of thing that they generally perceive, and one sort of deception they are prone to, then you have already prepared the ground for the sense datum theorist. He has already got things rocking with such admissions. A small push and over they go.

What about perceiving things directly? Moore argues at length that we never are directly acquainted with material objects. We have only indirect perception of them. They are known only by description as the things related to *this* directly perceived sense datum, in a relation which he doesn't know (Chapter 2, above). His account is quite unilluminating, though it looked persuasive when Moore offered it. But let us see what Austin has to say about the word 'directly'.

To begin with, 'directly' is a word with a special use which is stretched beyond recognition by the sense datum theorist. Consider its opposite, 'indirectly.' How do we use this word? Someone sees something indirectly if he sees it 1) through a periscope, 2) in a mirror. One might see someone directly (in person) or 3) indirectly might be seeing his shadow on the blind. One hears the music indirectly 4) over the radio. The first two cases have to do with the change in direction of the line of sight, but the second two do not. Again, hearing something indirectly might mean 5) that someone else told you. And again, is touching someone with a pole 6) touching him indirectly? There is no one thing which 'directly' and 'indirectly' mean, but a variety of things.

Once separate cases are examined, the sense datum theorist's notion that you see sense data 'directly' and objects 'indirectly' no longer looks so clear. What works with sight does not work so well with sound. With touch it works even less well, and with taste and smell one is hard-put even to form the dichotomy—I smell it—indirectly? in a mirror? through a facsimile? from the other direction? how?

Suppose we do speak of perceiving material objects indirectly. According to the sense datum theorist, we cannot, in principle, see them directly. But if this is so, if we can never perceive them directly, then we might want to deny that we ever do perceive them at all. Compare seeing a car indirectly in your rear-view mirror, which you might have seen directly had you turned around, with seeing beads of moisture in a Wilson cloud chamber. In the second case the subatomic particle is not perceivable at all. Would we want to say that we see it indirectly because we see what we take to be a sign of it? If not, why say that we see material objects indirectly when we see sense data which are their signs, but are forever barred in principle from seeing them?

Austin turns to the argument from illusion (20) which, according to him, is intended to induce people to accept sense data as what they perceive under abnormal conditions. It is then argued that the same thing takes place under normal conditions. Austin draws his arguments from Ayer, but Moore had used them also. Different observers see material objects differently on the same occasion, and on successive occasions the same observer sees changes in the object which cannot have occurred. Hence what they and he are seeing is not an object, but appearances of it: sense data. The straight stick partly immersed in water looks bent. But the stick could not have changed shape. Hence we are seeing a crooked sense datum of the stick.

According to Austin, this argument only seems to work because the sense datum theorist speaks as if three different sorts of phenomena were really the same at bottom, but we merely use three different ways to describe them. Once we notice this, the argument from 'illusion' no longer appears sound. For it proceeds by speaking of cases of normal perception as if they were illusory, and then going on to speak of *illusions* as if they were *delusions*.

What are illusions and delusions? Consider optical illusions. Every elementary psychology text contains several. Lines of equal length shaded in a certain way are made to look unequal; two parallel lines are made to look as if they would cross. An illusion is a case of seeing something which looks different from its normal appearance. (20) One can be on guard against illusions. Seeing the trick, as we say, enables us to see through the illusion. Looking carefully at the 'headless woman' on stage we discern that the illusion is created by a black bag covering her head so that it is lost against a black background. Measuring the lines and noting the shading, we see that they are really the same length and really parallel. We can dispel the illusion.

But delusions are different. In delusion something *unreal* is conjured up: the pink rats of the alcoholic or the delusions of grandeur of the aging actress. They are products of a disordered mind. One cannot rid oneself of them by being on guard; one cannot examine the delusion to get at its trick. Delusion is not a case of seeing something abnormally as illusion is, but a case of seeing, or thinking you see, what is not there.

Even if the argument from illusion got you to admit that seeing a stick as bent in the water is illusory, which it is not, there is a gap between illusion and delusion which the sense datum theorist's argument fails to bridge. He tries to go from his pseudo-illusions to the conjuring up of some totally nonexistent thing to satisfy his theoretical need.

Now, the standard cases which the sense datum theorist trades upon as illusory are really *normal* occurrences. From certain angles pennies look elliptical; mirror images look as if they are behind the glass. That is their *normal* state. If it is thought that perspective shows objects in an abnormal way, what would the normal way be like? Is it normal to look at pennies only with one's line of sight perpendicular to their surfaces? But they grow smaller and larger with distance. Is there a normal distance? If so, what is it and how is one to know?

It might be safer, in fact, to say that bent sticks half in and half out of water don't really look bent, or as if they are bent. Perhaps one might think they are bent if one didn't see the water or if one hadn't seen many such sticks. But it is not usual to think of them as looking like really bent sticks. As Austin says, "Does anyone suppose that if something is straight, then it jolly well has to *look* straight at all times and in all circumstances?" (29)

Now for the word 'real.' The sense datum theorist (Ayer again) makes free use of this word. One sees or does not see the *real* shape of the stick; one sees or does not see the *real* material body; one is or is not *really* seeing what one thinks one is seeing. Close examination of this word will reveal that it has many different uses which mark many distinctions that it can be used to make. By assimilating this variety to just a few uses, the sense datum theorist tries to make his case.

The first thing to notice is that 'real' is an ordinary word with a fairly established set of uses and meanings in our language. Philosophers cannot ignore these as they please, as if it were a technical word which only they use and to which, therefore, they may attach whatever meanings serve their purposes. If in our moments of theoretical flight we recall that 'real' is often used in expressions like 'real cream', we may be warned off saying ". . . or seeming to say that what is not real cream must be a fleeting product of our cerebral processes," (64) a sense datum of cream. In this case 'real' is not opposed to 'mental' or 'appearance', but rather to 'powdered', 'half-and-half', 'synthetic', and the like.

Consider the phrase, 'the real color of the thing'. The theorist is prone to say that it is the color that appears to the normal observer under normal conditions. But compare with: a) that is not the real color of her hair; b) that is not the real color of the wool. In a) one is saying that she dyes her hair and in b) that in daylight it will look different or that natural wool, unlike this, is a dirty greyish-white.

Again, what does saccharine *really* taste like? Sweet in your coffee, but bitter alone on your tongue. Does it make sense to ask the real color of the sun, the sky, a chameleon? What could standard conditions for these things be like? Consider paintings. As is well known to art students, moderately clever use of certain colors gives the effect of other colors. Austin's example of a *pointilliste* painting (one where the paint is applied in tiny dots rather than in strokes) can be made up of blue and yellow dots. What is the *real* color of the painting?

The same sorts of things may be said of shape. Pennies have a *real* shape to which sense datum theorists like to contrast their apparent shape. But what of clouds, rainbows, and animals? What is the *real* shape of these things? But compare with cases where 'real' is properly used. Is this *real* jewelry? Is that *real* caviar? For here we know what we are contrasting with 'real': paste jewelry and salmon's eggs, false jewelry and false caviar. But do clouds and cats have false shapes? Are their true shapes determined under standard conditions? What might standard conditions be for determining the shape of a cat?

Again, the word 'real' takes its primary sense from the negative use. We know what someone means when he calls something a real X, if we know with what he wished to contrast it. To say that something is a real X might mean that it is not fake, not synthetic, not a decoy, not a trap, not a forgery, not a counterfeit, not an impostor, not an impersonator, etc. This is unusual because for most words the affirmative use is primary. But the fact that there is such a variety of things the word 'real' might, on any occasion, be used to exclude is why ". . . the attempt to find a characteristic common to all things that are or could be called 'real' is doomed to failure. . . ." (70)[9]

If Austin's points are valid, and there is certainly a good case to be made for them, then though the sense datum theorist may still be able to make his case, he must do so with far more care and investigation of separate cases. If Austin has not destroyed the theory, and many theorists would deny that he has, then he has at least robbed it of one of its chief attractions—its charming simplicity—and has shown that there are far more questions to be answered than the theorist had led us to believe with his well-restricted set of examples and paradigm cases.

Does the criticism leveled against the sense datum theory by Ryle and Austin vitiate Moore's position? If it does, what of other possible versions of the sense datum theory? If we take Ryle's attack first we must say that insofar as the attack depends upon the general notion of categories, it seems to fail, for that notion is not very clear.

Ryle has denied that one can meaningfully conjoin or disjoin propositions about concepts belonging to different categories *(CM,* 22; see p. 184 above). But this is wrong. It is not the conjoining or disjoining of the propositions which gives absurdity, but the treatment of two things belonging to different categories as if they belonged to the same category. *Sometimes* the mere conjunction or disjunction of propositions about them gives the impression that two such things are being treated as if they belonged to the same category: i.e., ". . . he bought a left-hand glove, a right-hand glove, and a pair of gloves." *(CM,* 22) Here the conjunction makes it appear that 'pair of gloves' is a third thing over and above right- and left-hand gloves, and *sometimes* this is not true. But sometimes it is. Suppose you had two children one of whom lost his left-hand glove and the other of whom lost his right-hand glove, and you went to the store to replace the missing items. Then, if you bought yourself a pair of gloves in addition to buying replacements for the missing items, you could certainly legitimately say, 'I bought a left hand glove, a right hand glove, and a pair of gloves'.

Furthermore, one can surely say, 'this is Oxford University and that is a building belonging to the university'.[10] But Ryle argued in his examples that buildings and universities belong to different categories. In general, it does not seem possible to avoid category mistakes by the specification of a criterion, except the criterion that when you have said something which is absurd in a particular way you have committed a category mistake. There appears to be no further specification of this sort of absurdity; and so the notion is unhelpful. As Smart has argued (see p. 182 above), given any two concepts, one can almost always construct a sentence such that if it is taken as a sentence about one of the concepts it makes sense, while if that concept is replaced in the sentence by the second, the sentence becomes absurd. Do all concepts, or the words denoting them, belong to different categories?

There is more trouble with Ryle's examples. The only point that the example about battalions, divisions, squadrons, and batteries (16) could possible have made is that the child has made a category mistake in demanding to see a division in addition to battalions, squadrons, batteries, etc. Then divisions must belong to different categories from batteries and the like. But can't the commanding general assign to a particular sector of the front four divisions from the Third Army, three battalions from the Fifth Army, and twelve squadrons from the Tenth Army without making a category mistake?

When someone has made a category mistake, one appears to know this only on the basis of some prior knowledge of what things belong to different categories. And then, even if one commits a category mistake by talking in a certain way about two things, he may easily say a whole host of other things about them without committing one. But isn't it the case that the justification of such prior knowledge, and the question of what things can be said properly or improperly, are just the issues. And if so, then the notion of category, while it may be useful as a sorting device in exposition, can never be the *justification* for sorting out things or concepts in some particular way. If this is true, then it can never follow from the fact that to say something about one concept is absurd while to say the same thing about another is not, that the two concepts belong to irreducibly different categories. The logic of the two terms may be different, but that scarcely shows that the entities referred to by the terms are ontologically different. It does not show that we cannot say the same things about minds as about bodies.[11] We turn to other criticisms of the sense datum theory. First, both Ryle and Austin deride the notion of a sense datum as the product of a theory. The implication appears to be that getting tangled up in theory confuses the proponent of sense data, where a plain, hard look at the facts and the logic of the situation would reveal the true situation. But such criticism misses the point against Moore, for few men took plainer and harder looks at things than he. It misses another important point as well, for isn't it usually by means of theory that we explain things in the first place? The *plain* view is generally thought to be too plain to afford adequate explanation. What is really at issue is not whether or not the sense datum theory is a theory, but whether or not it is a good theory: whether or not it helps to explain the facts.

Second, consider two of Ryle's arguments: 1) the sense datum theorist gets to sense data by arguing as if the terms of observation were terms of sensation (pp. 185ff above). Ryle claims that we *observe* robins and shoes, but *sense* colors and pains. The first step on the false pathway to sense data is to argue as if we were also observing colors and pains and thus to make them into objects like shoes and robins. This is a mistake, for it makes no sense to speak of observing our sensations. We can, for example, improve our observations of things, but we cannot improve our sensing of pains. Moreover, observation consists in part of the having of sensations, so sensing cannot be a species of observation.

But suppose it were. 2) There would then be an infinite regress, for if seeing a robin were really seeing a color patch (that is, sensing it), then the seeing of the patchwork of colors must involve still a further seeing, and so on, *ad infinitum.* Thus no act of seeing could, on this account, ever take place. But, says Ryle, this is absurd.

I do not think these objections hold against Moore. Each of them depends upon saying that the sense datum theorist speaks of observing objects and sensing patchworks of colors as if they were the same sorts of operations. It is only in this way that the infinite regress can get started. As one of Ryle's own examples can be adapted to show, you would get into such a regress if, when you found that words were spelled with letters, you went on to argue that letters, too, are spelled, and that these further units of spelling were themselves spelled, etc. *(CM,* 206) Each further operation must be thought of as the same as the previous ones. But you don't, in fact, think this way. When you reach letters you stop. You do not ask how to spell *them.* Moore's argument, too, stops short of such a point. It stops short with the intuiting of color patches. (See pp. 24 f. above.) For Moore, our intuiting of color patches is not another kind of seeing, but a direct acquaintance which is different in kind from seeing.[12] As such, it avoids the crucial step necessary to start the regress.

Ryle attempts to counter such an objection by saying that to make this move we must speak of sensations as ". . . the *not* having any sensations. It avoids the imputed regress by the heroic device of suggesting that sensing is a cognitive process which does not require its owner to be susceptible of stimuli. . . ." *(CM,* 215) This reply is meant to show that once the sense datum theorist admits that he intuits or is directly acquainted with a color patch, he is just using different words to cover the fact that he is really sensing the patch, and so is still ripe for a fall down the infinite incline. But the reply merely says, without proving, that direct acquaintance, if it is anything, is a species of sensation. It is surely open to Moore to deny this, and further argument, not provided by Ryle, is required to show that he is wrong.

3. Austin, by making a great variety of distinctions and presenting us with a great variety of examples, seems to go further than Ryle in undermining the sense datum theory. Certainly, he presents many different cases from all sense modes which tend to show that it is not clear that we should say the same sorts of thing about each mode, or even clear just what different sorts of things we should say. By contrast with Moore, whose narrow range of cases seems to lead to only one possible conclusion, Austin shows that a correct analysis is not easily given. But does he show more than this? He does not seem to. What he shows is that in constructing a sense datum theory more is involved that first seems to be involved, and that some of the guiding motives of the sense datum theorists may have been wrong.

When Austin argues (page 192f above) that the sense datum theorist claims that we never have real certainty about the external world, it cannot be Moore whom he has in mind. Recall Moore's strong defense of common sense and of the fact that we *do* know that there are material objects, and his rejection of Hume's arguments (Chapter 2 above). For him, nothing is more certain than that the world exists as we think it exists. While it is true that we perceive sense data, it is also true that we perceive material objects. Moore's problem was not in doubting this fact, but in analyzing it. Austin charges the sense datum theorist with undermining our belief in the external world; but who could be less guilty of this than Moore? It is just as well to remember that there are many versions of the sense datum theory and that an attack upon one is not necessarily an attack upon all. Austin never claims to be refuting Moore, but in the excitment of his exposition it is easy to overlook this and to conclude that his arguments will do against any version of the theory.

4. Consider delusions. They are, according to Austin, the summoning up of unreal things. But *what* is summoned up? And how does one analyze them away? Surely not by the use of arguments designed to dispel the problems encountered by illusions—that pennies often appear elliptical without there being any elliptical things which appear, or that straight sticks don't jolly well always look straight even though there are no bent looks of things that we are seeing. What *is* happening with the unreal thing conjured up? Is one seeing it? Is he thinking that he is seeing it? Are there visual sensations occurring like those which occur when one really sees objects in the world? No analysis is provided by Austin. Ryle, in his chapter on imagination, tries to show that having an image or hallucination of *x* is thinking that you see *x*. But what is *that?* For reasons of physiology which are complicated in detail and which cannot be outlined here, this does not seem to be the case.[13] Until an analysis is provided which can explain these phenomena without using parts of some version of the sense datum theory, it seems premature to think the theory laid to rest.

Furthermore, some philosophers have argued that changing the language in which we describe perceptual phenomena does not solve the problems behind the sense datum theory. "It is true that one *could* describe these experiences in the language of appearing [as Austin attempts]. When I imagine a unicorn or a golden mountain I *could* describe the experience by saying, not that I have an image of such and such a sort, but that something appears in such and such a fashion. This way of putting the matter, however, leads us at once to the peculiar problems which the theory of appearing involves. For, in this language, we speak of *something* which appears. One may now ask, 'What is it that appears when I imagine a unicorn?' ('Is it a subsistent entity, or part of the brain, or parts of previously seen physical objects . . . etc?')"[14]

And Ryle, in his article "Sensations," wrote ". . . I confess to a residual embarrassment. There is something in common between having an after-image and seeing a misprint. Both are visual affairs. How ought we to describe their affinity with one another, without falling back on to some account very much like a part of the orthodox theories of sense-impressions? To this I am stumped for an answer."[15] We may safely conclude that not only is Moore not directly refuted by much of the criticism raised by Ryle and Austin, but that also though no version of the sense datum theory may, after all, be viable, a good deal of work remains before this can be shown.

3. W. V. O. Quine: Meaning and Reference

W. V. O. Quine is an American logician of considerable repute. In addition to his work in logic he has written much in recent years on epistemology and metaphysics. In particular he has been concerned with the metaphysical implications of logic, and this differentiates him from the logical positivists, for whom logic was a neutral tool which could be used with great effect just because it committed you to no ontology at all. Quine's views are nominalistic. He hopes to describe the universe by assuming only the existence of individuals. For him the best description would be one which did not use universals. Whether or not their use can be avoided remains an open question.

In his own phrase, Quine has a taste for desert landscapes,[16] And Strawson writes of him that "with a Roman ruthlessness he makes a solitude in which he can quantify peacefully over lumps of rock."[17] We shall sketch briefly and in part Quine's attempt to satisfy this craving. We deal first with his theory of ontological commitment, second with his rejection of the analytic-synthetic distinction, and last with his view of how science is constructed. These views are set out initially in nine essays contained in the above-mentioned book. We turn to the first essay, "On What There Is."

According to Quine we are committed to *saying* certain things *are* if our scientific theories say that they *are*. This is the outcome of his analysis of the problem of non-being. We recall from the account of Russell's theory of definite descriptions (Chapter 4 above) that some philosophers appeared to think that in the very act of denying being to something, since we name that thing, either it must *be* or we have not said anything. Consider the following argument: 1) Pegasus is not. 1) is a true sentence; therefore it is about Pegasus, for if it is not about Pegasus, then it is not about anything, and then it is not even significant, much less true. Therefore Pegasus *is*. (See below pp. 214f.)

Quine thinks this argument a bad one and he is right. In order to show that by the mere use of names we are not committed to the being of some entity, he adopts Russell's theory of definite descriptions for his own purposes. That theory applies to definite descriptions like 'the present king of France' and 'the author of *Waverley*'. In order to use it to rid ourselves of purported names it is necessary ". . . only to rephrase 'Pegasus' as a description, in any way that seems adequately to single out our idea; say, 'the winged horse that was captured by Bellerophon'. Substituting such a phrase for 'Pegasus', we can then proceed to analyze the statement 'Pegasus is', or 'Pegasus is not', precisely on the analogy of Russell's analysis of 'The author of *Waverley* is' and 'The author of *Waverley* is not'." (Quine 7) Thus we are not committed to an ontology containing Pegasus by the mere mention of the name 'Pegasus'.

What about universals? Are we committed to their being by the mere mention of their names? If we say there are red houses and red flowers does that commit us ontologically to what is common to them both: 'redness'? Not necessarily. Under a particular conceptual scheme it may, but under another it may not. Quine argues that we do commit ourselves ontologically to certain entities by the use of what is called in logic a 'bound variable'. Bound variables are expressed roughly in English by such phrases as 'there is (a something)', or 'there are (somethings)', where the part in parentheses stands for the things which *are*. Quine writes, "[b]ut this is, essentially, the *only* way we can involve ourselves in ontological commitments: by our use of bound variables." (12) We set up our theories or our conceptual schemes, and those entities referred to by the use of bound variables are the ones we are ontologically committed to. We may say 'some dogs are white' on this view without being committed to an ontology containing 'doghood' or 'whiteness', though we are committed to the existence of individual dogs which are white. But to say 'some zoological species are cross-fertile' is to commit ourselves ontologically to species. If we can devise a method of paraphrasing our statements to get rid of 'dogs' or 'species' then we shall no longer be ontologically committed to them.

We must note that Quine's criterion does *not* tell us what *is,* what things there are ontologically, but merely what things we are committed to *saying* there are ontologically. In Strawson's succinct phrase, "[y]ou say *there is* what you *say* there is; but if in saying, perhaps incidentally, that there is *x,* you can say what you want to say without saying that there is *x,* then in order to achieve your purpose, you need not say (are not committed to saying) that there is *x.* " ("A Logician's Landscape," 229) Your ontological commitments depend, then, upon your theories or conceptual scheme, always remembering that it is assumed that all theories or conceptual schemes are expressible in what Quine calls 'canonical notation' (roughly, a formal logical system) where it makes sense to speak of bound variables. This requirement may not always be satisfiable.

But after we know what we are committed to by *saying* that there is something, how do we go about finding *what* there is? For what there is does not depend upon words (Quine, 16) Then what does it depend upon? Quine says, "[o]ur acceptance of an ontology is, I think, similar in principle to our acceptance of a scientific theory, say a system of physics: we adopt, at least insofar as we are reasonable, the simplest conceptual scheme into which the disordered fragments of raw experience can be fitted and arranged. Our ontology is determined once we have fixed upon the over-all conceptual scheme which is to accommodate science in the broadest sense. . . ." (16–17) So the answer is that what *is,* is what we are committed to in the end by the best theories. These would be the theories which, pragmatically speaking, are the simplest and the most wide-ranging; which give the most comprehensive explanations. Which theories these are is an open question, and in a tolerant vein Quine counsels the experimental spirit: use competing conceptual schemes and see which, in the end, is best suited for your purposes. (19)

We turn to a brief view of Quine's notions on the analytic-synthetic distinction. Analytic statements are those held to be true independent of all experience (e.g., 'all bachelors are unmarried men'). This appears to follow from the meanings of the words alone. But synthetic statements are held to be true or false according as experience confirms them or not (e.g., 'this paper is white'). The distinction is an old one in philosophy, made in one way or another by Leibnitz, Hume, and Kant. It is essential to the formulations of the logical positivists, for their verifiability principle said that statements are meaningful if and only if either 1) they were analytic, or 2) they could be reduced to statements which could be confirmed or disconfirmed by some actual or possible sense experience. This allowed an empirical criterion of meaning for some sorts of statements, while allowing others to be meaningful if, like mathematical statements, they had no apparent empirical content.

In his second essay, "Two Dogmas of Empiricism," Quine attacks both the analytic-synthetic distinction and the thesis that all non-analytic statements can, if they are meaningful, be reduced to statements about sense experience. He does this, as we should now expect, by espousing a radical pragmatism which ends by blurring the 'supposed boundary' between natural science and speculative metaphysics. (20)

The analytic-synthetic distinction is attacked and abandoned for two reasons. The first is because it cannot be formulated without either circularity or dependence upon notions which require analysis as much as analyticity itself. For example, we might say that a statement is analytic if the relevant terms are synonymous. But what is synonymy? The second reason the distinction is abandoned is because it will be seen that as reductionism is false, there is no hard-and-fast distinction between those statements which will be held true in the face of all possible experience, and those abandoned in the face of disconfirming experience. We can keep or abandon any of them if our purpose warrants. In that case, there can be no analytic statements. The actual argument against the analytic-synthetic distinction is complicated, and I shall not outline it here. I shall move on to the last point, which leads directly to Quine's arguments about reductionism.

Quine turns to the verifiability theory of meaning. According to this theory, the meaning of a statement is its method of verification. So two statements will, on this view, be synonymous just in case they are both verified by the same method. If we can get the concept of the synonymy of statements, perhaps we can derive the concept of synonymy for words as well. And if we had that, then we could define analyticity. Thus, everything turns on this principle.

The verifiability principle can have many forms, as we saw in Chapters 7 and 8. Just how will we compare a statement with experience? The first possibility Quine calls 'radical reductionism'. It is the view that a statement is meaningful if and only if it is completely translatable into a statement or statements about our sense experience. This view may be attributed to Locke and Hume, who argued that all the ideas in our minds originate in sense experience or are compounds of ideas so originated. There are no other possibilities. There are many well-known objections to this view. We seem to have ideas which do not and cannot originate in sense experience. Knowledge would, on this view, be pictorial, a comparing of ideas or images in one's mind, and not propositional. As we saw, Moore argued against this view.

Quine points out further that radical reductionism is vague about what counts as a particular sense experience, and it is too restrictive, requiring that we break each idea down into individual sense bits for examination. He therefore moves on to a less restrictive version of this thesis. Full statements rather than individual ideas are to be accepted as the building blocks to be compared with experience. They must be translated into a sense datum language. This step he identifies with Frege and Russell. Its full elaboration begins with Carnap's *The Logical Structure of the World.*

Quine pays Carnap the tribute of saying that "he was the first empiricist who not content with asserting the reducibility of science to terms of immediate experience, took serious steps toward carrying out the reduction." (39) As we have seen, despite his accomplishments, Carnap failed in his main task for technical as well as epistemological reasons. Although he was more generous than Russell, allowing himself not only a sense datum terminology, but almost all of pure mathematics, he was unable to do without certain concepts which belong neither to a sense datum language nor to mathematics. (On this precise point see Quine, 40.)

So this ambitious effort failed also. We have got to this point. If we can specify what the method of verification of a statement consists in, then we shall be able to tell when two statements are verified by the same method. But if, as the verifiability principle holds, the meaning of a statement is its method of verification, then when two statements are verified by the same method, we will know that they have the same meaning. And if we know that, then we will know they are synonymous. And that is what we are after.

But from the evidence of the failure of reductionism to make a case for itself in detail, Quine draws the conclusion that single statements are not what is verified at all. Might it not be the case in principle that there was no set of possible sensory experiences which would always lead us to feel that an empirical statement was confirmed or made more probable? What Quine suggests is that empirical statements are tested not singly, but in a body. He argues that the dogma of the analytic-synthetic fed upon and is, in turn, fed upon by, the dogma of reductionism. The dogma holds that even if *some* statements are rendered true or false by experience, there are others which cannot be rendered true or false by any experience whatsoever. If some statements are reducible to sensory experience, some are not. "The idea of defining a symbol in use [compare Russell's incomplete symbols] was, as remarked, an advance over the impossible term-by-term empiricism of Locke and Hume. The statement, rather than the term, came with Frege to be recognized as the unit accountable to an empiricist critique. But what I am now urging is that even in taking the statement as a unit we have drawn our grid too finely. The unit of empirical significance is the whole of science." (42)

But this is a radical position. It surely seemed obvious that some statements were confirmed by experience and some were not. The stock of scientific statements was increased by finding interesting statements of the first kind: i.e., 'the earth is round', 'water is composed of hydrogen and oxygen', 'earthquakes are caused by geological faults', etc. If Quine rejects that, with what is he prepared to replace it? He writes that the totality of our knowledge is like ". . . a man-made fabric which impinges on experience only along the edges." (42) Changes at the border cause us to realign parts of the interior of the fabric. Our statements are interconnected and hence, changing some may result in changing others, but usually not all. However, what statements we change is a matter of choice, usually dictated by convenience. Single experiences may make border changes necessary, but rarely cause realignment deep in the interior, though they could.

To change Quine's metaphor, think of an army. At the front, in contact with the enemy, are the soldiers who get killed or wounded, or turned back. Behind them is the front-line command; it is less exposed to the danger of battle, but a heavy bombardment may strike there. Further back are the field commanders, generals. A real rout forces them to retreat, but this is rare. Further behind is the staff headquarters for the theater of operations. Disastrous planning in the field may cause us to remove the men in charge of planning here, but they are rarely shot at. Then there are the joint chiefs of staff and the president. Battles never rage in the Pentagon and in the White House. But poor results at the front may occasion the removal of a joint chief or two, or a president's failure to seek re-election. The battlefront rarely directly affects the government, but it can affect it indirectly. Such events contributed to Truman's decision not to run in 1952 and to Stevenson's defeat. They brought De Gaulle to power in 1958, and may have caused Johnson's decision not to run in 1968.

In the structure of science, then, logical laws and analytic statements occupy positions analogous to the president. Experience does not impinge upon them, but enough trouble up front and they can be changed. Such a view may be likened to Aristotle's. For him, certain logical laws, like the law of the excluded middle, are laws because reality is that way. Perhaps Aristotle was not as ready as Quine to think that things might change, but if they had, wouldn't-he have had to change his logic?

Quine's suggestion differs in several ways from Neurath's notion of how new sentences are co-opted into a scientific system (Chapter 7). First, as a conventionalist, Quine draws no hard-and-fast line between science and metaphysics. Second, therefore, he can refer to a substantial world behind our experience, even though the way we think of that world may have to be changed. Third, a sentence may be compared with experience as well as with the system in order to see whether to accept or reject it. For Neurath, only comparison with the system can be made. Fourth, therefore acceptance or rejection of the sentence is open to Quine on more grounds than to Neurath.

An example from nuclear physics might aid in illustrating Quine's notions and also show that science does, in broad outline, appear to work in the way which he suggests. In his book *The Structure of Science* Ernest Nagel gives the following account. (65–66) One of the principal laws of physics is the law of conservation of energy. It says roughly that in any interaction energy is neither gained nor dissipated, though it may change form. But experiments in beta-ray decay appeared to show that energy was, in fact, dissipated. Faced with this challenge, physicists did not deny the law, but posited a new particle—a neutrino—in order to account for the energy loss. Rather than take the beta-ray experiment at face value and reject a central pillar of our physical knowledge, it was decided to invent a new entity. Note that what was to be done in that case was a matter of choice, finally dictated by what was the most convenient thing to do.

In contrast to this, a few experiments were enough for physicists to reject the principle of parity, which says that ". . . in certain types of interactions atomic nuclei oriented in one direction emit beta-particles with the same intensity as do nuclei oriented in the opposite direction." (Nagel 66) But parity was not a central law in physics and it was comparatively easier to reject it rather than to go to any lengths to keep it.

Science, in Quine's view, is an invention of man and can be altered to suit his needs. It is true that "Any statement can be held true come what may, if we make drastic enough adjustments elsewhere in the system. Even a statement very close to the periphery can be held true in the face of recalcitrant experience by pleading hallucination or by amending certain statements of the kind called logical laws. Conversely, by the same token, no statement is immune to revision." (43) In fact, Quine notes that revision of the law of the excluded middle has been proposed because of fundamental discoveries in quantum mechanics.

If this view is a viable one, then the hard-and-fast distinction between many pairs of opposites may be blurred. A universe of events, like Whitehead's, may in the end be more suitable for scientific and metaphysical purposes than one of gross or of micro-physical bodies. It might even be the case that what worked in one part of science might not work in another. To think of scientific theories as being in a one-to-one correspondence with the bits and pieces of the world, like an architect's blueprint of a building so that just as when one strips away the unnecessary plaster, paint, and brick facing, the real structure of the building is exposed, so scientific theories reveal the true structure of the universe is to think of them incorrectly. They might better be thought of as rough predictive devices which never predict or describe with precise accuracy. New purposes and new ways of looking at things demand new adjustments in the theoretical structure. Quine's words sum up his position. "Each man is given a scientific heritage plus a continuing barrage of sensory stimulation; and the considerations which guide him in warping his scientific heritage to fit his continuing sensory promptings are, where rational, pragmatic." (46)

4. Peter Strawson: Meaning and Reference

Strawson's paper "On Referring" [18] is directed against Russell's theory of descriptions. Strawson begins by asserting that we use expressions of varying but different kinds in order to mention or refer to places, things, events, and the like. This use of expressions he calls 'the uniquely referring use'. He gives us four classes of such expressions, which by no means exhaust the possibilities: singular demonstrative pronouns ('this' and 'that'); proper names ('Venice', 'Napoleon', 'John'); singular pronouns 'I', 'you', 'it', 'he', 'she'); phrases beginning with the definite article followed by a singular noun ('the so-and-so'). All of these expressions do occur as subjects of what is considered in grammatical terms a singular subject-predicate sentence. It is this occurrence which Strawson will analyze. He is quite clear that this is not a unique use of these grammatical forms, and this might give us the clue that it is not in virtue of the grammatical form alone that Strawson will conduct his analysis. Our second clue that the analysis will not be given in terms of form alone is Strawson's use of the word 'utterance' in his example. He says, "It is obvious that anyone who uttered the sentence, 'The whale is a mammal', would be using the expression 'the whale' in a way quite different from the way it would be used by anyone who had occasion seriously to utter the sentence, 'The whale struck the ship'. In the first sentence one is obviously *not* mentioning, and in the second sentence one obviously *is* mentioning, a particular whale." (Flew 21)

Now in addition to making this point about mentioning, Strawson has implicitly made the point that a sentence needs something besides its bare form; it needs to be *used,* and his use of the word 'utterance' tells us this. For Russell—and I think this can be safely stated for all logicians—a sentence asserts some proposition, or statement, or has meaning in virtue of its form alone, whether that form is a series of marks identifiable as letters of the Latin alphabet forming words in the English language, or a well-formed formula of some logical calculus. For Strawson that is not enough. A sentence, so to speak, lies there and of itself it says nothing; to say something it must be used, much in the same way that one might say with a certain degree of accuracy that knives do not cut, they must be used in order to cut.

Thus far, Strawson has explicitly said that these referring expressions can be used in other ways. He now goes on to say that it is also possible to have more than one such expression in any one sentence as in 'the whale struck the ship', where one particular whale and one particular ship are mentioned and meant to be referred to, as in the eighty-fifth chapter of *Moby Dick*. Strawson wishes to examine only sentences where the referring expression occurs as the grammatical subject.

Russell's theory of definite descriptions concerns itself with expressions of the form 'the so-and-so', and according to Strawson it was, when he wrote "On Referring," still held up as the correct analysis of sentences containing these expressions. He will argue that the theory provides an incorrect analysis. The question is approached obliquely: why did Russell think he needed to invent a theory of descriptions? Consider the sentence 'the king of France is wise'. We should all agree that the sentence was significant (i.e., meaningful), but we know that there is no king of France now. Strawson feels that the theory is an attempt to show how such a sentence can be significant even though its referring expression does not refer to anything—that is, even though there is not now a king of France. Russell does this not only to save the significance of such sentences but also to discredit the answer given by some Platonistic inflationists. Meinongians[19] argued in the following way: let the sentence 'the king of France is wise' be called *S*. (23)

1) 'The king of France' is the subject of *S*.

2) To say 1) is to say that *S* is about the king of France.

3) If *S* is about the king of France then it is true only if the king of France *is* wise; and it is false only if the king of France *is not* wise.

4) But 2) and 3) could not be true unless there were a king of France.

5) Therefore, if *S* is significant there must *be* an object named the king of France.

We should note that neither Strawson nor Russell is prepared to say that *S* is not significant: which would certainly rid us of the problem. Russell wants to say that *S* is significant because its grammatical form is misleading and it really states a proposition that is quite different from the proposition that it appears to state. When we unpack such a sentence, we find that it really is a series of conjoined propositions that are being asserted, and that this series of conjoined propositions is meaningful even though it is often seen to be false.

On the other hand, what Strawson will assert is that while the *sentence* itself has meaning, only *uses* of it can be said to mention or to refer and to be true or false. Where the context of utterance justifies its use, the question of its reference or its truth arises; where the context does not justify its use, those questions do not arise. Russell holds that sentences are either true or false, or meaningless. But Strawson holds that sentences by themselves are either meaningless or meaningful. They need, however, to be used by someone to say what is true or false. It is not sentences but statements uttered in a context which are true or false. This will become clearer shortly.

Strawson continues the main stream of the argument by applauding Russell's rejection of the paradigm Meinongian argument quoted above. He deplores, however, the concessions that he feels Russell makes in rejecting it. Calling the referring phrase *'D'*, he summarizes Russell's argument: *D* is the grammatical subject of *S*, but it is not its logical subject and in fact S is not logically a sentence of the subject-predicate type, grammatical appearances notwithstanding. S is really a series of conjoined existential propositions, but the grammatical structure of our language hides this. In order properly to analyze S, it should be rewritten so as to expose its logical form. This is familiar from our discussion of Russell's theory in Chapter 4. Now Strawson holds that what Russell has so far said in answer to the 'Platonizing' arguments implies certain doctrines which we have already seen as the object of attack by Wittgenstein. Any sentence similar to S in these respects—i) grammatically of the subject-predicate form, and ii) where the subject fails to refer—can only be meaningfully analyzed by showing that they are not logically of the subject-predicate form. But this implies that if there is any sentence which is logically of the subject-predicate form, then its significance guarantees that the logical-grammatical subject actually refers to something which really exists. The argument follows by contra-position: let q be logical subjects having genuine (existent) references and p be sentences logically of the subject-predicate form. Then Russell's argument as Strawson puts it is: '$\sim q \supset \sim p$', but by contra-position '$p \supset q$', or sentences logically of the subject-predicate form imply that their logical subjects have genuine references. Strawson asserts that Russell implies that there are such sentences, for to be misled by grammatical appearances into believing that there are sentences of the subject-predicate form must indicate that there are sentences which are both logically and grammatically of the subject-predicate form. On Strawson's view Russell accepted these consequences, and this is shown by what Russell says about proper names and definite description: 1) Logically proper names alone can occur as subjects of sentences genuinely of the subject-predicate form. 2) Any expression supposed to be a logically proper name is meaningless unless there is some unique object for which it stands precisely because the meaning of such an expression *is* the unique object which the expression designates; to be a name is to designate something.

Now, the argument continues, if anybody believes 1) and
2), then the only way for him to save the significance of *S* is
to deny that it is logically of the subject-predicate form.
Short of actually Platonizing and filling the void with entities, a possibility which Strawson will not consider, this appears true. Recapitulating, then: Russell's error is to hold
that if a sentence which appears to be about some particular
entity is to be significant either i) its grammatical form is
misleading as to its logical form, or ii) its grammatical
subject is a logically proper name and designates a unique
individual which is its meaning.

Strawson is concerned to deny these two alternatives. He
wishes to assert that expressions used in a uniquely referring
way are *never* logically proper names or definite descriptions
—that is, analyzable on Russell's model. For him there are
no logically proper names and no descriptions in this sense
at all.

On Russell's analysis we have the following translation of
S:

1) There is a man who holds royal power in France
   (univocal use of 'is').
2) There is not more than one man who holds royal
   power in France.
3) There is nothing which is the man who holds royal
   power in France and not wise.

Strawson holds that Russell arrived at this analysis by asking
under what conditions the utterance of *S* could be said to be
a true assertion.

The whole real difference between Russell and Strawson
on this point is that Russell holds that a sentence *itself* refers
and is true or false; Strawson holds that only uses of sentences refer and are either true or false. Strawson admits that
1), 2), and 3) above describe the circumstances which are
necessary conditions of *S* being true. What he is concerned to
deny is that the translation of *S* provided by 1), 2), and 3) is
correct, or even partially correct, but incomplete.

Strawson adopts the following terminology:

An expression = df.   an expression with a uniquely
referring use.

A sentence = df.   a sentence containing such an
expression.

He also introduces the following distinctions:
A_1) A sentence.
A_2) A use of a sentence.
A_3) An utterance of a sentence.
and
B_1) An expression.
B_2) A use of an expression.
B_3) An utterance of an expression.

He considers our sentence *S*. We imagine it to be uttered
at various times in the course of history. It is one and the
same sentence uttered at different periods. In this sense he
uses the notion A_1. But two men may utter the sentence at
different times—during the reigns of Louis XIV and Louis
XVI, respectively—and in one case it might be held that the
sentence was being used to make a true assertion and in the
other case it might be held that it was being used to make a
false assertion. But if both men uttered the sentence in the
reign of Louis XIV it would be held that both men made
either a true or false assertion. In the former case a different
use was made of the same sentence upon each utterance. In
the latter case the same use was made of each utterance of
the sentence. Strawson holds that this is enough to show that
we ought not to speak of 'the sentence' being either true or
false, but rather of the sentence 'being used to make a true
or false assertion'. Likewise we ought not to speak of *the sentence* being about a particular person, for the same sentence
will be about different persons at different times; only a particular *use* of a sentence will be about a definite person. The
notion of 'utterance' is also made clear in the latter example
above when we say that two different men made two
different utterances of the same sentence about Louis XIV

and used it in the same way, i.e., to make either a true or a false assertion.

Analogously, we can make the distinction between an expression, a use of an expression, and an utterance of an expression. These distinctions are not precisely identical to those between a sentence, its use, and an utterance of it, for expressions do not make true or false propositions as sentences do, nor do expressions themselves talk about persons as sentences do. We must say rather that we use the expression to refer to a particular person in the course of using a sentence to speak about him. But in the same way 'the expression' cannot be said to refer any more than 'the sentence'. We must say that the expression has different mentioning uses. " 'Mentioning', or 'referring', is not something an expression does; it is something that someone can use an expression to do. Mentioning, or referring to, something is a characteristic of *a use* of an expression, just as 'being about' something, and truth-or-falsity, are characteristics of *a use* of a sentence." (Flew 29)

Strawson illustrates this notion by considering the word 'I' and the sentence 'I am hot.' Everybody can and does use (utter) this same sentence but no one can make the same use of it, in his sense of use, as anybody else. Strawson holds that to say this is, in a sense, to give the meaning of 'I' somehow by specifying the rules for its use. 'I' does not refer to a particular person; only a *use* of 'I' can do that. One might call 'I' the paradigm case for Strawson's position.

Strawson, recapitulating once again, considers the sentence *S*. Russell would say the following two things about *S:* 1) *S* is significant and anyone uttering it would be making a significant statement; 2) anyone now uttering *S* would be making a true assertion if and only if there now actually existed a king of France and he were wise. But Strawson holds that Russell would also say the following two false things: 1) anyone now uttering *S* would be making either a true or a false assertion; 2) part of what he would be asserting would be that there at present exists one and only one king of

France. Strawson has already given reasons why he thinks that 1) and 2) directly above are false. He now proceeds to add to those reasons by adducing one more locution from ordinary language. If someone told us that the present king of France was wise, we would not say that what he said was true or false. We would look a bit uncomfortable and if pressed for a reply we would not say 'yes' or 'no' but 'France is no longer a monarchy, and questions about the present king of France simply don't arise'. Strawson says that if a man persisted in asking this question, it would be evidence that he believed that France was still a monarchy.

It is on the same paradigm of ordinary usage that Strawson also disagrees with and corrects Russell's analysis of 'the', For him one of the functions of the definite article is to 'act as a *signal*' that a unique reference is being made. It does not act as an *assertion* that such is the case. This will arise only from the context. Thus to say 'the so-and-so' is to imply that there is a unique reference being made to actual so-and-so's, but Strawson holds that this is not to assert that there are so-and-so's. It implies, in some weak non-logical sense of 'implies', that Russell's existential conditions are fulfilled, but it does not state that they are: 'implies' in the sense of 'implies that the utterer believes'. Strawson calls this presupposing.

In his book *My Philosophical Development* Russell offers a sharp reply to Strawson which covers many points. I believe Strawson's account to be correct in the main and I shall deal here with only one of Russell's points. Russell writes:

> This brings me to a fundamental divergence between myself and many philosophers with whom Mr. Strawson appears to be in general agreement. They are persuaded that common speech is good enough, not only for daily life, but also for philosophy. I, on the contrary, am persuaded that common speech is full of vagueness and inaccuracy, and that any attempt to be precise and accurate requires modification of common speech both as regards vocabulary and as regards syntax. Everybody admits that physics and chemistry and medicine each require a language which is not that of everyday life. I fail to see why philosophy 'alone' should be forbidden to make a similar approach towards precision and accuracy. (241–42)

"Common speech" need not be nearly so bad as Russell makes out. Of course if he means by that phrase the speech of the street, or unthinking speech, then he is right. But he need not mean this. Suitably refined, common speech gives generally good service in law, commerce, diplomacy, history, literary criticism, etc. If we take medicine, Russell's own example, we should note that formalization and quantification of language has not proceeded nearly so far as it has in chemistry and physics. Presumably the doctors know what they are about and so it may well be the case that the subject does not lend itself to that degree of precision—at least in some of its aspects—necessary for successful formalization.

No one tries to formalize or mathematicize literary criticism. Why? In one sense this may be difficult to determine, but in another it is not. In the easier sense we may say that it just doesn't seem appropriate to try to do this for literary criticism. Aside from the stupendous task that would entail, it doesn't look as if the subject lends itself to the sort of idealization of cases and abstraction that physics does (e.g., all falling bodies have a few relevant features in common, etc.), nor is that degree of measurement and precision found in physics either possible or necessary in literary criticism. In order to gain precision, say in making deductions, an artificial language or formal system uses a small stock of types of primitive terms together with a few rules for combining these into formulae and a few rules for passing from one formula to another. For that precision it gives up breadth of expression. Literary criticism just does not seem to fit into such a mold, for it uses a great range of style and nuances of language to gain its effect. Its aims are essentially different from a formal language system. Besides being discursive and giving information, it is itself an object whose style and literary expression count in its appraisal.

Much of what I said about literary criticism holds for philosophy. It is true that individual points or arguments are often seen more clearly when spelled out formally. This is obviously true for points in the philosophy of logic and is often true in the philosophy of science. But whole positions or philosophic works would tend to become less and not more manageable if expressed in a formal language. Given the small primitive stock of rules and types of symbols, one would have to go to great lengths of ingenuity to try to write out all the intricate positions of Kant or Hegel or Aristotle, even if it could be done. The lengths of the strings of symbols and their complexity would be enormous. We saw that even such straightforward notions as fragility, which are genuinely parts of science, present problems not easily solved in their attempted translation.

For these reasons such an enterprise seems wrong-headed. To the objection that what couldn't be adequately formalized is best omitted as not being part of genuine philosophy, one must reply that this needs to be shown on independent grounds if it is not to beg the question. What seems best is to go on using common speech carefully and refining it as we go along. Where we can exhibit a formal pattern of argument we ought to do so if it helps clarify matters, but where we wish to avoid the ontological traps that careless use lulls us into, we ought in the first instance to look at the way in which we use words and how they do function, so as to set things right.

All this is by way of saying that Russell seems incorrect when he says that philosophy, like physics, needs its formal idiom. From the fact that physics has progressed in this fashion it does not follow that philosophy will also. And this brings us back to Strawson's approach. It seems true to say that people use phrases to refer but it seems false to say that the phrases refer in the absence of such use. If we adopt this view, then Russell's problem is solved not by asking what the formal conditions for a successful reference are, or what rules standard language ought to obey, but rather how and when people use phrases successfully to refer, and what standards language does obey.

11

Epilogue

Very generally, we might suggest that the history of a philosophic movement stands on a spectrum somewhere between the history of a scientific discipline and the history of a literary movement. Philosophy may exhibit progress, but not in the way a scientific discipline does, for philosophic problems are rarely solved in the way that scientific ones are. There is a vaccine against smallpox but none against universals. Yet the history of a philosophic movement is not just the bare outlines of works written, opinions held, and influences, as is literary history. New problems arise and new techniques are invented. One reads Descartes today not to get the solutions to contemporary problems, but out of historical interest. But it is not historical interest which impels us to read Shakespeare. His work does neither more nor less for us now than it might have done three hundred years ago. This is not generally true either in science or in philosophy.

I have traced some of the views of analytic philosophers from the beginning of the twentieth century to about the mid-1950's. The phases through which the account has passed could conveniently be listed as early realism and analysis, logical atomism, logical positivism, and ordinary language philosophy. It should now be obvious why it is possible neither to specify what all analysts have in common, nor who exactly falls into each phase, nor exactly where each phase begins and ends. In a way, notions like the notion of analytic philosophy or of each phase are ideal labels which are convenient for talking, but which do not necessarily denote specific traits. To borrow a phrase from Wittgenstein, they denote groups of men who are related to each other by family resemblances, and hence, the groups are open-ended. But the philosophers whose work has been discussed do have in common a desire to analyze and a preoccupation with language, if only with the aim of expressing themselves unambiguously. Moreover, they did address themselves to an interlocking series of problems, and often to each other.

In covering the nest of problems called the problems of sense data and of meaning and reference, it has become clear that not only do the different philosophers find different methods of attack and offer different conclusions, but they often view the problems themselves quite differently. Moore conceived the problem of sense data largely as the problem of finding out what it was that we perceived immediately. But Carnap and Russell were more interested in constructing our knowledge of the world from them. Ryle, Austin, and Wittgenstein conceived the entire enterprise as misguided: a series of language traps into which carelessness leads the unwary. They found less in the way of substantive problems and more in the way of linguistic confusion.

Can we discover any sort of progress between 1899 and the present? Are we any better off now than we were then? In one sense as philosophers we are clearly better off. Philosophers like problems, and there are more of them now than ever. Of course there are also more philosophers, but they seem to generate rather than solve problems. Nevertheless, there has been a kind of progress. First, symbolic logic was invented, and when a new discipline is invented that must count as progress. Second, with the aid of formal systems, problems in the philosophy of science have taken on a different and more precise character. This, too, is progress.

Third, standards of rigor in argument have tightened considerably. We are, perhaps, more alive to conceptual confusions which creep into arguments and more wary of what we count as a sound argument. Fourth, in connection with this we have become aware that some problems are empirical problems, some are generated by conceptual confusion, and some by the theoretical framework within which we work. Fifth, we are aware of the paths closed by previous analysis. Sixth, we have come less to the view that philosophy is a matter of a few great minds working in lonely splendor to create ideas over which the rest of us ponder, and more to the view that it is a matter of systematically attacking problems with the sort of group approach prevalent in many sciences. The old dichotomy was between great philosophers and students of philosophy. This may now have become the dichotomy between more and less skillful philosophers. But whether or not this is progress may depend upon your point of view.

What hope is there in the future for complete solutions to the problems of meaning and reference and sense data? Little, I think, for it does not at all seem to me that philosophic problems ever do get solved. But I do think that progress of the sort I have outlined will continue, and at the moment I think it likely to be made by those philosophers who work with scientific disciplines. In terms of our two problems, this means that solutions must be searched for on the basis of a knowledge of structural linguistics for the problems of meaning and reference, and on the basis of knowledge of psychology, physiology, and neurology for the problems of perception and sense data. This seems to be denied by Ryle and Wittgenstein, though Austin might have been open to it. Nevertheless, I believe it to be true, and I will sketch briefly why I think it is.

Generally speaking, one might look upon philosophy as a second-order discipline like criticism. Criticism cannot exist without something to criticize, and so works of art are necessary to it. In the same way, philosophy philosophizes about something. In the case of our first problem it philosophizes about language, and in the case of our second it philosophizes about perception and minds. Unlike critics, however, philosophers have often felt free to make up their subject matter as they went along. In some cases they had to do this. When Locke and Hume wrote on perception there was no science of psychology which studied that subject. They did their best, and it was quite good. They thought about what it had to be like if perception were possible, and they analyzed what they discovered. Their results were accordingly primitive. But it is no longer either necessary or desirable to follow such a procedure. Psychology and linguistics now exist. Though it may be a pleasurable intellectual exercise to try to reconstruct the world given Hume's analysis of perception, that analysis is no longer viable. Perception is far more complicated than Hume thought it was, and the people in a position to describe its mechanism are psychologists, physiologists, and neurologists. It will be said in reply that philosophic problems are not empirical problems, and this may even be true. But a shift in the accepted empirical data often places the locus of a philosophic problem in quite a different area; sometimes it may wipe out a problem altogether. To take a well-known example, Kant developed his philosophy in the first critique at least in part in order to account for what he thought was the absolute certainty of science. His problem was to explain how philosophy could become certain and exhibit a progress like science. But with the rise of the notion that science was not absolutely certain, at least the character of Kant's problem shifted, even if the problem was not altogether dissolved. It is, I think, significant that philosophers of science do not make up *a priori* patterns of scientific explanation, but look to see what the scientists think counts as explanation. Why should philosophers of language or mind do otherwise?

Proponents of structural linguistics are sometimes prone to make extravagant claims for the discipline. It will not, however, solve all previous philosophic problems. It will merely provide a basis upon which to build attempted solutions. At the very least, philosophers will have to try to analyze its basic concepts and characterize the nature of its theories and explanations. In discovering how language functions they may find solutions to some of their own problems as well. One cannot analyze the concept of motion unless one knows how bodies move. Zeno Vendler makes the point well (though for other and more intricate purposes), so I borrow it from him.

Since Ryle's discussion in *The Concept of Mind,* some obviously philosophical conclusions have been drawn from the fact that certain crucial verbs like *know, believe,* or *love,* unlike, say, *run, study,* or *think,* have no continuous tenses. While I can say that I am studying geometry, I cannot say that I am knowing geometry. For this and similar reasons, philosophers have concluded that while studying and the like are actions or processes, knowing and the like are states or dispositions. The trouble, however, is that this distinction cannot be made in German or French—or, indeed, in most of the Indogermanic languages. And how should one know that other arguments of this kind will hold in languages other than English? What shall we say then? That, for instance, knowing is not a process in English? But what sort of a philosophical thesis is this? Or shall we do comparative linguistics before making a philosophical claim? What we definitely should not do is to say what Ryle does in "Ordinary Language": "Hume's question was not about the word 'cause'; it was about the *use* of 'cause.' It was just as much about the *use* of 'Ursache.' For the use of 'cause' is the same as the use of 'Ursache,' though 'cause' is not the same word as 'Ursache.' "[1] This is an incredible claim. How does Ryle know, without an exhaustive study of both languages, that the use of *Ursache* is the same as that of *cause?* How, moreover, can two words ever have the same use in two different languages that do not show a one-to-one correlation of morphemes and syntactic structures? Anyway, insofar as Ryle's claim is understandable it is obviously false: the word *cause* is both a noun and a verb. *Ursache,* on the other hand, is never a verb. And this, I say, is quite a difference in use.[2]

Sometime back in Chapter 2, I made the point against Moore that he examined too narrow a range of cases, and I suggested that acquaintance with psychology *might* have opened wider vistas to him. While it is true that Austin counters with such a range, it is also true that if that range is relevant it would be better to get the whole thing straight at once and be done with it; it is psychologists who have such information. In another instance, Ryle, in his chapter called "Imagination," attempts to analyze away hallucinations and mental images by saying that to have a hallucination of *x* is to think you see *x* when, in fact, you don't. Aside from the difficulty of going on to analyze 'think' there is the further difficulty that the psychological literature is full of cases which actually deny this. Experimentally hallucinated people rarely think that they are seeing something and sometimes even paranoids and schizoids fail to think they are seeing something when they are hallucinating. But this evidence seems to vitiate an important point in Ryle's analysis. One surely cannot settle the matter without examining it.

Other cases could be developed, and much needs to be done. I am not making the claim that philosophic questions are all empirical questions or that philosophic problems will all be solved empirically. I am not even saying that empirical findings are relevant to all philosophic questions. Many philosophic questions about value may not be so related. It may even be plausible to argue that no empirical finding is relevant to the question of the relations of philosophy with empirical science. I want merely to deny the claim that no empirical findings are relevant to philosophic questions about language or minds. I want to claim that they are far more important than has often been realized.

Notes

CHAPTER 1

[1]Quoted as a motto in J. Katz, *The Philosophy of Language* (New York, 1965). Translation mine.

[2]*An Enquiry Concerning Human Understanding*, Sec. II, paragraph 14. ed. by L. A. Selby—Bigge, second ed. Oxford, 1902 *OUP*.

[3]"The History of Analysis," in R. Rorty, ed., *The Linguistic Turn* (Chicago, 1967).

CHAPTER 2

[1]In P. A. Schilpp, ed., *The Philosophy of G. E. Moore* (Evanston, Ill., 1944), p. 14.

[2]In *Philosophical Papers* (London, 1959), pp. 32–59. Hereafter referred to as *PP* and *ADOCS*.

[3]London, 1953. Hereafter referred to as *SMPOP*.

[4]*Philosophical Studies* (London, 1922), pp. 31–96. Hereafter referred to as *PS*.

[5]For a critique, see ch. 10, sec. 2 on Austin.

[6]See, e.g., "The Nature and Reality of Objects of Perception," *PS*, 70 f.; and *SMPOP*, 67, 111. But see also the statement in "The Status of Sense-Data," *PS*, 76–77.

[7]See ch. 4 for Russell's theory of definite descriptions.

[8]In R. Swartz, ed., *Perceiving, Sensing and Knowing* (New York, 1965), pp. 130–37. Originally published in C. A. Mace, ed. *British Philosophy in the Mid-Century*. London, 1957.

[9]See pp. 22–3.

[10]See ch. 10, sec. 2.

[11]See ch. 10, sec. 1.

CHAPTER 3

[1]*Mind* (1899), pp. 176–93. Hereafter referred to as "NJ."

[2]Bk. IV, ch. XIV, 3.

³See Moore, *Principia Ethica* (Cambridge, Eng., 1903), sec. 5–14. Work referred to hereafter as *PE*.

⁴E.g., in the *Parmenides*.

⁵On this see A. R. White, *G. E. Moore: A Critical Exposition* (Oxford, 1958), chapters II–VII.

CHAPTER 4

¹*My Philosophical Development* (New York, 1959), p. 62. Hereafter referred to as *MPD*.

²*Introduction to Mathematical Philosophy* (London, 1919), p. 169. Hereafter referred to as *IMP*.

³"The Theory of Objects" in R. Chisholm, ed., *Realism and the Background of Phenomenology* (Glencoe, Ill. 1960), p. 82.

⁴See Russell, "Meinong's Theory of Complexes and Assumptions," *Mind* (1904), p. 204.

⁵Fuller accounts of Meinong's position may be found in: G. E. Moore, "The Subject-Matter of Psychology," *Aristotelian Society Proceedings* (1909–10); R. Chisholm (above n.), Introduction and selection 4; H. Spiegelberg, *The Phenomenological Movement* (The Hague, 1960), vol. I, 98–101; J. N. Findlay, *Meinong's Theory of Objects and Values* (Oxford, 1966, 2nd ed.); Leonard Linsky, *Referring* (New York, 1967), ch. II.

⁶"On Sense and Reference" in M. Black and P. Geach, eds., *Translations from the Philosophical Writings of Gottlob Frege* (Oxford, 1952), pp. 56–78.

⁷Russell, "On Denoting," *Mind* (1905), p. 484, reprinted in Marsh p. 47.

⁸ See pp. 97–98 for truth functional connectives; specifically, p. 97 for conditional statements.

⁹For a fuller account of Frege's theory see his article "On Sense and Reference" in Black and Geach; W. and M. Kneale, *The Development of Logic* (Oxford, 1962) pp. 493 f.; and Linsky, ch. III.

¹⁰See pp. 96–98, for these connectives.

¹¹London 1919, pp. 167–80.

¹²This is not always true for all types of propositions, even on a purely formal analysis. See Linsky (above note 9), pp. 70 f.

CHAPTER 5

¹*Our Knowledge of the External World* (London, 1914), p. 82. Hereafter referred to as *OKEW*.

²In *Mysticism and Logic* pp. 140–73. (Garden City, N.Y. 1957).

³For fuller accounts of the comparison between Wittgenstein's and Russell's views see: L. Wittgenstein, *Tractatus Logico-Philosophicus* (London, 1921, new trans. 1961); Russell, *My Philosophical Develop-*

ment, chs. IX and X; J. O. Urmson, *Philosophical Analysis: Its Development between the Two World Wars* (Oxford, 1956); D. F. Pears, *Bertrand Russell and the British Tradition in Philosophy* (New York, 1967) G. Pitcher, *The Philosophy of Wittgenstein* (Englewood Cliffs, N. J., 1964). See the bibliographies in these works for a listing of the vast literature dealing with this area.

⁴Originally in *The Monist* (1918-19); reprinted in R. C. Marsh, ed. *Logic and Knowledge* (New York, 1956), 175-282. All references are to Marsh.

⁵But see pages 93, 129ff. for the problem of solipsism which it raises.

⁶"The Ultimate Constituents of Matter" in *Mysticism and Logic* (above n.), p. 125.

CHAPTER 6
¹London, 1936; rev. ed. 1946. Hereafter referred to as Ayer 1936, 1946.

²I. A. Richards, *Science & Poetry* (New York, 1926).

³For a full account of the Circle and its early members see V. Kraft, *The Vienna Circle* (New York, 1953 rev. 1968); and J. Jorgensen, *The Development of Logical Empiricism* (Chicago, 1951).

⁴See M. White, *Toward Reunion in Philosophy* (Cambridge, Mass., 1956), pp. 19 f.

⁵See Schlick, "Positivism and Realism" (1932), in A. J. Ayer, ed., *Logical Positivism*, (New York, 1959), p. 107. Book hereafter referred to as Ayer, 1959.

⁶For a complete table of those whom the positivists counted as their intellectual forefathers see Jorgensen, p. 6. For a brief account of the contributions of Peirce and Einstein see W. P. Alston and G. Nakhnikian, eds., *Readings in Twentieth Century Philosophy* (New York, 1963), pp. 385-86; and M. Schlick, "Positivism and Realism" in Ayer, 1959, pp. 89-90.

⁷Reprinted and revised in his *Aspects of Scientific Explanation* (New York, 1965), pp. 101-22. Hereafter called Hempel, 1965.

⁸For a detailed treatment of Hempel's work with criticisms see I. Scheffler, *The Anatomy of Inquiry* (New York 1963).

⁹For extended treatment of this notion see K. Popper, *The Logic of Scientific Discovery* (New York, 1959); and I. Scheffler, *The Anatomy of Inquiry*, (New York 1963) pt. II.

CHAPTER 7
¹1928 (in German); Los Angeles and Berkeley, 1967 (trans. into English by R. George). Hereafter referred to as *LSW*.

²In parts of the book Carnap presents arguments for the epistemic primacy of the solipsistic point of view, and within that point

of view, for the epistemic primacy of elementary experiences. These are presented in more compact form in his paper "Pseudo Problems in Philosophy," which is reprinted in the same volume.

[3](London, 1935). Reprinted in Alston and Nakhnikian.

[4]See, e.g., M. Merleau-Ponty, *The Structure of Behavior* (Boston 1958) *The Phenomenology of Perception* (N.Y. 1962); P. McKellar, *Imagination and Thinking* (London 1957); S. Hampshire, "Review of Ryle's *The Concept of Mind,*" *Mind* (1950); G. Meyers, *Philosophical Psychology.* (this series 1969); J. Gibson, *The Senses Considered as Perceptual System* (Boston 1966); J. Singer, *Daydreaming* (N.Y. 1966).

[5]"Testability and Meaning," reprinted in R. Ammerman, ed., *Classics of Analytic Philosophy* (New York, 1966), p. 188.

[6]For further comment, see the work of Carnap, Hempel, and Scheffler mentioned in the Notes (p. 000). Additional bibliographies will be found there.

CHAPTER 8

[1]London, 1921; new trans. 1961. Hereafter referred to as *Tractatus.*

[2]There is an enormous literature in this area and we cannot go into it here. See the selected items in the Bibliography on Wittgenstein.

[3]Oxford, 1953, 1958. Hereafter referred to as *PI.*

[4]G. Warnock, *English Philosophy Since 1900* (London, 1958).

[5]Sec. 23. Numbers refer to sections in *PI,* pt. I.

[6]*PI,* pt. I, sec. 1. Wittgenstein is unfair. Augustine criticized this view at great length and in a very modern way in his *De Magistro (On the Teacher,* trans. by George Leckie, New York, 1938). (I owe this reference to the Rev. Thomas Munson, S. J.)

[7]P. 223. Page numbers refer to pt. II of *PI.*

[8]G. Pitcher, *The Philosophy of Wittgenstein* (Englewood Cliffs, N.J., 1964), p. 243.

[9]See the *Republic,* bk. I; *Charmides; Laches; Theatetus.*

[10]"Review of *Philosophical Investigations*" in Pitcher, ed., p. 26.

CHAPTER 9

[1]For extended bibliographies in the area see the notes to J. Passmore, *A Hundred Years of Philosophy* (London, 1957), ch. XVIII; the articles and books on this topic listed in Pitcher, 1964 and 1966; Pitcher's own analysis in 1964; and J. Hartnack, *Wittgenstein and Modern Philosophy* (New York, 1965), ch. IV.

[2]For a contrary interpretation of Wittgenstein, see Donagan, "Wittgenstein on Sensations" in Pitcher, 1966.

CHAPTER 10

[1]Warnock, 1958, ch. VII; Hampshire's review, *Mind* (1950); and J. Hartnack, 1965, ch. V. Sec. 1.

[2]*The Concept of Mind* (New York, 1949), p. 7. Hereafter referred to as *CM*.

[3]*Proceedings of the Aristotlean Society* 1937–38; reprinted in A. Flew, ed., *Logic and Language,* Second Series (Oxford, 1953). Pages cited in Flew.

[4]See J. J. C. Smart, "A Note on Categories," *British Journal for the Philosophy of Science* (1953).

[5]This last part, at least, of the claim appears false. See pp. 198 f. for a criticism.

[6]In his *Philosophical Papers* (Oxford, 1961).

[7]Further accounts of Austin's uniqueness may be found in Warnock, 1958, pp. 147–54; Urmson, "The History of Analysis" in Rorty, ed., 1967, pp. 294–301; and J. Passmore, 1966. See especially the bibliographical notes in Passmore.

[8]Oxford, 1962. It is a continuous writing-out of what were in some cases very fragmentary passages. Mr. Warnock claims that the substance of the argument is Austin's, though the detail and phrasing cannot be.

[9]Compare with Moore's papers, "The Nature and Reality of Objects of Perception" and "The Conception of Reality" in *PS*.

[10]I owe this point to Professor Arnold Levison.

[11]This point is made for another effect by U. T. Place, "Are Sensations Brain Processes?" in V. C. Chappell, *The Philosophy of Mind,* Englewood Cliffs, N.J., 1962.

[12]See Laird Addis, "Ryle's Ontology of Mind," *University of Iowa Publications in Philosophy* (1956), pp. 58 f. for a similar point.

[13]See M. Shorter, "Imagination," *Mind* (1952) in Gustafson, ed. *Essays in Philosophical Psychology,* (Garden City, N.Y. 1964), S. Hampshire, "Review of *CM*" (1950).

[14]R. Chisholm, "The Theory of Appearing," in Swartz, p. 184; originally in Black, ed., *Philosophical Analysis* (Ithica, N.Y. 1963). See also H. H. Price, "Appearing and Appearances," *American Philosophical Quarterly* (1964).

[15]In Swartz, p. 203; originally in H. D. Lewis, ed., *Contemporary British Philosophy* 3rd series (London 1956).

[16]*From a Logical Point of View* (Cambridge, Mass., 1953), p. 4. Hereafter referred to as Quine.

[17]"A Logician's Landscape," *Philosophy* (1955), p. 229.

[18]*Mind* (1950); reprinted in Flew, 1956. Pages cited are to Flew.

[19]See Chapter 4 above.

CHAPTER 11 EPILOGUE

[1]"Ordinary Language," *Philosophical Review,* 1953, p. 171.

[2]Zeno Vendler, *Linguistics in Philosophy* (Ithaca, N.Y., 1967), pp. 11–12.

Selected Bibliography

General Accounts

Ayer, A. J., et al., *The Revolution in Philosophy* (London: Macmillan, 1956). A highly readable account of the analytic movement taken from BBC broadcasts made by eminent contemporary philosophers.

Mehta, Ved, *The Fly in the Fly Bottle* (Baltimore: Penguin, 1968). The first half of this book originally appeared in the *New Yorker* magazine in 1963. It is written from the human-interest point of view.

Passmore, J., *A Hundred Years of Philosophy* (New York: Basic Books, 1966). The best history of the rise of the movement, beginning with John Stuart Mill. It contains very detailed references.

Urmson, J. O., *Philosophical Analysis: Its Development between the Two World Wars* (Oxford: Clarendon Press, 1956). A detailed account of logical atomism, its origins, and its eventual dissolution.

Warnock, J. G., *English Philosophy since 1900* (London: Oxford University Press, 1958). A brief overall account touching the high spots of major doctrines and methods.

White, M., *Toward Reunion in Philosophy* (Cambridge: Harvard University Press, 1956). An attempt to outline original solutions to major philosophical problems with many historical excursions into the origins of analysis.

Collections of Essays

Alston, W. P., and G. Nakhnikian, eds., *Readings in Twentieth-Century Philosophy* (New York: Free Press, 1963).

Ammerman, R., ed., *Classics of Analytic Philosophy* (New York, McGraw-Hill 1965).

Ayer, A. J., ed., *Logical Positivism* (New York: Free Press, 1959).

Flew, A., ed., *Essays in Conceptual Analysis* (London: Macmillan, 1956).

——————, ed., *Logic and Language,* First and Second Series (Oxford: Blackwell, 1952, 1953; reprinted 1960, 1961).

Marsh, R. C., ed., *Logic and Knowledge* (London: Allen & Unwin, 1956).

Rorty, R., ed., *The Linguistic Turn* (Chicago: University of Chicago Press, 1967).

Swartz, R., ed., *Perceiving, Sensing, and Knowing* (New York: Doubleday, 1965).

Gustafson, D., ed., *Essays in Philosophical Psychology* (New York; Doubleday, 1964)

Individual Philosophers or Movements
G. E. Moore

Moore, G. E., "The Nature of Judgment," *Mind* (1899).

——————, *Principia Ethica* (Cambridge: University Press, 1903).

——————, *Philosophical Studies* (London: Routledge & Kegan Paul, 1922).

——————, *Some Main Problems of Philosophy,* 1901–11 lectures (London: Allen & Unwin, 1953). Available as a Collier paperback.

——————, *Philosophical Papers* (London: Macmillan, 1959). Available as a Collier paperback.

————————

Schilpp, P. A., ed., *The Philosophy of G. E. Moore* (Evanston: Northwestern University Press, 1944).

White, A. R., *G. E. Moore: A Critical Exposition* (Oxford: Blackwell, 1958). The major secondary source on Moore; contains complete and detailed bibliographies. Because of the detail, it is a difficult book to read.

Keynes, J. M., *Two Memoirs,* (London, 1949) Contains a witty and charming portrait of Moore by the great economist, who knew him.

Bertrand Russell

Russell, Bertrand, "On Denoting," *Mind* (1905).

——————, "The Relation of Sense Data to Physics" (1914) and "The Ultimate Constituents of Matter" (1915), in *Mysticism and Logic,* (Doubleday Anchor Garden City, New York 1959).

——————, *Our Knowledge of the External World* (London: Allen & Unwin, 1914). Available as a Mentor paperback.

—————, "The Philosophy of Logical Atomism," *Monist* (1918–19). Reprinted in Marsh (above).

—————, "Descriptions," in *Introduction to Mathematical Philosophy*, (Allen & Unwin London 1919).

————— *My Philosophical Development* (New York: Simon & Schuster, 1959).

Pears, D.F., *Bertrand Russell and the British Tradition in Philosophy* (New York: Random House 1967). A major secondary source on Russell: a very readable, detailed, and profound account of his work from 1905 to 1919 with appropriate historical background.

Schilpp, P. A., ed., *The Philosophy of Bertrand Russell* (Evanston: Northwestern University Press, 1944).

Logical Positivism

Ayer, A. J., *Language, Truth, and Logic* (London: Gollancz, 1936; rev. ed. 1946). Available as a paperback.

Carnap, R., *The Logical Structure of the World and Pseudo Problems in Philosophy*, trans. into English by R. George (Berkeley: University of California Press, 1967) Originally published in German in 1928.

—————, *Philosophy and Logical Syntax* (Kegan Paul Trench, London: Trubner, 1935). Reprinted in Alston and Nakhnikian (above).

—————, "The Physical Language as the Universal Language of Science" Reprinted in Alston and Nakhnikian (above).

—————, "Testability and Meaning" Reprinted in Ammerman (above).

Schilpp, P.A., ed., *The Philosophy of Rudolf Carnap* (La Salle, Ill.: Open Court, 1963). Secondary sources on Carnap.

Hempel, C. G., "Empiricist Criteria of Cognitive Significance: Problems and Changes." Reprinted and revised in his *Aspects of Scientific Explanation* (New York: Free Press, 1965).

Neurath, O., "Protocol Sentences" Reprinted in Ayer, 1959 (above).

Schlick, M., "Positivism and Realism," (1932–33) and "The Foundation of Knowledge" (1934). Reprinted in Ayer, 1959 (above).

———

Kraft, V. *The Vienna Circle* (New York: Philosophical Library, 1953).
Jorgensen, J., *The Development of Logical Empiricism* (Chicago: University of Chicago Press, 1951).

Ludwig Wittgenstein

Wittgenstein, L., *Tractatus Logico-Philosophicus* (London: Routledge & Kegan Paul, 1921; new trans. 1961).
——————, *Philosophical Investigations* (Oxford: Blackwell, 1953; 2nd ed., 1958).

———

Hartnack, J., *Wittgenstein and Modern Philosophy* (New York: NYU Press, 1965). A very brief outline.
Pitcher, G., *The Philosophy of Wittgenstein* (Englewood Cliffs, N.J.: Prentice-Hall, 1964). A detailed account, concise and easy to follow.
Pitcher, G., ed., *Wittgenstein,* (New York: Doubleday, 1966) A collection of contemporary papers.

Other Directions

Austin, J. L., *Philosophical Papers* (Oxford: Clarendon Press, 1961).
——————, *Sense and Sensibilia* (Oxford: Clarendon Press, 1962).
Quine, W. V. O., *From a Logical Point of View* (Cambridge: Harvard University Press, 1953).
Harmon, G., "Quine on Meaning & Existence, Pt. I and Pt. II," *Review of Metaphysics,* 1967. See also the Quine edition of *Synthèse,* Dec. 1968 for articles on Quine's work.

———

Ryle, Gilbert, "Categories" (1938–39) *Proceedings of the Aristotlean Society.* Reprinted in Flew, 1953 (above).
——————, *The Concept of Mind* (New York: Barnes & Noble, 1949).
——————, "Sensations," *Contemporary British Philosophy,* ed. H. D. Lewis (London: Allen and Unwin, 1956). Reprinted in Swartz (above).

Strawson, P. F., "A Logician's Landscape," *Philosophy* (1955).
—————, *Individuals,* 2nd. ed. (New York: Barnes & Noble, 1965).
—————, "On Referring," *Mind* (1950). Reprinted in Flew, 1956.

INDEX

Alston, William P., 133
Analysis
   horizontal, 99
   results of, 62–65
Analytic, 109ff., 207
Aquinas, St. Thomas, 22
Aristophanes, 74
Aristotle, 74, 144, 211, 222
Artificial language, 16–17
Atomic facts, 101–102
Atomism, logical, 13, 84-85, 98–105
Augustine, Saint, 149
Austen, Jane, 19
Austin, John, 14, 18–19, 42, 89, 224,
   225, 227
   on sense data, 189–204
Autobiography (Moore), 22–23
Ayer, A. J., 107, 109–113, 116, 118–
   121, 123, 125, 127, 137, 191, 195

Behaviorism, 166–167, 170–171
Being, 48
Berkeley, George, 10, 25, 30, 89
   on sense data, 25, 26
Berkeley (Moore), 191
Beta-ray decoy, 211–212
Bradley, F. H., 11, 12, 44, 45

Carnap, Rudolf, 107, 110, 122, 124,
   128–140, 209, 224
Cartesianism, 166–170
Categories, 181–185
"Categories" (Ryle), 182
Church, Alonzo, 121
Comte, Auguste, 108
Concept, 45–50, 58, 62
Concept of Mind, The (Ryle), 18, 165–
   166, 180, 182, 227
Confessions (St. Augustine), 149

Connections, truth functional, 96ff.
Content, 34–35

"Defense of Common Sense, A"
   (Moore), 23–24, 26–27, 29, 55
Denoting phrases, 74
Descartes, René, 166, 183, 223
Descriptions, 177–178
   definite, 78
Descriptive phrases, 74

Einstein, Albert, 137
"Empiricist Criteria of Cognitive
   Significance, The: Problems and
   Changes" (Hempel), 111
Empiricist language, 138–140
Energy, conservation of, 211–212
Epistemological priority, 131
Epistemologically primary, 131
Epistemologically secondary, 131
Essay concerning Human Understanding,
   An (Locke), 45
Ethics (Spinoza), 144
Existence, 48, 49, 50
Experience, stream of, 128–132
Extensionality, thesis of, 98ff.
External world, 39–43, 126–127

Facts
   atomic, 101–102
   general, 102–103
   intensional, 104
   negative, 103–104
Feigl, H., 107
Foundations of Empirical Knowledge,
   The (Ayer), 191
Frege, Gottlob, 14, 70–72, 75, 209,
   210

Galileo, 183
General facts, 102–103
Gödel, K., 107

Hahn, H., 107
Hampshire, Stuart, 180
Hegel, G. W. F., 222
Hempel, Carl, 111, 113, 114–116, 119, 122, 138–139
Hilbert, David, 135
Horizontal analysis, 99
Hume, David, 10, 12–13, 25, 39–42, 89, 108–109, 202, 207, 208, 210, 226, 227
   on sense data, 25, 26
Husserl, Edmund, 91–92

Imprecise language, 17
Incomplete symbol, 74
Individuals, 100–101
Intensional facts, 104
Introduction To Mathematical Philosophy (Russell), 76

James, William, 19, 108
Journal of Symbolic Logic, The, 121

Kant, Immanuel, 44, 108, 144, 156, 207, 222, 226
Knowledge, basis of, 123–140
Kraft, V., 107

Language, 9–20, 150–154, 156, 189–191
   areas of concern about, 9–10
   artificial, 16–17
   empiricist, 138–140
   functions of, 146–149
   imprecise, 17
   physical, 132–138
   relativity of philosophical theses in regard to, 134
Language, Truth and Logic (Ayer), 107
Leibnitz, Gottfried Wilhelm von, 10, 89, 108, 207
Linsky, Leonard, 230
Locke, John, 10, 11, 12, 25, 44, 45, 129, 188, 208, 210, 226
Logic, symbolic, 9, 13, 15, 96ff.
Logical atomism, 13, 84–85, 98–105
Logical positivism

meaning and reference, 106–122
   complete verifiability, 111–118
   verifiability principle, 110–111
   weak verifiability, 118–122
sense data, 123–140
   empiricist language, 138–140
   physical language, 132–138
   the stream of experience, 128–132
Logical Structure of the World, The (Carnap), 128, 209
"Logician's Landscape, A" (Quine), 206

Material bodies, relation of sense data to, 35–38
McKellar, Peter, 232
Meaning, 160–163, 208
Meaning and reference (See Logical positivism)
   Moore on, 44–65
      the concept named, 58–61
      early view, 44–55
      later view, 55–58
      the object named, 58–61
      as the object of understanding, 61–62
      as the result of analysis, 62–65
   Quine on, 204–213
   Russell on, 66–82
      Frege's position, 70–72
      Meinong's position, 68–70
      preliminary notions, 72–75
      theory, 75–82
   Strawson on, 213–222
   Wittgenstein on, 141–158
Meinong, Alexius, 68–70, 71, 75
Mendeleev, Dmitri, 113
Mental acts and sensations, 159–179
Merleau-Ponty, Maurice, 232
Mill, John Stuart, 11, 108
Milne, Edward Arthur, 137
Mind, 15, 18, 64
Minds, relation of sense data to, 30–35
Monadology, 89
Moore, G. E., 9, 11–16, 19, 21–65, 67, 69, 83, 86, 87, 91, 93–96, 102, 107, 123, 128, 137, 151, 156, 159,

186, 189, 191, 192, 194, 195, 198, 200–202, 208, 224, 227
  on meaning and reference, 44–65
    the concept named, 58–61
    early view, 44–55
    later view, 55–58
    the object named, 58–61
    as the object of understanding, 61–62
    as the result of analysis, 62–65
  on sense data, 21–43
    the external world, 39–43
    how it arises, 21–26
    material bodies and, 35–38
    our minds and, 30–35
    problem of, 21–26
    what they are, 26–30
My Philosophical Development (Russell), 67, 83, 90, 220

Nagel, Ernest, 211–212
Nakhnkian, George, 133
Names, 73–74, 100
"Nature of Judgment, The" (Moore), 44
"Nature and Reality of Objects of Perception, The" (Moore), 27
Nausea (Sartre), 144
Negative facts, 103–104
Neurath, Otto, 107, 137, 211
Nietzsche, Friedrich Wilhelm, 144
Notebook of Malte Laurids Brigge (Rilke), 144

Occam, William of, 66
Occam's razor, 66–67, 85
"On Denoting" (Russell), 15
"On Referring" (Strawson), 213, 214
"On What There Is" (Quine), 204
"Ordinary Language" (Ryle), 227
Our Knowledge of the External World (Russell), 86

Parity, Principle of, 211–212
Parmenides (Plato), 46
Pascal, Blaise, 144
Peano, Giuseppe, 135
Pears, D. F., 99
Peirce, Charles Sanders, 19, 108

Perception (Price), 191
Philosophical Analysis (Urmson), 84
Philosophical Investigations (Wittgenstein), 17, 18, 142–146, 180
"Philosophy of Logical Atomism, The" (Russell), 84–85, 86
Philosophy and Logical Syntax 3 (Carnap), 133
Physical language, 132–138
"Physical Language as the Universal Language of Science, The" (Carnap), 133
Pitcher, G., 151
Plato, 10, 15, 45, 46, 49, 50, 53, 60, 68, 74, 144
"Plea for Excuses, A" (Austin), 189
Popper, Karl, 116
Positivism, logical (See Logical positivism)
"Positivism and Realism" (Ayer), 111–112, 123, 125
Pragmatism, 213
Principia Ethica (Moore), 58
Principia Mathematica (Russell and Whitehead), 15, 84, 95, 98
Principles of Logic, The (Bradley), 44
Propositions, 44–58, 62, 72, 79–80, 82, 99–100, 125
  characteristics of, 55–58
  truth functional, 96–98
"Protocol Sentences" (Neurath), 137

Quine, W. V. O., 19
  on meaning and reference, 204–213

"Refutation of Idealism, The" (Moore), 31
"Relation of Sense-Data to Physics, The" (Russell), 84, 86, 94
"Reply to My Critics" (Moore), 62
Richards, I. A., 107
Rilke, Rainer Maria, 144
Russell, Bertrand, 9–19, 36, 38, 43, 60, 64, 66–105, 106, 107, 114, 124, 129, 130, 135–137, 141–143, 145, 151, 157, 159, 179, 186, 189, 205, 209, 214–217, 219–222, 224
  on meaning and reference, 66–82
    Frege's position, 70–72
    Meinong's position, 68–70

preliminary notions, 72–75
theory, 75–82
on sense data, 83–105
logical atomism, 98–105
problem of, 86–93
truth functional propositions, 96–98
what they are, 93–96
theory of descriptions, 67
Ryle, Gilbert, 14, 18, 19, 43, 89, 165–166, 189, 198–204, 224, 225, 227, 228
on sense data, 180–189

Sartre, Jean Paul, 91–92, 144
Schlick, Moritz, 107, 108, 113, 114–115, 118–119
Science and Poetry (Richards), 107
Sensations, 166–179
mental acts and, 159–179
"Sensations" (Ryle), 203–204
Sense data
Austin on, 189–204
Berkeley on, 25, 26
five subclasses of, 28
Hume on, 25, 26
logical positivism, 123–140
empiricist language, 138–140
physical language, 132–138
the stream of experience, 128–132
Moore on, 21–43
the external world, 39–43
how it arises, 21–26
material bodies and, 35–38
our minds and, 30–35
problem of, 21–26
what they are, 26–30
Russell on, 83–105
logical atomism, 98–105
problems of, 86–93
truth functional propositions, 96–98
what they are, 93–96
Ryle on, 180–189
Sense and Sensibilia (Austin), 19, 191
Sense and Sensibility (Austen), 19
"Sense-Data Are Physical" (Russell), 94
Sentences, 134, 137–138, 211, 213–214
three kinds of, 133

Shakespeare, William, 223
Socrates, 49, 74
"Some Judgments of Perception" (Moore), 36
Some Main Problems of Philosophy (Moore), 22, 24, 39, 50–51, 55
Sophist (Plato), 10, 50, 68
Spinoza, Baruch, 144
"Status of Sense Data, The" (Moore), 28, 30, 31
Strawson, Peter, 18, 19, 72, 155, 204
on meaning and reference, 213–222
Stream of experience, 128–132
Structure of Science, The (Nagel), 211–212
Synthetic, 109ff., 207
System of Logic, A (Mill), 11

Theatetus (Plato), 10, 60
Tractatus Logico-Philosophicus (Wittgenstein), 141, 142, 143
Truth functional propositions, 96–98
"Two Dogmas of Empiricism" (Quine), 207

"Ultimate Constituents of Matter, The" (Russell), 86
Understanding, 163–166
the object of, 61–62
Wittgenstein on, 163–166
Urmson, J. O., 13, 84

Variables, 72–73
Vendler, Zeno, 227
Verifiability principle, 110–111, 208
complete, 111–118
weak, 118–122
Vienna Circle, 16, 107, 137
"Visual Sense-Data" (Moore), 38

Waismann, F., 107
Warnock, G., 145, 180
Warnock, J. G., 191
Watson, J. B., 166
Whitehead, A. N., 15, 84, 135, 136, 137
Wittgenstein, Ludwig, 10, 13, 14, 16, 17–18, 19, 43, 60, 82, 84, 89, 106, 107, 109, 180, 187, 189, 216, 224, 225
on meaning, 160–163

on meaning and reference, 141–158
on sensations, 166–179
on sensations and mental acts, 159–179

on understanding, 163–166

Xenophon, 74

Zilsel, F., 107